GETTING IT PRINTED

GETTING IT PRINTED

How to Work with Printers
and Graphic Arts Services
to Assure Quality,
Stay on Schedule,
and Control Costs

Mark Beach, Steve Shepro, Ken Russon

COAST TO COAST BOOKS
PORTLAND, OREGON

Library of Congress Cataloging in Publication Data

Beach, Mark, 1937-
Getting it printed

Bibliography: p.
Includes index.
  1. Printing, Practical. 2. Graphic Arts.
3. Publishers and publishing. 4. Self-publishing.
I. Shepro, Steve, 1945-   II. Russon, Ken, 1939-
Z243.A2B4   1986   686.2   85-70831
ISBN 0-9602664-7-X Soft Cover
ISBN 0-9602664-8-8 Hard Cover

Manufactured in USA.

Coast to Coast Books

Coast to Coast Books is a publishing company specializing in books about the graphic arts and communication. On many occasions, publisher Kathleen Ryan used her good humor, common sense, and red pencil to help shape the content of this volume. Susan Brady and Warren Sendek helped keep the company running smoothly during the last year that *Getting It Printed* was being created.

The Authors

Mark Beach is a writer and publisher with 25 years of experience. His previous books in the graphic arts include the nationally-acclaimed guide *Editing Your Newsletter*. He teaches workshops and consults about producing and marketing newsletters and books.

Steve Shepro is a sales representative for one of the Northwest's leading printers. During his 24 years in the graphic arts, he has also been a production manager, estimator, platemaker, press operator, and production artist for printing companies and publishers.

Ken Russon is a graphic arts consultant for one of the nation's largest paper distributors and also teaches workshops throughout the country about printing papers. He has spent 23 years in sales and management for printing companies and paper merchants.

Editing

Susan Page-York, of Page-York Written Communications, edited the text for structure, substance, and style. Her precise thinking and skill at organizing improved the manuscript at every stage of its development.

Design

John Laursen of Press-22 devoted his expertise to this project from its inception. His 15 years of experience designing and producing high quality books made his technical advice and editorial contributions invaluable; his eye for detail set demanding standards. John designed this volume and coordinated production of art and type, pasteup, printing, and binding.

Production

Cherry Britton of Industrial Illustrators produced the technical illustrations; Susan Applegate of Publishers Bookworks made the charts and did much of the pasteup. Bill Nordstrom of Color Imaging did the color separations. Lis DeMarco of DeMarco Studio designed the cover and Aaron Jones assisted with photography. Blair Jones and his associates at Beaver Engraving made the die in the photo.

Getting It Printed was written and edited on a Xerox 820 II computer using Wordstar. ITC Garamond type was set on a Mergenthaler V-I-P by Martin White and Patti Morris of Irish Setter.

This book was printed at Publishers Press and bound at Mountain States Bindery, both in Salt Lake City, Utah. Hard covers are Smythe sewn, soft covers are burst perfect bound. We appreciate the interest and professional skill of Bruce Bracken, sales representative for Publishers Press, whose commitment to quality added greatly to this book.

Acknowledgments

We appreciate the encouragement we received while writing this book and want to thank the many people who added to our knowledge of the graphic arts.

Sheridan Barre, Ruth Christensen, Karen Davis, Louise Kasper, Bob Lander, Mimi Maduro, Mary Ruhl, Bob Shaw, Connie Shepro, and Hans Veeder gave generously of their time to evaluate a fourth draft of the manuscript. Bob Bengtson, Lis DeMarco, Holly Derderian, Jack Derderian, Gary Hottel, Steve Johnson, Howard Klug, Ron Martinolich, Verni Moore, Patti Morris, Bill Nordstrom, Chet Percival, Susan Post, Rich Sanders, Jean Speece, and Martin White reviewed parts of other drafts.

Elizabeth Anderson, Dan Barkley, Neal Buchanan, Rich Harrison, Chuck King, John Lowes, Polly Pattison, John Trachtenberg, and Gary Wilcuts helped us understand areas of the graphic arts industry in which they specialize.

We are grateful to printers Susan Post at Kaleidoscope Graphics and Sheridan and Marlene Barre, Dave Hancock, and Mary Midkiff at PIP #73 for their special attention throughout the writing of this book. We also appreciate the care with which Mimi Maduro of Groupware Systems read the entire book in layout.

For permission to reproduce copyrighted material, we thank Color Imaging Company, Graphic Arts Technical Foundation, and International Typeface Corporation.

Contents

GETTING IT PRINTED

Introduction

Many people find printing a mystery. Their concept of type and presses comes from textbook accounts of the Gutenberg Bible. Today's customer needs to understand graphic arts photography and offset lithography, the foundations of most modern printing.

Customers who do not grasp the fundamentals of printing give printers too much responsibility. Too many customers prepare materials incorrectly and set unreasonable deadlines; too many printers salvage jobs without telling customers how to do better next time. Better communication between customers and printers would lead to more satisfactory results, on-time deliveries, and lower costs.

Printing is a blend of art, craft, and industry. Effective layout requires artistic vision; proper preparation and press work call for skilled crafting; timely production demands industrial efficiency. We describe the technical and business requirements needed to make this blend work well for you.

This book is for everyone who plans, designs, or pays for printing. We wrote it to help you increase control throughout the production sequence. Readers who are not professionals in the graphic arts will find a useful introduction to all types of printing. Graphic arts professionals will learn both how and why their work must conform to technical specifications.

With almost 30,000 commercial and 80,000 in-plant shops, printing is one of the nation's most widely dispersed industries. Shops range from neighborhood businesses run by one person to corporations with hundreds of employees and national clientele. Many printing companies specialize in product categories. For example, only 800 printers make 90% of all business forms and about 1,000 plants make most of the nation's books and large catalogs.

For the customer, the variety, number, and specialization of printers has both good and bad aspects. On the plus side, the business is highly competitive. Shopping pays. On the negative side, it is often hard to judge which printer is right for which job and even harder to know when a printer has given reasonable quality at a fair price.

In this guide we tell you how to find the right printer at the right price for each job.

Matching printers to jobs is especially important with regard to quality standards. We define four categories of quality: basic, good, premium, and showcase. The categories give you and your printers precise language for discussing quality and to help you decide what quality you want for a particular printing job.

We organized this book to follow the sequence of most printing jobs from idea through delivery. Chapter One deals with planning and supervision. In Chapters Two through Five we describe the visual elements of most printed pieces and how they are prepared to go on press. These four chapters cover type, camera-ready copy, photographs, graphic arts negatives, and printing plates.

In Chapter Six we interrupt the sequence of preparation through press work to discuss paper and ink. The chapter explains how mills make paper and defines paper characteristics such as weight and bulk. It describes how to choose papers and how to tell printers what papers and ink colors you want them to use.

Chapters Seven and Eight are devoted to printing processes. Chapter Seven deals with offset lithography, the most popular method of commercial printing. It describes how presses work and the functions of press operators and supervisors. Text and visuals explain what can go wrong with jobs on press, how to keep problems to a minimum, and what to look for when examining products printed to various quality standards. Chapter Eight consists of short descriptions of other printing methods such as letterpress, thermography, and gravure.

Regardless of the method of printing, most jobs require folding, binding, and other finishing steps. Chapter Nine deals with those steps, telling how to prevent problems and monitor quality during the last crucial phase of a job.

Chapter Ten is concerned exclusively with locating, evaluating, and working with printers. It portrays the various kinds of printers and tells how to identify those that are suitable for specific jobs. It explains how to evaluate the final bill and analyse printing trade customs.

At the end of this book are several appendices. Appendix A presents production tips about 110 printed products such as catalogs, labels, and newsletters. For further information, we have included as Appendix C an annotated list of books, periodicals, and trade associations. The three forms in Appendix E are ready to photocopy for your own use in organizing and specifying jobs and recording equipment and services at printing companies.

This volume presents information in several ways in addition to text. Illustrations, examples, and photographs convey concepts that seem most understandable in a visual format. Forms help readers pinpoint needs and record individual information. Checklists relate to quality standards and help spot problems with items such as mechanicals and transparencies. Charts present data in a format allowing for easy comparison when planning or shopping.

For ease of reference, we refer to all illustrations, forms, checklists, charts, examples, and photographs as "visuals." Each visual is numbered by chapter and sequence. For example, Visual 5-5, a checklist about how to evaluate proofs, is the fifth visual in Chapter Five.

A few graphic arts terms, such as "keyline," have different meanings in different parts of the country. In addition, some terms, such as "reverse," that have technical meanings in the graphic arts have other, non-technical meanings. We limited each term to only one meaning, its definition in the glossary, and avoided using a word in any sense other than its technical one. The glossary with definitions of more than 500 graphic arts words may be found as Appendix B.

Graphic arts professionals in the United States use inches to describe distances. Because the inch is standard, we omitted inch marks when writing paper sizes. Persons needing to write specifications using metric units or the ISO system will find instructions and conversion tables in Appendix D.

The three of us have spent much of our lives working in the graphic arts on behalf of ourselves and our clients. During that time, we have heard thousands of stories about every aspect of design and production. To help capture the creative flavor of the profession, we have reproduced 55 of those stories in the words of the people who told them to us. These anecdotes are scattered throughout the book wherever their content seemed appropriate.

We hope you enjoy reading our book and find its information useful. If there are ways you believe this book could be improved, we would appreciate learning your views in a letter addressed to the publisher.

Mark Beach
Steve Shepro
Ken Russon

1

Whether you are a customer of a printer, a graphic arts professional, or both, planning even the most simple printing job requires many decisions. Complex projects may demand hundreds. Each decision affects all the others in the sequence from concept to finished product.

Careful planning is essential to controlling the quality, schedule, and cost of printing jobs. Planning gives a clear vision of the final product, promotes communication among people involved in production, and helps avoid costly changes made after production begins.

Making decisions about printing jobs involves both business and technical information. This chapter focuses on business considerations as a framework for technical decisions. We describe the four types of graphic arts services most commonly used to coordinate printing jobs, explain how work may be affected by copyright laws, and present twelve questions whose answers are keys to effective planning. The chapter includes an explanation of job specifications and why they are crucial to effective management of printing jobs.

In this chapter we include two forms as aids to planning. The Printing Job Organizer helps identify the tasks required to complete most jobs and who will handle them. The Request for Quotation is a specifications form. Both forms are filled out with information about a real printing job and are slightly reduced in size to fit our format for visuals. The forms appear in Appendix E at full size and

Planning Your Printing

ready for you to photocopy and fill out for your own printing jobs.

To fill out either planning form in this chapter requires more technical knowledge than many readers may have as they begin this book. We introduce the forms here to make clear the number and kinds of decisions that managing printing requires. By the end of the book, you will have the knowledge you need to complete the forms.

As a further aid to planning, we introduce in this chapter four categories of printing quality. We refer to these categories frequently throughout this book and summarize their characteristics in Chapter Seven. Let us emphasize that the categories of quality are to classify printing, not to judge it. Controlling costs and schedules includes selecting which quality category is appropriate for a specific job.

Job Coordinators

Getting printing done at the right quality level, on time, and within budget requires careful supervision of each step of the process. For people who must get a specific job done but lack the time or skill to coordinate it, the graphic arts industry has several categories of professionals who can do the work for them.

Printers. Most graphic arts specialties, such as design and typesetting, were once handled exclusively by printers. Many printers still offer these services in addition to printing.

Printers who offer in-house design and typesetting can often produce the entire job, starting with your rough copy and thumbnail sketch.

Other printers subcontract some steps in the production sequence. They may rely on separate businesses for type, color separations, and bindery work. They may even subcontract printing itself instead of working overtime or running a job on a press that would be inefficient for the job.

A few printers build their businesses around the concept of full service. They begin a job when it's only an idea and take it all the way through writing, photography, design, and production. Some full service printers also handle distribution and maintain mailing lists.

Printing brokers. Printing brokers are independent business people who make their living by coordinating printing jobs. Their staff may include a typesetter or production artist, but their profit comes mainly from markups added to the cost of the printing.

"Two years ago I printed circulars for some people planning to exhibit at a trade show. They were just going into business, and they had no way of knowing how many they would need. I suggested they order a conservative amount and promised to keep the plates until after the show. Sure enough, they called me during the middle of the second day to ask for 5,000 more. I delivered circulars the next morning and sealed a business relationship that's been great ever since."

Brokers are specialists in shopping for printing, so may get jobs done for less money than their clients could. They may also get wholesale prices or prices based on their high volume of patronage. Brokers depend on these price advantages to allow them to add their markup while remaining competitive with printers' representatives.

Unlike brokers in many other fields, printing brokers take their fees from the buyer, not the seller. Their business depends on providing satisfactory printing jobs. When evaluating a specific printing broker, ask for references to previous customers.

Advertising agencies. The function of an ad agency is to build an overall plan that may range from corporate logos to television commercials, then carry out the plan by contracting with media and producing messages. Clients hiring an agency assume the campaign will involve some printed products, but may have no specific ideas in mind.

Not all ad agencies deal knowledgeably with printing. Some specialize in broadcast media and others in public relations. If you have printed pieces in mind as part of your ad campaign, make sure an agency you are considering has printing buyers with local experience.

The staff at ad agencies that handle a lot of printing includes copywriters, graphic designers, production artists, and at least one person, either the art director or the production manager, who works with printers. In addition, ad agencies subcontract work to free-lancers.

Graphic designers. Graphic designers build on customers' ideas to create and produce printed messages. The "graphic" part of graphic design refers to art that communicates; the "design" part means planning for efficient, economical production at the appropriate level of quality.

"People who don't know what they are doing with a large printing job could really help themselves by hiring an experienced graphic designer for a few hours as a consultant. It might cost a couple of hundred dollars to get proofs examined or help with doing a press check, but the investment could save thousands."

Like printers, printing brokers, or ad agencies, graphic designers subcontract for services and pass the charges on to clients along with a markup. Often, however, designers stop short of contracting for the printing itself. Not many design studios have sufficient cash flow to broker major printing jobs; most prefer to have the customer contract directly with the printer.

If you are not a graphic arts professional and are coordinating printing for yourself, be sure your graphic designer and printer consult with each other. Unless you have agreed differently, your designer's responsibility stops when you accept mechanicals. To assure appropriate quality at reasonable costs, and to keep alterations to a minimum, the designer must know about the stripping, press, and bindery requirements of the printer.

Working with Coordinators

Few rules or customs govern the relationship between clients and the professionals who coordinate printing on their behalf. Clients cannot assume the coordinator they hire will be responsible for quality, price, or schedule, so must be as clear about what they expect as if they were dealing directly with the printers. Moreover, accountability for the accuracy of final copy lies with the client. Conscientious professionals in the graphic arts ask clients to approve and sign all proofs.

Brokering printing, whether done by a broker, ad agency, or design studio, takes a lot of work, a good credit rating, and faith in the customer's ability to pay. The professional doing it is entitled to a profitable markup. Clients, however, should occasionally ask to see job specifications, quotes, and other evidence that brokers are keeping printing costs competitive.

People in your industry or line of work can recommend local brokers, ad agencies, and designers. So can sales representatives for printers and graphics consultants for paper distributors. Because these people routinely call on agencies and designers, they can recommend services suited to your needs.

Classified directories list ad agencies under categories such as "advertising—direct mail" and "advertising agencies and counselors." Most graphic designers are listed only under their own classification. When you call, state your needs and ask about the kinds of work in which they specialize.

When you talk with previous customers about their experience with a printer or graphic arts service, ask about business practices as well as artistic expression. Find out if the designer keeps appointments and prepares work according to specifications. Learn if the account executive meets deadlines and works well with others. Ask about the average gap between original estimate and final bill.

Agencies and designers soliciting business want to show you their portfolios. When examining samples in a portfolio, remember that they are the best the person has to offer, not the average. Avoid being impressed too quickly.

Hiring expertise in design and production does not exempt you from answering the planning questions outlined later in this chapter. To get the best work from designers and agencies, you must explain your goals and audiences and give them rough ideas about format and budget. If the people who want your business don't ask you planning questions, ask yourself how helpful they will really be. On the other hand, don't waste their time and your money because you have no idea what you want.

There is a fine line between being specific enough to get what you want and general enough to stimulate creativity. Take time to tell a designer or agency about yourself and your organization. The conversation may reveal needs you didn't know you had. For example, if you want presentation folders for a convention, a designer may suggest you also get nametags and notepads with coordinated artwork.

Open-ended discussion with a creative service adds to your control over quality and cost. Be honest about your quality needs. You pay for quality not only at the printer, but in how the designer or agency conceives of the job and prepares it. Describe what you consider appropriate quality for the job by showing samples of other work you find satisfactory.

Agencies and designers charge for their services either by the hour or by the job. Some agencies also commonly charge a retainer which may or may not include hourly rates, but certainly will not include costs of printing. Finally, an agency or designer may mark up printing costs 15% or more.

Some local trade associations of designers and agencies suggest rates for various kinds of work, but most people simply charge what their market will bear. When dealing with a graphic arts professional, ask for an estimate of costs as early in the process as possible. Recognize that you are paying for help with planning, so precise costs cannot be known until the planning is done. Insist, however, on a detailed cost projection before authorizing production to begin.

Although we advise getting cost estimates from agencies and designers, we do not recommend getting competitive prices for every project. On the contrary, we urge that you build long-term business relationships with creative services. These services should be constantly monitored and occasionally compared to alternatives, but the best work will come from people who become familiar with your goals, organization, and staff.

Experienced printing buyers know when they need professional help. Whether or not you are a graphic arts professional, specific jobs may have unfamiliar or time-consuming aspects that someone else should handle. Looking at Visual 1-6 will help identify the production stages of most printing jobs. By using this form, you can establish a production schedule and pinpoint who is responsible for each stage.

Printing jobs involve many people. Each person's duties affect how others do their work. Most printing jobs also involve changes between idea and production. When a change is made, everyone working on the job should learn about it immediately. Using the Printing Job Organizer will remind you of everyone who must know about changes as the job progresses.

"I thought I was pretty smart designing a rack brochure 9¼ inches high to stick out above the others. I realized my mistake when it was time to mail them to last year's visitors. My oversized brochures were too big to be machine-stuffed into #10 envelopes."

Planning Jobs

Getting printing done at the quality level you want and within your budget and schedule calls for answers to many questions. Details will emerge as plans develop, but the general outline should remain.

What is your purpose? You may want the printed piece to entertain, warn, sell, or inspire. Maybe it is for keeping records, impressing clients, recruiting members, or gaining customers. A list of goals will help you answer questions about design, quality, quantity, and cost. For example, a brochure intended to build membership in a trade association might include a postpaid response card.

Who is your audience? Your message may be for customers, members, employees who know you already, or for readers who have never heard of you. Your readers may be old or young, men or women, active or sedentary.

As you define your audience, think of traits which affect design. A poster advertising a rock concert should look very different from one announcing a philosophy lecture. If your average reader is older than 50, give extra thought to how type size may affect legibility.

What is your competition doing? Every printed message competes for the attention, memory, and action of readers. If you're preparing a catalog, try to imagine it completed and on a shelf or coffee table along with other catalogs. Yours needs the right colors and size to stand out. Your promotional calendar's design, paper, and ink must look good when compared to others from organizations similar to yours.

"I was supposed to make our newsletter look better, but didn't know how. I'm a good secretary, but I'm not an artist at all. Someone in marketing helped me persuade my boss to let me hire a graphic designer. The designer made us a nameplate that we preprint for color, developed a format that I use every month, and helped us make an annual printing contract. I worked with the designer to create a format that would be efficient on my word processor. With that professional help, our newsletter not only looks better but gets done faster and costs less. What a relief!"

Thinking about the competition suggests what quality you need. Engraved, watermarked stationery may seem pretentious if everyone else is using the local quick printer. If you are an aspiring doctor, however, a quick-printed letterhead might encourage patients to think speed is your approach to surgery, too. Stay consistent with the best standards set by others similar to yourself.

Competition is a fact of life. Recognize that fact by thinking about the vast number of other messages trying to reach your readers. Even the solitary skywriter on a cloudless day must somehow attract people to lift their eyes.

What will the printed piece say? With communication goals clearly in mind, try to imagine specific words, photos, illustrations, and graphics. Good content is easy to discuss in the abstract, but difficult to produce in the concrete. Take plenty of time to write, then to test the writing on typical readers.

Poor writing can ruin a printed piece as easily as poor design. Equally important, a red editing pencil applied to a manuscript cuts production costs faster than any other tool. Every word, sentence, or paragraph eliminated saves on typesetting, paper, and printing. Be careful, however, that information is complete and accurate. Changes during later stages of production are expensive.

How will the piece look? Words carry information, but design transmits image. Even in the earliest phases of planning you have some ideas about design. You imagine a handsome annual report, efficient form, or enticing catalog. You have in mind size and approximate page count. Knowing goals, audience, and budget shapes your vision.

Your concept of yourself, your business, organization, or client also affects design. Should your audience perceive you as dignified or informal, conservative or speculative? Do you offer products, sales, or services? Answers to questions such as these help stimulate the creative processes of writing and designing. The answers also influence decisions about ink colors, papers, and printing quality.

Good design builds effective communication. The right mix of type and visuals makes

Sample Production Schedule for Stationery

Weeks	1	2	3	4	5	6	7	8
Design logo/typography	▓							
Approve design		▓						
Specifications to printers		▓						
Final art and typesetting		▓						
Paste up mechanicals			▓					
Proofread mechanicals			▓					
Correct mechanicals			▓					
Select printer			▓					
Camera work/stripping			▓					
Make blueline proofs			▓					
Proofread bluelines			▓					
Plate and die making				▓				
Printing/embossing				▓				
Bindery work				▓				

1-1 Sample production schedule for stationery. Visual 1-1 could be a schedule to produce 2,500 letterheads with matching envelopes and 500 business cards, all printed with two colors and embossed. Production is in the good quality category. The 20-working-day schedule begins with designing the logo and layout.

messages clear, complete, and memorable. Designers must, however, also consider costs.

Few projects have unlimited budgets. Costs can be kept under control by sticking with standard sizes and formats. For example, standard paper and press sizes are based on multiples and divisions of 8½ x 11. File folders, report covers, and #10 business envelopes are built around this size. A poster might be 17 x 22 (four times 8½ x 11) printed two up on a 23 x 35 sheet (eight times 8½ x 11 plus an extra inch for press grippers and trimming). Books and catalogs are most efficiently printed with page counts in multiples of four, eight, or sixteen.

Many printed pieces are custom designed, but others look fine on preprinted layouts. Colorful award certificates, for example, need only artful lettering of names and dates. Off-the-shelf business and legal forms often have perfectly functional designs and the space for imprinting individual information.

When do you need the job delivered? Customers often do not allow enough time for jobs to be at the printer. Some customers imagine that commercial or specialty printing will take only a little longer than quick printing.

A routine job at a commercial print shop typically takes about ten working days, starting when you deliver camera-ready mechanicals. Typesetting and layout can easily add another two weeks. Writing, editing, and approvals can add another two weeks before that. For complicated jobs and when things go wrong, these times can easily double.

Visuals 1-1 through 1-5 show possible production schedules for five common jobs. The times shown are based on the assumption that everything goes smoothly. Printing jobs, however, especially complex ones, rarely go smoothly. Your schedule could possibly be 50% or even 100% longer for any of the jobs shown.

A printer's ability to deliver on schedule

Sample Production Schedule for a Poster

Weeks	1	2	3	4	5	6	7	8
Write copy/design	▓							
Type copy/make headlines	▓							
Paste up mechanicals	▓							
Proofread mechanicals	▓							
Make photocopy proof	▓							
Platemaking	▓							
Printing	▓							

1-2 Sample production schedule for a poster. Quick printing would be appropriate to produce 400 two-color, 11 x 17, basic quality posters. The 5-working-day schedule represented above begins with writing copy and assumes using a typewriter for body copy, transfer lettering for headlines, and border tape for rules.

depends on many factors. Customers control some of them: submitting mechanicals on time and in good condition, reading proofs promptly, keeping alterations to a minimum, handling payments as agreed. Printers control others: scheduling jobs through various departments, ordering paper and ink early enough, and maintaining good business relationships with trade shops, binderies, and other subcontractors. Sometimes fate steps in: the printer's number one account demands priority press time, blizzards block all roads from paper mills, or proofs show a photograph featuring an employee who just got fired.

Printers are constantly juggling jobs within the shop to assure more efficient use of machines and people. Good customers may get priority, but "first in, first out" is the rule of thumb for most shops.

Realistic scheduling demands honesty between you and your printer. If your mechanicals may be late, say so. Also be fair. If you can accept a partial shipment, don't insist on full delivery; if Monday morning is soon enough, don't insist on Friday afternoon.

Keep in mind how delivery methods may affect schedules. Mailing services require two or three working days to address, bundle, and get materials to the post office. First class mail takes another two or three days to reach its destination, but third class bulk mail may require two weeks. Figure for weekends and holidays, too. U.S. mail moves at least a little bit every day of the week, but many commercial carriers work only five days.

To stay on schedule, set your final deadline in consultation with your printer and stick to deadlines that apply to you. For every day you are late with mechanicals, expect your job to be delayed by at least one day. If you miss deadlines, your job may be rushed too fast to achieve the quality you want or you may be charged for overtime rates. Dependable customers get dependable service.

When planning how long it will take to produce your printed piece, keep in mind the time required to write copy. Writing may take longer and cost more than printing, but the time and money must be taken into account as part of the overall job. In practice, the writing and design schedules often overlap.

How many pieces do you need? A wrong decision about quantity raises costs. Because of additional setup charges, going to press a second time makes unit costs higher than printing all you need in one run. Also, unit price goes down as quantity goes up, so one large order costs less per piece than several consecutive small orders. For example, 5,000 maps might cost $2.75 each if run all at once. Printing 3,000 now and 2,000 later might increase the unit cost of the entire 5,000 to $3.90.

Sample Production Schedule for a Newsletter

Weeks	1	2	3	4	5	6	7	8
Edit copy/write headlines	▓							
Make rough layout	▓							
Fit copy	▓							
Crop and scale photos	▓							
Typesetting	▓							
Proofread galleys		▓						
Correct type		▓						
Paste up mechanicals		▓						
Proofread mechanicals		▓						
Correct mechanicals		▓						
Camera work/stripping			▓					
Make blueline proofs			▓					
Proofread blueline			▓					
Correct negatives			▓					
Platemaking				▓				
Printing				▓				
Bindery work				▓				
Addressing/mailing				▓				

1-3 Sample production schedule for a newsletter. Producing 5,000 copies of an 8½ x 11, two-color, eight-page newsletter with 15 halftones might take 21 working days if everything went smoothly. Bindery work includes drilling for loose-leaf binding and folding to fit #10 business envelopes. Production is in the good quality category. The schedule assumes that copy is already written, format established, and type specified, and that the printer is the same one contracted during previous issues. It begins with editing and getting approvals for copy.

Generously estimating needs might save money, especially because next year printing will probably cost more than this year. Yet today's cost of the job is important. Large quantities are wasted if new information makes your piece obsolete or your market turns out to be smaller than anticipated. Cash tied up in printed inventory might be better invested elsewhere.

Choosing the right quantity is one of the toughest judgments about any print job. To help decide, ask people who will use the product for their best guess about how many they need. Remember to account for damage during packing, transit, or storage. Think also about circumstances that could mean needing either more or less than what now seems like enough. Finally, get prices for printing two or three quantities greater than your immediate needs. You might discover a price break, a number over which unit costs drop significantly.

We recommend being conservative about quantities. More customers regret having too many than wish they had more. A year's supply of most products is plenty and is often too much. New forms might be revised in two months; established forms might be obsolete in six months.

Although the matter of quantity may be largely guesswork, it does have a bright aspect. Once the guess is made, it can be expressed clearly. No one should be confused when you state the number you want printed. But be careful. Most printers follow the trade custom allowing delivery of 10% over or under the amount ordered. If you need 1,000 folders and will be in trouble if you get only 950 or even 975, make this clear when you place your order.

How will readers use the printed piece? People read books gradually, but signs at a glance. Readers sort quickly through newsletters and direct mailings, more slowly through brochures and catalogs. Considering how printed pieces will be used leads to decisions about quality of paper, ink, binding, and protective coatings. A menu must be strong at the fold, resist spills and greasy fingers, and be readable in low light.

Thinking about use includes considering life expectancy. One loose-leaf binder may be used only during a weekend workshop, while another must last years as a reference tool. If your catalog must serve two years, consider a separate price sheet that can be changed every few months.

How will other businesses work with the printed piece? Printed pieces must often coordinate with other products and services. Labels must fit bottles and instruction sheets fold to fit boxes. Show a dummy to people who will handle your piece to be sure it meets their needs.

Printing customers often run into problems when they take their products to mailing services. Machines for folding, inserting, addressing, and sealing may not handle the pieces. If you are managing printing for direct mail advertising, be sure to coordinate carefully with your mailing service.

"The most important thing I learned during my first year as advertising manager was how many dollars it takes just to get complicated jobs ready for printing. We can spend thousands on writers, photographers, editors, typesetters, and designers, and then thousands more for mechanicals, proofs, and plates. Now I'm experienced enough to be alert to those expenses ahead of time. If some department wants elaborate work but only a small quantity, I make its people convince me that those high unit costs are really justified."

How will the piece reach your audience? Perhaps the message will be included in an envelope with other printed pieces such as a business reply envelope and flier. If so, you may need matching papers and coordinated sizes. When planning stationery or direct mailings, remember that envelopes in standard sizes and colors cost less and are more readily available than custom-made envelopes.

Materials for mailing must meet requirements of size, shape, weight, folds, colors, and seals. A business reply card must be rectangular, in a light color that contrasts with the bar codes, and no less than .007 inches thick. Most brochures do not have to be sealed, but their folded edges must face right to accommodate right-handed sorting procedures.

Before making final decisions about design, show a dummy of your piece to a postal official and ask for a signature affirming that it meets the standards of the class of mail you have in mind. The official who signs your dummy should work at the post office where you plan to mail. Avoid being unhappily surprised by a regulation you never heard of or a worker at another post office who interprets rules differently.

Some products need special packaging. Books with plastic comb bindings must be carefully alternated within boxes to prevent crushing the bindings. Paper goods must be protected from moisture. If the standards of your industry are to ship in dozens, tell your printer to pack in boxes with 12, 24, or 36 units. Consider box weight and size. Shippers have a variety of requirements which, if not met, mean they can turn down your goods.

What is your budget? During early planning, it may be impossible to say how much you will spend for a specific job. It should be possible, however, to develop some rough estimates. Experience with previous jobs and knowledge of local rates will help you make educated guesses about the cost of many products.

It's easy to underestimate the cost of design and other work done on a project long before it gets to the printer. Professional writers, photographers, illustrators, and graphic designers cost money, whether they are on your staff or are free-lancers. The money that they cost is

Sample Production Schedule for a Catalog

Weeks	1	2	3	4	5	6	7	8
Make comprehensive layout	▓							
Approve comp		▓						
Specifications to printers		▓						
Specify type		▓						
Typesetting		▓						
Proofread galleys			▓					
Correct type			▓					
Select printer			▓					
Paste up mechanicals			▓					
Proofread mechanicals				▓				
Correct mechanicals				▓				
Separate transparencies				▓	▓			
Approve separations					▓			
Camera work/stripping						▓		
Make blueline proofs						▓		
Proofread blueline							▓	
Make 4-color proofs							▓	
Examine 4-color proofs							▓	
Correct negatives							▓	
Platemaking							▓	
Printing							▓	▓
Bindery work								▓
Delivery								▓

1-4 Sample production schedule for a catalog. A schedule to produce 20,000 copies of a 16-page, 8½ x 11, 4-color process catalog involves many variables. The catalog represented in this example is printed in the premium quality category and has 31 color separations. It includes a separate, 4-page cover and an order form and will be saddle stitched. The 38-working-day schedule assumes that photography and copy are already done and approved. This catalog is the same product planned in Visual 1-6 and specified in Visual 1-8.

appropriate for all jobs which must read well, look good, and print efficiently, but should not be overlooked when computing the total cost of the job.

Experienced printing buyers keep budgets in perspective by thinking about fixed and variable costs. Fixed costs stay the same whether you print one copy or one million and include design, typesetting, and printer preparation. Variable costs include the price of paper, press time, and bindery operations that go up or down as quantities change.

Fixed costs must be taken into account when determining unit price. For example, $1,000 for a nameplate design to appear on 1,000 newsletters means the nameplate costs a dollar per copy. Putting the same nameplate on 50,000 newsletters cuts the unit cost to two cents. The designer that seemed a luxury for 1,000 copies is a bargain for 50,000.

One way to approach budget planning is to estimate how much the job is worth to you when properly done. A brochure that sells $30,000 cars is worth far more than one that sells $30 books. Even if the product you have in mind doesn't lead directly to financial profit, you hope it will produce specific results. You must decide how highly you value those results and what you are willing to pay to achieve them.

Quality Expectations

The market for printing ranges from simple, one-color fliers and forms to complicated, full-color books and art reproductions. Few individual printers, however, try to handle jobs spanning the entire range of quality levels. Most printers limit themselves to working within one or two of the quality categories described in the following paragraphs.

Because the range of quality among printed pieces and printers is so great, planning printing requires decisions about how good the product must be. Customers who know exactly what quality they want can plan realistic schedules and budgets and select printers who can do the work properly.

Throughout this book we refer to four categories of printing quality. We define the categories here and elaborate on the definitions in many other places. Visual 7-8 gives details about 14 features of each quality category.

"When we opened the new store on the east side, sales representatives from two printers were among the first people to walk through the door. One thought I would buy printing because the two of us could swap fishing stories. The other arrived with samples of our own brochures and catalogs from previous printings and showed me how we could raise our quality and still cut costs. That rep had done plenty of homework before getting to my office. You don't have to guess who has had most of our business ever since. And she doesn't take us for granted, either. We still get great service."

Basic printing. Basic quality printing gets the job done reasonably well without losing legibility. Basic quality pieces are usually in one ink color only; photographs are recognizable, but may have lost detail from the originals. Conscientious quick printers produce basic quality as their everyday work. Political or advertising fliers, business forms, and newsletters are usually printed basic quality.

Good printing. Good quality printing involves standard materials and quality control. Colors are strong, color photos pleasing, black and white photos crisp, register tight but not perfect. Most commercial shops do good printing routinely. Average direct mail catalogs, most hardcover books, retail packaging, and magazines such as *Time* and *Newsweek* show good quality printing.

Premium printing. Premium quality printing requires careful attention to detail and high-grade materials. Color photographs almost match original transparencies and black and white photos appear very sharp. Products printed in the premium category have few flaws and seem almost perfect to people who are not graphic arts professionals. Many commercial printers can do premium printing when schedules and budgets permit. This category includes the better direct mail catalogs and magazines such as *National Geographic.*

Showcase printing. Showcase quality printing combines the best machines and materials, and artisans who give scrupulous attention to detail. Everything from design to paper is first class. Color photos come as close as possible to matching objects or original scenes. The category of showcase printing consists of products which themselves are forms of art that only a few printing buyers can afford or printers can achieve. It includes museum grade art books, brochures advertising very expensive automobiles, and the finest annual reports.

Each printing job has its own appropriate quality level. There is no reason to take a simple catalog to a printer specializing in showcase quality annual reports or to pay a $100 per hour graphic designer to coordinate basic quality printing. We devised this system of quality categories to help you decide what level of printing

Sample Production Schedule for a Book

Weeks	1	2	3	4	5	6	7	8	9	10	11	12	13	14	15	16	17	18	19	20
Edit manuscript	▒	▒																		
Author reviews editing			▒																	
Author/editor negotiations				▒																
Prepare photos and art		▒	▒	▒																
Final editing					▒															
Proofread manuscript						▒														
Design book			▒	▒	▒															
Design cover				▒	▒															
Specify type					▒															
Typesetting						▒	▒													
Write printing specifications					▒															
Printers prepare quotes							▒													
Proofread galleys							▒													
Correct type							▒													
Lay out text								▒	▒											
Revise type									▒											
Prepare index									▒											
Typeset index										▒										
Select/contract printer										▒										
Paste up mechanicals										▒	▒	▒								
Proofread mechanicals												▒	▒							
Correct mechanicals														▒						
Camera work/stripping															▒					
Make blueline proofs																▒				
Proofread bluelines																	▒			
Correct negatives																	▒			
Platemaking																	▒			
Printing																		▒		
Bindery work																			▒	
Shipping																				▒

1-5 Sample production schedule for a book. A schedule to produce 5,000 copies of a 192-page, 5 x 8 book with 18 halftones and 10 line drawings would be expressed in weeks, not days as with other schedules in this series. The book has a two-color cover, is perfect bound, is produced to good quality standards, and is shipped 1,000 miles from printer to publisher. The 18-week schedule begins with editing manuscript and assumes that author, publisher, and typesetter all deal with the manuscript electronically via modem. It also assumes an experienced job coordinator, not one who oversees a book only occasionally. The book you are reading was written and edited using a word processor and took about three years to complete, beginning when the authors agreed to collaborate.

you want, select printers who can produce to that standard, and keep materials and production skills consistent throughout the job.

Once you have chosen a printer, you must decide whether you want your job treated routinely or with special care. Routine work might be suitable for your directory, but not for your convention program. You must tell the printer how much attention you want and recognize that extra attention will raise the price.

It is imperative to understand that we use these four quality categories to classify printing, not to criticize or praise it. Criticism is for the printer who promises work created to a certain standard, then doesn't produce it; praise is for the printer who honestly describes what the shop can make, then delivers exactly what the customer was led to expect.

All components of a printing job should be kept within the same category of quality. By components we mean specific features such as type, paper, print quality, and design. Components below the average quality level for the job drag down the others; components above average don't look as good as they should, thus are a waste of time and money.

Consider a poster advertising an arts festival. The poster includes photographs and lettering from top professionals who planned their work to appear on premium paper. Using ordinary paper would be false economy because it would not reflect the quality of the other components. It makes sense to use a premium paper and to work with a printer who has precision equipment and a reputation for extra attention to detail.

Quantity needs, costs, and deadlines, as well as quality requirements, affect which printers are right for your job. The arts festival poster could be printed to the same quality by a small, medium, or large commercial printer. The small printer might give the best unit price for 2,000 posters, the medium-sized printer be

"I've taken my last two jobs to ABC Litho without even getting prices from other printers. ABC costs more, but those projects had absolutely no room for error. I'll always pay a few extra dollars for dependable work."

most efficient for 10,000, and the large printer best for 50,000. The printer with the lowest price, however, might not be able to get the job done most quickly.

Organizing Jobs

Many people can be involved in getting a printing job from idea to finished piece. A list of tasks and who is responsible for them helps keep the job on schedule and may point up potential problems or delays.

Visual 1-6 is a form on which to identify everyone involved in production. The sample information written onto the form deals with a catalog for a fictitious company owned by Angela Williams. John Brighton is marketing manager for the company and David Netsuka is his assistant. Susan Preston is a graphic designer whose studio works with Brighton and his staff.

When using this form, it is important to know who the job coordinator is. In this example, John Brighton is coordinator because he is marketing director of the company publishing the catalog. Had Susan Preston been employed by the company instead of being free-lance, she might have coordinated the job.

Notice that it's the responsibility of the coordinator to keep track of every aspect of the job. John Brighton involves his boss Angela Williams at appropriate points. He manages his staff and works with Susan Preston.

The Printing Job Organizer is designed to fit the requirements of a variety of printing jobs. Many jobs will not call for all the activities listed on the form, but others may require several more. You can see that the summer catalog will not have illustrations or charts, but will involve mailing services. When you fill out the form for your own job, start by striking out the activities not relevant to the job and adding those not printed on the form.

During the early planning of many jobs, you do not know who will do the printing or perform some of the other graphic arts services. In our example, the color separation service and paper distributor as well as the printer will be chosen later in the process. All we could show here was who will make the selection.

Job Name SUMMER CATALOG   Coordinator JOHN BRIGHTON   Date 1-9-87

Function	Person Responsible	Supplier
Write copy	DAVID NETSUKA	
Edit copy	JOHN BRIGHTON	
Proofread copy	NETSUKA	
Approve copy	ANGELA WILLIAMS	
Make rough layout	BRIGHTON	PRESTON DESIGN
Approve rough layout	BRIGHTON	
Make comp and dummy	BRIGHTON	PRESTON DESIGN
Approve comp and dummy	WILLIAMS	
Choose typesetter	SUSAN PRESTON	
Specify type and mark up copy	PRESTON	
Set type	PRESTON	DIGITYPE
Proofread type	BRIGHTON + PRESTON	
Create illustrations		
Create charts, graphs, maps		
Create/select photographs	BRIGHTON	CRONISE PHOTOS
Approve visual elements	WILLIAMS	
Miscellaneous camera work	PRESTON	AD CAMERA

1-6 Printing job organizer. Even small printing jobs involve many of the tasks shown above. Large jobs may require them all plus more. Use this list to help plan for effective management. The job described above is the catalog scheduled in

Function	Person Responsible	Supplier
Choose production artist	PRESTON	
Paste up mechanicals	PRESTON	PRESTON DESIGN
Proofread mechanicals	BRIGHTON	
Approve mechanicals	WILLIAMS	
Choose/specify trade services	BRIGHTON + PRESTON	
Make halftones/separations	PRESTON	?
Approve proofs of photographs	WILLIAMS + BRIGHTON	
Select paper	BRIGHTON + PRESTON	?
Write printing specifications	BRIGHTON + PRESTON	
Select possible printers	BRIGHTON + PRESTON	
Obtain bids from printers	BRIGHTON	
Choose printer	BRIGHTON + PRESTON	
Contract with printer	BRIGHTON	
Approve proofs from printer	WILLIAMS + BRIGHTON	
Do printing	BRIGHTON	?
Approve press sheets	BRIGHTON	
Do bindery work	PRINTER	?
MAILING	BRIGHTON	QUICK-OUT MAILING
Verify job done per specifications	BRIGHTON	
Verify charges for alterations	BRIGHTON	
Verify mechanicals and art returned	BRIGHTON	
Pay printer and trade services	WILLIAMS	

Visual 1-4 and specified in Visual 1-8. In this fictitious example, John Brighton is marketing director for a company using Sandra Preston as graphic designer. A full-size, blank version of this form appears in Appendix E.

Copyright Laws

Clients and graphic arts vendors must be aware of how copyright laws affect business agreements. Free-lance writers, graphic designers, illustrators, and photographers own rights to their creative works. A logo, technical drawing, or photograph is the property of the artist who made it, even when the image was made on commission for a client, unless the contract between client and artist has a specific provision to the contrary.

Copyright protection extends to services that may not be regarded as creative because they are not perceived as artistic. For example, commercial printers may do design work and always make negatives as they prepare a job. They own rights to the design and own the negatives as physical property. If a typesetter writes a computer program to interface with a personal computer, the typesetter owns rights to the program even if a customer paid for the work.

Often clients assume incorrectly that paying for creative work automatically entitles them to use it any way they wish. Under copyright law, clients buy licenses to use creative work with specific products. For example, if you hire a photographer to make a series of photos for an annual report, the photographer has the right to an additional fee when the photos are used in a brochure. Of course, the photographer could agree to sell you "all rights" instead of merely "annual report rights," but might charge more to give up potential future income from the photos.

Writers, artists, and photographers should protect their own interests and help clients avoid disappointment by dealing with copyright issues early in negotiations for new jobs. As graphic arts vendors help clients define needs, they should also inform them about how copyright laws might affect the work under discussion. Vendors and clients are free to negotiate any transfer of rights they find mutually agreeable, but should express their agreement clearly in writing before work begins.

For people who have created work that they want to copyright, the procedure is easy. They are legally protected simply by putting their name, the copyright symbol, and the year of creation on the work itself. For example, art appearing on a banner might include in small lettering "© 1987 Outdoor Design Group." A form designed by the owner of a small business could include the notice "Copyright 1988 Quick Muffler Shop." The fact that a creative work carries copyright information when it appears in public means that it is protected.

To establish an exact date of copyright, you can fill out a form available from the Copyright Office, pay a small fee, and send examples of your creation for official registration. The formal procedure is necessary before defending a copyright in court or to have it honored in other countries. U.S. copyright laws are administered by the Copyright Office of the Library of Congress, Washington DC 20559.

For detailed information about copyright laws, consult the books by Norman Beil, Tad Crawford, Leonard Duboff, William Strong, and Ben Weil cited in Appendix C.

Involving a Printer

For any but those jobs you consider routine, talk with a printer as early in the planning as possible. When planning a large or complicated job, consult with more than one printer.

Discussing possible jobs with customers is part of a printer's marketing. Describe your needs and ask whether your piece can be printed practically. Consider suggestions about alternate papers, design changes, and other ideas about how to save time and money. Every job is unique and every printer has an individual mix of equipment, skills, and materials. A printer may even find ways to do the job better and cheaper than you thought possible.

"Two years ago we paid a commercial artist to airbrush a scene for the cover of our university catalog. I had specified exactly what I wanted in the illustration. Last month I saw the image used in a corporate annual report. I felt cheated. I always thought that the university owned art and photos that we commissioned. Not so. Our lawyer told me that artists usually hold the copyright and can sell their work to other clients."

thumbnail rough

comprehensive layout, or comp

folding dummy

Although discussing jobs with printers is useful, remember that they want your business. By suggesting changes which take advantage of particular presses or papers, a printer may be shaping your job to fit that shop. Keep in mind that you are getting consultation and may not be ready to write specifications.

When talking with a printer, it's useful to have a dummy to help visualize the final printed piece. Depending on your experience and planning needs, the dummy might be anything from a simple thumbnail rough to a comprehensive layout that looks much like the final product. The printer can keep the dummy for a few days as one basis for estimating prices.

A dummy showing bindery needs can be made by folding one or two sheets of paper to simulate the format you want. On larger jobs, such as books and annual reports, a paper distributor will assemble and bind a dummy to your specifications. If you need a dummy of 128 pages, 8½ x 11, 60# ivory vellum, perfect bound with a 10 point cover, ask for it from your printer or paper representative.

A kind of dummy known as a thumbnail rough can be made by sketching in areas of type, art, and photos. You could even create a dummy looking nearly like the finished piece by making it to the exact size and adding colors and transfer type. This comprehensive layout, known simply as a "comp," tells the printer precisely how you expect the job will look.

Examining roughs, comps, and other dummies helps anticipate production problems. Dummies help printers think about practicalities such as ink coverage and accuracy of folding. A printer looking at exactly what you have in mind may suggest printing smaller solids or point out that borders may not line up properly when sheets are assembled.

1-7 Dummies. Making a thumbnail rough helps plan a production schedule and budget. The next stage of development, the comp, shows type and colors to help clients and supervisors visualize the final product. A folding dummy also helps make your needs clear to postal officials, production artists, printers, and people at binderies and mailing services.

As you look at a dummy with a printer, some specifications will already be clear in your mind. You'll probably know at least how many copies you want and when. The printer's comments will help pin down other facts such as what kind of paper you need. When discussing ink colors, both you and the printer should refer to a color matching system as described in the ink section of Chapter Six.

To get the quality you want, tell the printer what you expect. If you demand close register and vivid colors, say so. If you wonder about the printer's ability to hold shadow detail in photographs, ask. Also ask for examples of the printer's work that are similar to your job. Study them carefully, knowing that they represent the shop's best work, not its average.

Writing Specifications

Every printing job, even the most simple and routine, should be specified in writing. Written specifications assure clear communications between you, the printers that you ask for prices, and the printer to whom you give the job. The kind of information required for good specifications is written on the Request for Quotation form, Visual 1-8.

Good specifications are complete, accurate, and written in language printers understand. They are important for several reasons.

Assure accurate comparisons. When each shop quotes on the same specifications, you can compare prices accurately and fairly.

Look professional. Clear, carefully written specifications convey to printers that you know what you are doing and that you expect quality and attentive service.

Provide a checklist. Specifications help you review the entire production sequence and save you time in getting quotes. They make it obvious if you forgot an important detail.

Keep costs down. Specifications written on a form which is then photocopied notify printers that you are soliciting competitive bids.

Reduce guesswork. With good specifications, printers can figure costs exactly, identify ways to save money, and spot potential problems in the production sequence.

Help monitor changes. Almost every set of specifications changes at least a little as the job goes through the production process. With the original specifications as a guide, you can keep track of alterations.

Make payment easier. By comparing the final bill to the specifications, you can see exactly what was called for, what was done, and how alterations affected the final price.

Good specifications do not prevent printers from making suggestions. In fact, good specifications encourage thinking about options. Even though you welcome alternatives, insist on knowing a price based on your original specifications. That dollar figure is an important basis for comparing printers.

We cannot overemphasize the need for clear specifications set forth in writing and accompanied by a dummy, rough, or photocopy of mechanicals. Even the most simple job can run into problems, so don't make printers guess about anything. Make everything clear by writing it down and, when you can, by providing an example.

Requesting Quotations

There is no standard specifications form in the graphic arts industry. Many printing buyers have developed their own. The form shown as Visual 1-8 is based on the numerous forms we have seen. It is filled out with specifications for the summer catalog job described in the Printing Job Organizer.

The Request for Quotation form, the example information entered on it, and our instructions about how to fill it out use technical terms that may be unfamiliar. All the terms are defined in the glossary and are discussed in detail in subsequent chapters.

"I had to argue in staff meetings for a year before being authorized to send specifications for our catalogs to several printers for their bids, but finally got approval. My boss was amazed at the results. There was a 50% cost difference between the highest and lowest quotations. I know professional printing buyers who consider that percentage typical."

When you fill out this form, begin by identifying the job and the printing buyer. A simple job name will work for purposes of discussion and information retrieval. Write a convenient name such as "Western directory" or "Riverfront brochure." Give the job a number only if needed for your records or procedures. The printing company will assign the job a number for its own records.

The contact person is the person responsible for discussing the specifications with printers. Usually it's the person filling out the form. The business name is that of your organization, and its address and phone number are where the contact person can be reached.

The first date called for is the date the form is being filled out. The date the quote is needed is the day on which you need to know estimates from all printers receiving the specifications. The date the job goes to the printer is when you estimate mechanicals and loose art will be completely ready for the printer, final specifications decided, and work by the printer authorized to begin. The date the job is needed is when you need the job delivered. Be realistic in setting this date. A tight schedule could increase cost or decrease quality.

On the line asking what kind of quote you need, check whether you need a firm figure or would be satisfied with a rough estimate; whether you would be satisfied with a conversation or need a price in writing. If you are asking for a firm quote, get it in writing.

The job is new if it has never been printed. It's an exact reprint if the printer has done it once and has negatives or plates on file. If this job is a reprint with changes, write a brief note about the changes. Use the space at the bottom of the second page if you need more room.

The quantity line allows for several options. The first number should be your ideal quantity. The other quantities you specify may help you find a price break. Ask for prices on other quantities only if you would seriously consider printing that many. The end of the line allows asking the cost of additional 100s or 1000s above the highest number specified. Prices for additional 100s or 1000s are for printing them as part of this job, not for printing them as a repeat job at some future date.

To specify quality, use the categories developed earlier in this chapter. For more precise descriptions of those categories, see Visual 7-8. Use the lines for miscellaneous instructions at the end of the form to write comments about special quality considerations.

The format of the job should be described in standard terms such as "business card" or "rack brochure." A job consisting of a single, flat sheet should be described by its trim size, such as 8½ x 11 flier. If a single sheet will be folded, give its folded size, such as 8½ x 3¾. Items such as books, catalogs, and magazines, should be described by the dimension of their pages after being bound and trimmed.

When writing the number of pages, remember that every sheet, or leaf, in a bound item, such as a directory or book, counts as two pages. Even leaves with no printing on them must be included in this count. An 11 x 17 sheet folded in half makes an 8½ x 11 piece with four pages. Books, catalogs, magazines, and other bound products have a number of pages divisible by four.

Self-cover means that the cover consists of the same paper as the inside pages. If the cover paper is different from paper inside, the product is said to be "plus cover."

If the printed piece consists of anything in addition to a cover and inside pages, refer the estimator to miscellaneous instructions at the end of the form. Additional items might include a separate order form or envelope insert.

On the design features line, indicate whether there will be bleeds, tints, or reverses

"All the really good printers in town know that our studio works with clients that always demand top quality, but that we also provide mechanicals and specifications they can depend on. We are professional enough never to cost a printer extra money. When I send out requests for quotations, I tell all the sales reps that I plan to accept a quote somewhere near the middle of the range of bids for the job. I don't want some estimator to quote under cost to win my business, and then try to rush the job through or have to cut corners on quality in order to make a profit."

Job name ___SUMMER CATALOG___   Date _3/2/87_

Contact person ___JOHN BRIGHTON___   Date quote needed _3/9/87_

Business name ___WILLIAMS MARKETING___   Date job to printer _3/19/87_

Address ___919 SECOND AVENUE, ANTELOPE USA 10123___   Date job needed _4/15/87_

Phone __800-282-5800__ Please give ☑firm quote ☐rough estimate ☐verbally ☑in writing

This is a ☑new job ☐exact reprint ☐reprint with changes _____

Quantity 1) _25,000_   2) _30,000_   3) _40,000_   ☑additional _1,000_ s

Quality ☐basic ☐good ☑premium ☐showcase comments _CRITICAL FABRIC MATCH_

Format product description _CATALOG WITH ORDER FORM INSERT_

flat trim size ____ x ____   folded/bound size _8½_ x _11_

# of pages _16_ ☐self cover ☑plus cover

Design features ☑bleeds ☑screen tints # _60_ ☑reverses # _20_ ☑comp enclosed

Art ☑camera-ready ☐printer to typeset and paste up (manuscript and rough layout attached)

☐plate-ready negatives with proofs to printer's specifications

trade shop name and contact person _____

Mechanicals color breaks ☐on acetate overlays ☑shown on tissues # pieces separate line art _4_

Halftones ☐halftones # ____ ☐duotones # ____

Separations ☑from transparencies # _30_ ☑from reflective copy # _1_ ☐provided # ____

finished sizes of separations _5@3×5; 8@8½×11; 10@4×4; 8@5×8_

Proofs ☐galley ☐page ☑blueline ☑loose color ☑composite color ☐progressive

Paper	weight	name	color	finish	grade
cover	80#	SUPERCOTE	WHITE	GLOSS	COVER
inside	70#	SNOWLIGHT	WHITE	GLOSS	COATED BOOK
INSERT	70#	RYAN OPAQUE	CREAM	VELLUM	UNCOATED BOOK

☐send samples of paper ☐make dummy buy paper from _RIVER PAPER_

1-8 Request for quotation. Accurate, written specifications are essential to controlling quality, schedule, and cost. Use this form to record specifications so that printers and other services have a precise description of the job they are

Request for Quotation (continued)

Printing   ink color(s)/varnish   ink color(s)/varnish

cover   side 1 4-COLOR+ SILVER +VARNISH   side 2 4-COLOR + VARNISH

inside   side 1 4-COLOR+ VARNISH   side 2 4-COLOR + VARNISH

INSERT side 1 BLACK + ONE COLOR   side 2 BLACK + ONE COLOR

_____ side 1 _____   side 2 _____

Ink ☐ special color match   ☑ special ink METALLIC SILVER ON COVER ☐ need draw down

coverage is ☐ light ☑ moderate ☐ heavy ☑ see comp attached ☑ need press check

Other printing (die cut, emboss, foil stamp, engrave, thermograph, number, etc.) _____

_____

Bindery

☐ deliver flat press sheets   ☐ round corner   ☐ pad   ☐ Wire-O

☑ trim   ☐ punch   ☐ paste bind   ☐ spiral bind

☐ collate or gather   ☐ drill   ☑ saddle stitch ☐ perfect bind

☐ plastic coat with _____   ☑ score/perforate   ☐ side stitch   ☐ case bind

☑ fold _____   ☐ plastic comb   ☐ tip in _____

comments SCORE COVER; PERFORATE INSERT

Packing ☐ rubber band in # ___ s ☐ paper band in # ___ s ☐ shrink/paper wrap in # ___ s

☐ bulk in cartons/maximum weight ___ lbs ☑ skid pack ☐ other _____

Shipping ☐ customer pick up ☑ deliver to QUICK-OUT MAILING SERVICES

_____

☐ quote shipping costs separately ☐ send cheapest way ☐ other _____

Miscellaneous instructions PRINT 500 EXTRA COVERS; SHRINK WRAP

100 CATALOGS IN 10'S; DELIVER EXTRA COVERS AND CATALOGS

TO SUSAN PRESTON WHEN RETURNING MECHANICALS

AND PHOTOS

_____

quoting. The job described in the above example is the catalog planned in Visual 1-6 and scheduled in Visual 1-4. You may photocopy and use the full-size, blank version of this form in Appendix E.

and state how many. If the design includes any of these features, providing a comp along with specifications will let the printer know exactly what is required.

The art that you provide refers to production, not aesthetics. Most jobs are submitted camera-ready or prepared for the printer to paste up. Supplying plate-ready negatives and proofs means that a trade camera or color separation service is doing the work that a printer's preparation department would usually do, so the printer and the service must communicate.

For multicolor printing, the printer must know whether color breaks are indicated on tissue overlays or made using acetate overlays. If you will be giving the printer maps, illustrations, or other line copy not part of the mechanicals, enter how many pieces there will be.

Photographs will be reproduced as halftones, duotones, or separations. Black and white prints for halftones and duotones are usually given to the printer at the same time as mechanicals and charged by the number needed, regardless of size. Simply telling how many there will be is sufficient. Charges for color separations, on the other hand, depend on size, quality, quantity, and whether originals are transparent or reflective. When entering sizes of separations, write how many of each size you expect to need.

While entering information about photos, note whether any need masking, enhancing, or special effects. Enter that information as part of the miscellaneous instructions at the end of the form. Also use that section to describe any non-photographic reflective art or materials that must be separated.

When specifying proofs, you will usually ask for a blueline plus other kinds appropriate to the specific job. If you think you may need multiple copies of proofs or second proofs, enter that information as an instruction at the end of the form.

Paper for the job should be specified after consulting with a printer or a representative of a paper distributor. Printers work with a variety of paper suppliers, so don't hesitate to instruct your printer to use a specific distributor for your job. For examples of properly-written paper specifications, see Visual 6-14.

Use the open lines in the paper section to specify stock for miscellaneous items that will be part of the printed piece. If those items will be printed elsewhere and supplied to your printer for binding, note that information.

When you write information about inks, be specific. Use a name and number from a color matching system. Note whether varnish should be gloss or dull and whether it will be flood or spot coverage.

If ink for the job must be opaque, resist fading, or have other special characteristics, write the information here. Asking for a draw down means you can see the ink applied to the actual paper specified for the job.

To complete the ink section, give the printer a rough idea of ink and varnish coverage expected on the press sheet. Moderate coverage would be inking on 25% to 65% of the sheet.

If your design calls for printing in addition to or instead of offset, you may need to add details at the end of the form. Check with a printer to be sure you have all the necessary data.

Almost any of the boxes you check in the bindery section call for more details. Use the comments line to make your needs clear and provide a dummy along with the specifications.

You can specify what kind of packaging you want and how many should be in each package. If you simply want bulk packing in standard cartons and do not give a weight limit, each carton will weigh about 40 pounds. If you specify skid packing, be sure your receiving system can handle the pallets.

The printer needs to know where and how to deliver the job. Printers normally deliver locally at no extra charge, but add charges to the invoice for long-distance delivery. If you need to analyze shipping costs, ask that they be quoted separately. ❧

2

For hundreds of years, typesetting was exactly what the name implied. Printers set individual wooden or metal blocks with raised letters next to each other in a tray, called a galley. Blocks with no letters yielded spaces between words; thin strips of lead separated one line of words from the next. The first sheet printed from the finished assembly was the galley proof.

The old terms survive, but no longer describe what happens. Most modern type is set photographically from copy and format instructions entered at a keyboard. Output for inspection is still called a galley proof, but is in the form of black characters on photographic paper. After being corrected and assembled with other visual elements, type is photographed by the printer as the first step in making plates.

Type and its placement on the page govern how well printed pieces achieve their goals because how words look affects how their message is received. Thorough knowledge of type results in effective communication as well as sound management of printing jobs.

In this chapter we describe the machines and techniques used to set type for modern printing. We tell how to specify type, examine it for quality, and work with typesetters to achieve quality and service at reasonable cost. We include among the visuals a checklist of type quality and a glossary of key terms used by typesetters and printers.

This chapter begins with technical information that some readers may not need just to

Sources of Type

Type Fonts

Selecting and Specifying Type

Type Quality

Working with Typesetters

Typesetting

get typesetting done. Furthermore, advances in computer technology are changing typesetting faster than other aspects of the graphic arts. If your interest is mainly in buying type rather than understanding how it is made, we suggest you skim the first section of this chapter.

Sources of Type

In the graphic arts, type is letters, numerals, and other symbols such as punctuation marks that will be reproduced by printing. There are five kinds of type commonly used in the production of printed pieces. Which kind is appropriate for a specific job depends on needs for quality, speed, and economy.

Strike-on type. Machines that make strike-on type include typewriters, computer printers using ribbons, and the IBM Composer.

Typewriters and daisywheel printers make type appropriate only for basic quality printing unless the product is designed to have type that looks typewritten. Even the best of these machines produce type with fuzzy edges and offer limited choices among typefaces.

Although IBM stopped making Composers in 1983, thousands of type and in-plant print shops still use this machine for many jobs. Operated much like a typewriter, it has 125 fonts in 11 type families and produces proportionally spaced characters. The Composer is limited in versatility and speed, but its type is suitable for printing at the good quality level.

Although many computer users have printers that use elements, daisywheels, or thimbles, most strike-on computer printers form characters from dot patterns created when tiny needles hit a ribbon. The pattern of dots they make can look either loose and washed out or tight and dense. The density of a dot pattern is known as its resolution.

Dot resolution is expressed in numbers of dots per inch horizontally and vertically. A resolution of 90 dots per inch makes characters of the quality commonly seen on paychecks and address labels. As resolution gets tighter, the quality of images increases.

Inexpensive computer printers are limited to loose dot patterns, making type barely acceptable even for basic quality printing. More costly printers have better resolution, but output speed decreases as patterns tighten. Some printers can be adjusted to a medium-speed

"I wish more people knew all the things we could do for them with our typesetting equipment. If they would design with our capabilities in mind, we could save some of them hundreds of dollars a year in pasteup costs plus get their mechanicals to their printers much faster. For example, we can make page repros for the average newsletter complete with borders and floating rules. The designer just draws rough lines on a layout and specifies how thick and long to make them. Our machines do the rest. People who've never even seen a technical pen can get perfect work."

graphics mode (180 dots per inch) and a slow-speed letter mode (360 dots per inch). Even so-called letter quality dot printers, however, do not make type suitable for printing better than basic quality.

To look more like typesetting, strike-on type can be proportionally spaced using a computer printer operating with word processing software. If you want a personal computer printer to do proportional spacing, be sure you can get software and have a printer that can handle it. Software and printers that can proportionally space are currently available for only a few personal computers.

The paper used in a printer influences how legible strike-on type will be when reproduced. Erasable bond smears; light weight paper may wrinkle during handling; colored stock may yield insufficient contrast. For better results, use bright white, smooth paper that is at least 60# book or 24# bond.

Transfer lettering. Also called rub-on or press-on, transfer lettering offers the greatest range of typefaces for the least money when making headlines, advertisements, and other copy with only a few large words. Materials come in a wide variety of prices and quality. High quality letters rub off smoothly and can be enlarged up to 200% without losing sharpness. To assure best results, use transfer sheets within a year after purchase.

Because of the hand-positioning required, transfer lettering is more suited to display type than text type.

The lettering machines made by Kroy Inc. produce type similar in concept to transfer lettering. These popular and versatile machines make type on a tape which is then used for pasteup, signs, and labels. Type for offset printing should be set on Kroy's photo quality tape.

"When I first went into advertising, I wasted a lot of time running between my office and my typesetter. Finally I began to proofread copy for small jobs on the spot. Now I consult with my typesetter, find any mistakes, and agree on new schedules right at the type shop. It takes an extra couple of minutes at the counter, but it ends up saving me hours in the long run."

Metal type. Machines such as the Linotype set individual lines of metal type, sometimes called hot type. When introduced a century ago as the first automated typesetters, line-casting machines revolutionized the printing industry. By today's standards, the machines are slow and offer a limited choice of styles and sizes. They are still used, however, for routine letterpress jobs and by a few printers who specialize in short runs of specialty books.

Phototype. Today's highest quality typesetting machines create characters photographically by projecting light onto light-sensitive paper. Depending on the machine, each letter is set by hand (photolettering) or set automatically using a keyboard (typesetting).

Photolettering machines, often called headliners, make characters by projecting light through negatives. Image areas in the film create the characters as light passes through the film and strikes the paper. Photolettering machines produce results suitable for good, premium, and showcase quality printing, depending on the quality of the machine and the care with which it is operated.

Because they are relatively inexpensive, photolettering machines are found at many print shops, ad agencies, and design studios, as well as at type shops. They are ideal for fast turnaround situations because they make high quality type quickly.

Typesetting machines commanded from keyboards are computer-controlled. In these systems, text is kept in electronic memory, called onto a screen for editing, and printed out on demand. This method of typesetting is similar to word processing, although it requires more complicated formatting commands.

All computer-controlled typesetters rely on electronic memory devices to store copy and formatting instructions. Disks and magnetic tape are the most common memory media.

Typesetters consist of input and output systems. Input systems include keyboards and disks or other memory devices. Output systems include fonts for holding characters and a light source and mechanism for forming them. The mechanism for forming characters might be a strike-on or laser printer for making proofs or a photo printer for making the type itself.

There are three basic output systems. In the first, characters are formed by projecting light through negatives. In the second, equipment based on cathode ray tubes (CRTs) scans characters formed on the screen and transmits them to photo paper. The third system uses lasers to form characters from thousands of tiny lines made by a moving pinpoint of light.

Both CRT and laser typesetters create characters as composites of dots or lines and are called digital typesetters.

Photomechanical and digital machines are both capable of producing type suitable for printing at any quality level. The differences between the systems determine their speed, versatility, and relative cost.

Photomechanical typesetters function less quickly than digital machines, are not as versatile, and may cost less to operate. Small amounts of type such as for advertisements and fliers probably cost less from them than when produced by newer, more sophisticated systems. Customers who need large amounts of type, however, might seek type shops with digital equipment that can output faster. That equipment might also be able to produce graphics and integrate them with text.

The resolution of dots or lines affects both the quality and speed of output from digital typesetters. As a general rule, quality goes up and speed goes down as resolution gets tighter.

Some typesetting machines have adjustable resolution. By knowing their quality requirements, customers can reduce the time and cost of some output by requesting that it be done at lower resolution.

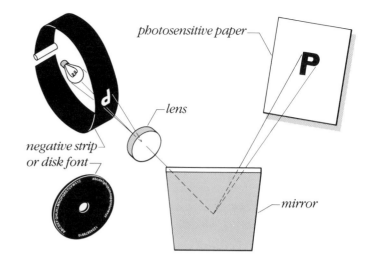

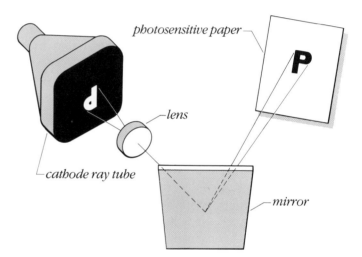

2-1 Phototypesetting. These drawings represent three ways that phototypesetting machines generate characters. The top drawing shows a photomechanical process using a negative strip as a font; the middle illustration represents characters displayed on a CRT; the bottom illustrates characters formed by a laser beam. Both the CRT and the laser devices are digital processes based on computer technology. All three kinds of machines project characters as light through a lens onto photosensitive paper.

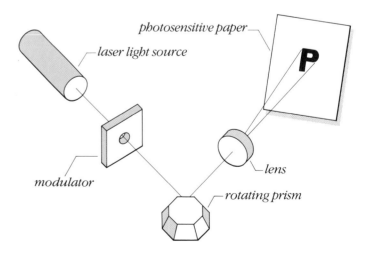

Electrostatic laser type. Laser printers are relatively inexpensive output devices that couple lasers with xerography to form characters from dots or lines. The images are created as toner, a powder, sticks to those areas of paper carrying an electric charge that has been placed there by a laser beam.

Laser beams are far more precise than the needles in mechanical dot printers, thus can produce more dots per inch without losing speed. Standard resolution from laser printers is currently 300 dots per inch.

Laser printers operate extremely fast because the beam pulses at rates up to several million times per second. The fastest laser printers currently available print about 2,000 characters per second while the slowest, desktop models work at about 300 characters per second. Those speeds compare to 50 characters per second from a fast daisywheel printer or a mechanical dot printer working at letter quality.

Electrostatic laser printers have the drawback that they use technology similar to photocopying to place characters on paper. They use plain bond paper and toner and, compared to phototypesetting, have relatively loose resolution. Output from laser printers is suitable only for basic and, in cases such as business forms, good quality printing.

Inexpensive laser printers coupled with personal computers put simple typesetting into the hands of writers and editors. For example, Apple Corporation licenses typefaces from Allied Linotype for use on its LaserWriter printer. The LaserWriter is most versatile when driven by an Apple computer, but can be driven by other personal computers as well.

"Whenever I needed new catalog sheets, I used to spend hours staring at my old catalogs, measuring point sizes, and getting a headache. One day I went to a meeting of the ad council and sat next to an art director who showed me some layouts. They had detailed type specifications written all over them. Now that I know how to spec type and have started keeping good records, I just get out photocopies of my old galleys. They have all the information that I need, even including character counts, right there in my own handwriting."

Xerographic laser technology is extremely useful for making proofs of type because it works so much faster and less expensively than phototypesetting. Customers can proofread electrostatic type that is almost identical to type that will be output later by the higher quality phototype processes.

Laser printers are valuable when making mechanicals for basic quality printing because they can output any combination of type and graphics that can be generated on a computer screen. The software that drives some laser printers is also valuable for preparing higher quality output. For example, pages composed on some Apple computers can be output on a LaserWriter, proofed and corrected, then output at typeset quality by a Linotronic 300.

Type Fonts

A type font is a complete assortment of characters of one typeface in one style. For example, the 11 point ITC Garamond Light you are currently reading is from one font. The subheadings in this volume are 14 point ITC Garamond Book, so are made using a font different from the one holding text type. Technically speaking, type balls, daisywheels, and even sheets of transfer letters hold fonts.

Phototypesetting machines use two kinds of devices to hold fonts. Photomechanical machines such as the one used to set type for this book use negative strips in which characters exist as clear areas. Light passes through the negative to strike photosensitive paper. Digital machines have characters on disks or tapes that instruct pinpoints or beams of light to strike the paper. With both kinds of equipment, light and photochemistry produce characters.

Computers and typesetting machines vary greatly regarding how many fonts they can access at one time. Costs for changing from one font to another are quite different from shop to shop. Because of machinery at a specific shop, you may have far more design flexibility than you thought—or far less.

Most type shops have fewer fonts than offered by the manufacturer of their machines. If you want a typeface, style, or size that your shop doesn't have, ask for it. Typesetters often buy fonts for big jobs and regular customers.

Fonts for the same typeface from different manufacturers may vary slightly with regard to fractions and special symbols and even design of the letterforms themselves. If you must switch fonts while staying with the same typeface, ask to see complete font printouts so you can compare characters.

Manufacturers of typesetting equipment will custom make fonts, although the work is very expensive. You could design your own typeface or add unique symbols or logos to fonts of existing typefaces. Type shops with scanners may also be able to add images to digital fonts on the premises.

Selecting and Specifying Type

Art applied to letterforms is as ancient as writing itself. Today there are almost 5,000 published typefaces. Only about four dozen, however, are commonly used.

Every commercial source of fonts offers sample sheets or books showing its range of typefaces. Fonts for typewriters and computer printers come in a much more limited variety than those for transfer letters and typesetting machines. Catalogs from transfer material companies show several hundred styles and sizes. Typesetters and many printers have type specimen books or posters showing the typefaces available from them.

Deciding what typeface is right for a specific job calls for judgments about design that are beyond the scope of this book, but there are some rules of thumb. Printing that is difficult to read or not pleasing to the eye often has not followed these rules.

Use a type family with variety. A type family is a group of type styles visually related to one another by the shape of their characters and other design traits. Baskerville, Futura, Palatino, and Souvenir are examples of commonly used type families.

If your printing job calls for captions, quotes, and several levels of subheads, be sure the type family you like includes an appropriate variety of weights, both for roman and italic,

Garamond Light
Garamond Book
Garamond Bold
Garamond Ultra
Garamond Light Italic
Garamond Book Italic
Garamond Bold Italic
Garamond Ultra Italic
Garamond Light Condensed
Garamond Book Condensed
Garamond Bold Condensed
Garamond Ultra Condensed
Garamond Light Condensed Italic
Garamond Book Condensed Italic
Garamond Bold Condensed Italic
Garamond Ultra Condensed Italic

2-2 Type in this book. The typography in this book uses four faces of ITC Garamond, a type family that includes 16 faces. Captions are set in Light 10/12, while text is Light 11/13½; names of publications are Light Italic; headings are various sizes of Book; anecdotes are Book Italic. Many type families offer more variety than would be appropriate for a single project.

and perhaps small capitals as well. Build variety by changing size, weight, and slant, not by switching the type family except under rare circumstances. Using only a few typefaces also may cut costs by saving the time some machines require to switch from one font to another.

Communication Arts magazine asked leading designers which type families they would retain if all the rest were to vanish. The consensus: Times Roman, Helvetica, Caslon, Goudy Oldstyle, and Garamond. We would add Optima to the list, but the point is that a small number of type families could suffice to meet most design needs.

Type specifications must also take readability into account. When planning headlines or other display type, remember that words set in all capital letters are more difficult to read than those set in upper and lower case. Words

AA. Author alteration; any change or correction made by the customer after type has been set.

Ascender. Portion of a lower case letter rising above its x height.

Base line. Imaginary rule running under each line of type. Base lines touch the bottoms of most letters.

Body copy. Copy set in text type. Also the bulk of a story; not its headline or subheads.

Bullet. Bold dot used for emphasis.

Callout. Descriptive word part of an illustration.

Cap height. Height of the capital letters of a typeface.

Caption. Identifying or descriptive text accompanying a photograph or other visual element.

Centered. Type with the middle of each line at the mid line of the column.

Character. Any letter, numeral, symbol, punctuation mark, or space between words.

Character count. Number of characters in a pica, inch, line, column, or page. It is different for each typeface and size and varies with extending or condensing.

Cold type. Alternate term for *Strike-on* or *Phototype*.

Compose. To set type.

Composition. Type that has been set.

Condensed type. Characters narrow in proportion to their height, thus seeming tall and tightly-spaced.

Copy. All written material needing to be typeset.

Copyfit. To use character counts and editing to plan so that type fits space alloted by the layout.

Descender. Portion of a lower case letter falling below its base line.

Digital type. Characters, such as from a laser printer or phototypesetter, made up of thousands of lines or dots positioned by a computer.

Dingbat. Symbol used for emphasis or decoration.

Display type. Type of 14 points or over.

Em space. A space whose width equals the point size of the type being set.

Extended type. Characters wide in proportion to their height, thus seeming fat and loosely-spaced.

Flush left or right. Type aligning vertically along the left or right side of the column.

Folio. Page number. Low folio is the left hand page, high folio the right.

Font. Complete assortment of upper and lower case characters of one typeface.

Galley. Tray used to hold metal type assembled ready for printing.

Galley proof. Proof of typeset copy.

Gothic type. Type without serifs.

Hard copy. Copy on paper.

Headliner. Machine that sets display type positioned individually by hand.

Hot type. Type made from metal.

Italics. Characters that slant to the right.

Justified type. Flush both left and right.

Kerning. Negative letterspacing that makes certain letters appear better fitted together.

Leader. Row of dots guiding the eye across a page.

Leading. Amount of space between lines of type, expressed in points.

Letter spacing. Amount of space between letters, usually adjustable.

Ligature. Two letters that, because of their design, may be typeset as one character. The letters "fi" and "fl" form ligatures in many typefaces.

Line measure. The width of a line of type.

Lower case. Letters that are not capitals.

Makeup. To arrange type and graphics into their proper pattern using layout as a guide.

Mark up. Using standard symbols and proofreader marks, to write instructions on copy or proof telling how it should be prepared or corrected.

Page proof. Type output in page format complete with headings, rules, and numbers.

2-3 Type terms. Graphic arts professionals use standard terms and units of measure to describe typography and specify type. Some of the terms have precise meanings, while others are more subjective. The meanings of a few terms vary from

Phototype. Type created by projecting light onto photosensitive paper.

Pica. Unit of measure equalling ⅙ of an inch often used to express line measure or column width.

Pi font. Font with math symbols, dingbats, and other characters for special needs.

Point. Unit of measure equalling ¹/₁₂ of a pica and ¹/₇₂ of an inch always used to express type size and leading.

Press-on type. Alternate term for *Transfer type*.

Proofreader marks. Standard symbols and abbreviations used to mark up manuscripts and proofs. Most dictionaries and style manuals include charts of proofreader marks.

Ragged right or left. Characteristic of type not flush right or left.

Repro. Type with corrections made and elements in position ready to reproduce by printing.

River. Distracting pattern of white space running down through text type.

Roman type. Type with serifs. Also type that is upright (not italic).

Runaround. Type set to conform to the outline of a photograph or illustration.

Sans serif type. Type without serifs.

Serif. Short line crossing the ending strokes of most characters in some typefaces.

Serif type. Type with serifs.

Set solid. Type set with no leading between lines.

Small caps. Capital letters approximately the height of lower case letters.

Soft copy. Copy in electronic memory.

Spec type. To write type specifications.

Specifications. Instructions about typeface and size, line measure, indentations, headlines, etc. Type size and leading are expressed as the upper and lower numerals in a fraction, with the points for leading measured baseline to baseline. Type 10/12 means 10 point type with two points of leading.

Straight copy. Copy that contains no charts, tables, formulas, or other elements that make typesetting complicated and time consuming.

Strike-on type. Characters, such as from a typewriter, made when a key or needle hits a ribbon coated with ink or carbon.

Swash. Curved flourish on selected letters.

TA. Typesetter alteration; any change made because of typesetter error.

Text type. Type of less than 14 points.

Transfer type. Type that can be rubbed off of its backing sheet onto another surface.

Typeface. Set of characters with design features making them similar to each other.

Type family. All the styles of a specific typeface.

Typesetter. Machine or person that sets type.

Type shop. Typesetting business.

Type size. The height of a typeface measured from the bottom of its decenders to the top of its ascenders, expressed in points.

Type specimen book. Book showing examples of all typefaces available from one type shop.

Type style. Italic, condensed, bold, and other variations of a typeface that form a type family.

Typo. Short for typographical error.

Typography. The art and science of setting type. Also the style and arrangement of type on a printed piece.

Unjustified. Alternate term for *Ragged*.

Upper case. Capital letters.

Weight. Characteristic of type determined by how light or dark it appears when set.

Widow. A single short line ending a paragraph as first line of a column or page. Also, a single or partial word appearing as the final line in a paragraph.

Word spacing. Amount of space between words, usually adjustable.

x height. Height of lower case letters without their ascenders or descenders, which is height of the letter x.

shop to shop or city to city, so it pays to check whenever using a new typesetter. If you and your typesetter are not speaking the same language, it can lead to errors that take time and money to correct.

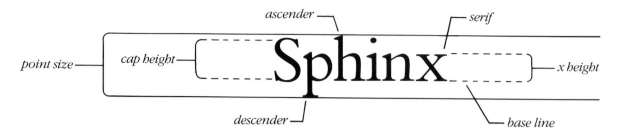

2-4 Standard features of type. Because lower case letters appear far more often than capitals, their size greatly affects how type appears. The x height of a typeface refers to the size of its lower case letters. The ratio of x height to point size varies greatly from one type face to another. The length of ascenders and descenders must be taken into account when planning spacing between lines. The example above is 48 point type.

formed from lower case letters have unique outline patterns, so familiar words are read as a whole. Words in all caps have no distinctive outline and force readers to slow down to grasp their meaning.

Efficient reading is also affected by line length. Research shows that the average reader takes in three or four words per eye movement and comprehends best when making two eye movements per line. Thus, the ideal line length is seven or eight words. Figuring an average of six characters per word, lines containing between 45 and 55 characters work best for the average reader.

Materials such as books and magazines that will take more than a few minutes to read call for a typeface with serifs. Serifs are the tiny lines that cross the ending strokes of letters and lead the eye from one letter to the next. Serifs make type more readable and reduce eye fatigue during long periods of reading.

While type printed as a reverse can be eyecatching, it can also cause problems. Lines less than half a point thick may fill with ink when reversed, reducing legibility. Text type always becomes less legible when reversed, whether or not the typeface has fine lines.

Specifying typefaces can be confusing when different manufacturers give different names to typefaces that seem identical. Helvetica, for example, looks similar to Helios, Claro, Newton, or Megaron. Furthermore, typefaces that have identical names may in fact be slightly different among manufacturers. The differences are small, but will show up in overall appearance of a page of text.

Character counts often provide an example of the variations among typefaces that seem the same. Different machines or fonts produce different counts based on identical specifications. For example, 10 point Claro by Alphatype and 10 point Helios by Compugraphic are each 2.4 characters per pica, but 10 point Helvetica when set on a Mergenthaler VIP is 2.7 characters per pica.

When selecting a typeface, consider long-range needs. If you'll need more type next year, from another typesetter, or in another part of the country, be sure you can match the typeface you are picking now.

If you are planning a large job such as a catalog or directory, ask your type shop to estimate the number of lines you would need for differing sets of specifications. When you know line length and number of lines per page, the type shop should be able to estimate the total length of most documents within about 5%.

Digital typesetters may be adjusted to set type in virtually any size and to change spacing between letters and words and leading between lines. If 9 point type is too small and 10 point too large, the machine can set 9½ point. Customers are no longer limited to traditional increments, such as 10, 12, and 18.

Digital typesetters can manipulate the shape and angle of type as well as its size and placement. The machines can slant letters to make oblique or italic type, squeeze them to make condensed type, and elongate them to make extended type. Digital machines can also automatically make reverses similar to those seen on some computer screens.

Type Quality

For basic quality printing, type from almost any source will communicate adequately. For good, premium, and showcase printing, type should meet quality standards appropriate to the job. These standards are attainable by any type shop where people take pride in their work and good care of their equipment.

Type that is fuzzy at the edges is less legible than type that is sharp. Fuzzy type can come from strike-on printers using cloth instead of carbon ribbons, dot matrix printers that are out of alignment, and typesetting machines that are out of alignment or focus. Of course, even properly maintained strike-on and laser printers do not make type as sharp as a typesetting machine.

Broken characters also make type less easy to read. They can come from worn keys, poor quality press-on lettering, scratched font negatives, and digital disks with flawed sectors.

14 point bold type reversed
14 point medium type reversed
14 point light type reversed

12 point bold type reversed
12 point medium type reversed
12 point light type reversed

10 point bold type reversed
10 point medium type reversed
10 point light type reversed

8 point bold type reversed
8 point medium type reversed
8 point light type reversed

2-5 Reversed type. Because the eye is accustomed to seeing dark type on a light background, reversed type may be difficult to read when made too small or used too much. In addition, fine lines, even on bold type, may disappear because they fill with ink during printing. To be effective, reverses should be used sparingly and carefully.

Type should appear dense and consistent. Phototype is more dense than type made on electrostatic printers.

All systems that set type have mechanisms to feed paper through the machine. If the paper goes through with uneven tension, lines of type may not be parallel to each other.

Paper itself can be a problem if type must stay camera-ready more than a few weeks. Many type shops use stabilization paper designed to be reproduced, then discarded. If you need type or mechanicals that are more permanent, ask for output on RC (resin coated) paper. Factors such as developing procedures, adhesives used for pasteup, and storage conditions also affect the useful life of type.

Working with Typesetters

Whether you have typesetting done through a printer, at an independent type shop, or in-plant, you need answers to several questions. Some of the answers will help in choosing where to have type set.

In what form should you deliver copy to be typeset? Handwritten material takes longest to keyboard, thus costs the most to typeset. Handwriting also increases chances of error and misinterpretation. For efficiency and accuracy, you should provide typed manuscript that is double-spaced and has wide margins for notes and corrections.

When you need type for books and other extensive materials, explore electronic options such as direct entry from word processor disks or transmission via modem. Be sure to make several tests to double-check with the type shop how machinery will interface. You may have to translate your disks into ASCII or some other standard code or use a media conversion service to make disks from your machine readable by typesetting equipment. You may also learn that file length, disk capacity, or disk formatting in your computer is different from what the type shop can use.

Studies by the National Composition Association show that interfacing word processors with typesetting machines can cut typesetting costs. The reduction can be almost 50% because keyboarding and proofreading amount to almost half the cost of the average typesetting job. When keyboarding is done on a word processor and proofread before typesetting begins, the work of the typesetter is kept to a minimum.

In addition to saving money, typesetting from a word processor can cut turnaround time. With editorial keyboarding complete, type might be set for a book in a few days instead of a few weeks.

Typesetting from word processing has drawbacks as well as advantages. Setting type is a professional skill. Taking typographic decisions away from typesetters increases chances of errors that will raise costs and reduce the visual quality of the printed piece as a whole.

Reading word processing disks or receiving information from modems may require programming at the type shop that is cost effective only for large amounts of copy. The text of this book, for example, was written on a word processor and given to the type shop on disks. All other material, including captions and callouts, was output on paper and given to the type shop for keyboarding.

We recommend that people interfacing word processors with typesetting machines stick to editorial matters and let typesetters enter the formatting commands. This policy means you would transmit text electronically, but still give the typesetter a manuscript showing instructions about type styles and sizes.

Those readers who keyboard on computers capable of electronic page assembly might ignore the above advice. Some companies making computers, typesetters, and software have developed ways for their products to interface. This cooperative effort is putting true typesetting and electronic page assembly into the hands of writers and editors. Taking advantage of this opportunity, however, requires a capable computer, extensive practice, and thorough understanding of both computers and typesetting.

How long will your job take? The answer depends on length and complexity. Straight copy goes quickly; footnotes and captions mean more time; charts and graphs take even longer. Discuss deadlines honestly. If you want the typesetter to respect the deadline you've agreed to, deliver the work when you promised.

An example of cloth ribbon typewriter type.

An example of standard dot matrix computer type.

An example of letter quality dot matrix computer type.

An example of laser-printed computer type.

An example of strike-on typesetting.

An example of phototypesetting.

An example of digital phototypesetting.

2-6 Type quality. The quality of type when printed depends heavily on the quality of original characters. Type made by typewriters and by dot matrix devices with relatively loose resolutions looks fuzzy, especially when enlarged. The edges of characters made by typesetting machines are more precisely defined. The words "An example" are enlarged to 250%. The type in the rest of the line is as it came from the machine that made it.

Normal service may mean two or three working days for small jobs. Some type shops specialize in overnight service; most will rush things when asked. It costs more, but it's the only way if the deadline is tomorrow morning.

What does the shop offer in addition to type? More and more typesetting equipment can make borders, rules, graphs, charts, and forms. Ask what specific machines can do. Type shops also may do design and pasteup, make photostats, and often pick up and deliver.

As typesetting becomes increasingly computerized, shops offer new services saving you time and money. Some can run your copy through a program that will check and correct spelling. Others can output fully assembled pages integrating graphics with type. Still others can scan art such as calligraphy, logos, and even photographs into digital memory systems, manipulate the images to change size and shape, then output them camera-ready.

Digital typesetters can make precise lines, thus can make keylines for photographs faster than a production artist using technical pens. Many machines can also make very dense areas that substitute for masking material to make windows. Either lines or windows can be integrated into text if you specify coordinates.

These computer capabilities fall into the general category of electronic page assembly. The service requires more sophisticated equipment than found at many type shops, but is becoming readily available in most urban areas.

Electronic page assembly means fully composing pages on a screen rather than pasting up blocks of copy. When dealing only with line copy and black and white photographs, some type shops and in-plant facilities offer the service as an extension of typesetting. Color photographs and electronic page assembly are handled by color separation services and are discussed in Chapter Four.

Camera-ready output from electronic page assemblers that includes only line copy is suitable for printing at any quality level, but output that includes scanned halftones is suitable only for basic quality work. The halftone positives on typesetting paper are about the same quality as they would be if made by the PMT process.

Size	
6 point	Alphabet
7 point	Alphabet
8 point	Alphabet
9 point	Alphabet
10 point	Alphabet
11 point	Alphabet
12 point	Alphabet
14 point	Alphabet
16 point	Alphabet
18 point	Alphabet
20 point	Alphabet
24 point	Alphabet
36 point	Alphabet
48 point	Alphabet
60 point	Alphabet
72 point	Alphabet

2-7 Type sizes. How big type seems when it is reproduced is influenced not only by its size but by its design, boldness, and spacing. In addition, typefaces with identical sizes may have different character counts. It pays to be familiar with how type of various sizes looks and fits when laid out.

Typesetters often help customers choose typefaces and sizes. To take best advantage of their advice, make a rough layout of your design in addition to the written copy. Show both to the typesetter who will make suggestions about type and specifications.

Most type shops offer complete pasteup services. Coupling these services with typesetting and consultation about design, they can

---

Specifications. Confirm that type was set at the point sizes, leadings, and measures you requested.

Sharp edges. Examine a random sample of letters under a magnifier to be sure of consistent sharpness.

Density. Inspect characters to be sure they are dense and uniformly black.

Unbroken characters. Use a magnifier to check for cracks and nicks.

Straight lines. Put a ruler under a few sample lines to be sure they are straight. There should be no hills or valleys.

Parallel lines. Scan lines to make sure they are parallel with each other.

Even justification. Lay a ruler vertically down the right and left edges of a few paragraphs of text type. Beginning and ending characters should properly abut the line.

Sensible hyphenation. Make sure that words are divided correctly. With ragged copy, words should be divided to prevent awkward gaps.

White paper. Type should appear against a pure white background without stains or flaws.

Stable paper. Verify that the typesetter used resin coated or fully fixed paper if type must stay camera-ready more than a few weeks.

Consistency. Check that features such as density, point sizes, and line widths stayed identical with type set on different days or by different machines. New lines or blocks of copy used for corrections or updates should stay consistent with original type.

2-8 How to check type. To be legible, type must be sharp and dense and have high contrast with its background. Using this list as a guide, examine type to be sure it is legible and meets the standards of quality you have for the specific job.

prepare your manuscript as camera-ready copy. Some shops carry the full service concept even further by offering printing. Typically they can print small jobs on the premises and will subcontract for larger jobs.

Typesetters are graphic arts professionals whose expertise can translate into convenience when they coordinate design, type, pasteup, and printing. They are also business people who mark up services. The typesetter, however, may get trade prices (similar to wholesale prices) on printing, whereas you as the customer would pay full fare. Whether or not an individual printing job would cost more if your typesetter managed it or if you managed it yourself depends on the nature of the job, the typesetter's markup, and how skillfully you would select a printer and handle the job.

What kinds of proofs can you get? Most type shops provide photocopies of galley proofs. Making galley proofs, however, can be expensive. To avoid this cost, some shops can make a plain paper printout from a daisywheel printer with line breaks and spacing identical to the finished type. A few shops can make a plain bond, laser printout similar to a photocopy of the type itself.

Photocopies and printouts provide inexpensive ways to proofread and make changes for copyfitting, but do not replace the need to inspect the actual type. When you see the type output, examine it for quality as well as to be sure that changes were made correctly.

What proofreader's marks should you use? Standard dictionaries and style books show symbols used to write typesetting instructions and indicate corrections on manuscripts. Specific symbols, however, vary from shop to shop. For best communication, consult with your typesetter about which symbols to use.

How will costs be figured? Every typesetting job is unique. Condition of the copy, amount of keyboarding required, complexity of text (charts, footnotes, formulas, etc.), deadlines, and font changes make pricing difficult. Some typesetters charge by the hour, others by the job, still others by character count. To keep costs down, specify type accurately. Describe requirements, then get estimates.

Typesetters vary greatly in their approaches to service and personal attention. Some proofread carefully, produce short jobs overnight, and make minor changes at no charge. Some keep your routine specifications on file and know your editing tastes well enough to spot errors. Some will pick up and deliver. Shops with these extras get top dollar for their work and are worth it.

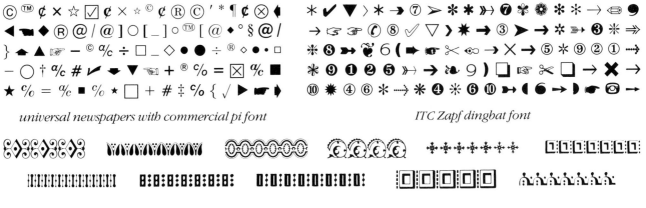

universal newspapers with commercial pi font

ITC Zapf dingbat font

borders

2-9 Miscellaneous fonts. Type shops have fonts with dingbats, math symbols, foreign letters, and other characters for emphasis or special purposes. Some fonts are part of a type family, others stand alone. Typesetting machines can also create a wide variety of rules and decorative borders produced in position with text.

In addition to differences in service, type shops vary in how rapidly their machinery works. Older, negative font machines may output as slowly as 20 lines per minute; newer, laser machines 100 times that fast. Faster output makes little cost difference when buying type for a simple advertisement, but can save hundreds of dollars with books and catalogs. If a typesetter charges by the hour, ask how long it will take to output your work and how much they charge per hour for output.

Who pays for changes? Typesetters and customers each pay for their own mistakes. Clear, detailed specifications and carefully prepared copy keep confusion low and accountability high. Clear specifications also cut costs.

Equipment operators at type shops vary a great deal in their keyboarding accuracy. If the cost of making corrections will be billed to you, an accurate operator could save you a great deal of money. Even if the shop pays to correct its own mistakes, corrections always cost you time.

What happens to keyboarding once the galleys are made? Keyboarding at most type shops is saved on a disk that the shop may erase and use again after the job is done. If your job is a catalog, directory, or guide that might need updating, ask that they save the disk. Computers are lifesavers with jobs using lots of data that change very little from one printing to the next. As an extra precaution, ask for a backup disk. A few dollars spent on disks now could save you much more next year.

Who owns materials and creative work done at the type shop? Typesetters are developing trade customs based on those used by printers. The typesetters' customs deal extensively with ownership of computer programs, formatting codes, working negatives, and similar ideas and products developed for specific customers. The legal and commercial status of this kind of work is similar to creative work by graphic artists and photographers: it is owned by the typesetter unless there was a prior agreement in writing granting ownership to the customer.

Questions about ownership have implications for insurance. Trade customs adopted in 1983 by the Typographers Association of New York deal with customer property such as manuscripts, art work, and magnetic media. The customs state that type shops are not liable for damage from fire, theft, and other causes beyond the control of the typesetter.

If you are concerned about insurance coverage of your property while in a type shop, check with both the typesetter and your insurance agent. Make very clear who owns the property in question and who is liable if it is damaged or destroyed.

Whether or not you are insured, never give a type shop your only copy of a manuscript, disk, or layout. Always keep a backup.

3

Printers think of the visual elements of printing jobs as either line copy or continuous-tone copy. Line copy is high contrast, usually black on white. It includes all type, rules, and clip art, plus many other illustrations. Continuous-tone copy has dark and light areas, but also has many intermediate shades and hues. It includes all photographs and some illustrations.

This chapter is primarily about line copy, although it includes a brief discussion of photographs as camera-ready copy.

Copy for every printing job must be prepared in accordance with the technical requirements of graphic arts photography. The preparation involves making mechanicals (also called keylines, artboards, or pasteups).

Printers use mechanicals, usually provided by customers, as the starting point for making printing negatives and plates. Mechanicals may be as simple as a sheet of typed copy. For complicated jobs, mechanicals would be type and graphics pasted to sturdy mounting boards and might include overlays of acetate or tissue.

Customers who understand the relationship between mechanicals and the negatives and plates can have a great deal of control over the quality, schedule, and cost of their printing.

In this chapter we describe how printers use photography to transfer line copy from mechanicals to negatives and plates. We present technical information about process cameras and graphic arts film to explain the meaning of camera-ready copy. We discuss screen tints,

Process Cameras

Scaling

Rules

Screen Tints

Charts, Graphs, and Maps

Illustrations

Photographs

Mechanicals

Camera-Ready Copy

illustrations, and other graphics and tell how to give printers instructions about cropping, scaling, and placing photographs. Finally, we describe the characteristics of good mechanicals.

Correct mechanicals are the practical aspect of design. Good layout, design's artistic aspect, is also essential to effective communication, but lies outside the scope of this book. Nor do we teach pasteup, the art of making mechanicals, but leave that instruction in technique to other authors who have already done it well.

We divide printers into the two general categories "quick" and "commercial." The distinction is based on both technical and business differences and has many implications for preparing camera-ready copy. Keeping the two categories in mind will help you understand much of the information in this book.

Many of the differences between quick and commercial printers are shown in the flow charts on the following two pages.

Process Cameras

The "camera" part of "camera-ready copy" refers to process cameras, devices that lie at the heart of preparation for offset printing and for most other printing methods as well.

Process cameras are optically similar to personal cameras for taking photographs. With both, operators control the amount of light passing through the lens and focus images onto the film.

Understanding the differences between process and personal cameras helps make clear the relationship between process cameras and mechanicals. Lenses in personal cameras have good depth of field: part of a scene can be close and part far away, but both parts will be in focus. Lenses in process cameras, however, have little depth of field, which is the reason why mechanicals must be flat.

The film used in process cameras is different from the film for personal cameras. Personal photographic films make continuous-tone images by responding to the full range of colors and intensities. After exposure and developing, emulsion on personal film has varying densities which will transmit light of varying intensity. High contrast graphic arts film is made specifically to produce line negatives. Portions of line negatives are either black (transmit no light) or clear (transmit all light). High contrast film records light grays as white and dark grays as black; there is no middle ground for intermediate tones or shades.

"My old boss figured that time was more important than money. If we had a chart or headline ready at the last minute, we might give it to the printer loose instead of putting it on mechanicals. The print shop would finish our pasteup or double burn a plate, depending on how late we were. My new boss figures that money is more important than time. Every mechanical that goes out of here now must be complete."

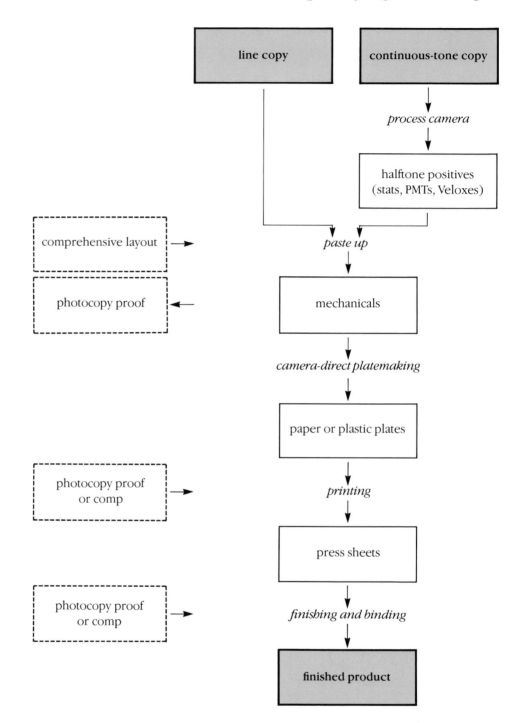

3-1 and 3-2 Production sequences for quick and commercial printing. Quick printers give fast service because they can have plates ready to put on press almost instantly after photographing mechanicals. Commercial printers need more time to make plates because they must make and assemble negatives and proofs first. By making negatives as an intermediate step to making plates, commercial printers can prepare high-quality jobs involving many design features.

In these charts the processes are in italic type and terms for the objects created are enclosed in boxes. The dotted boxes enclose names of proofs and guides. Their placement indicates when the proofs are made and used in the production sequence.

Production Sequence for Commercial Printing

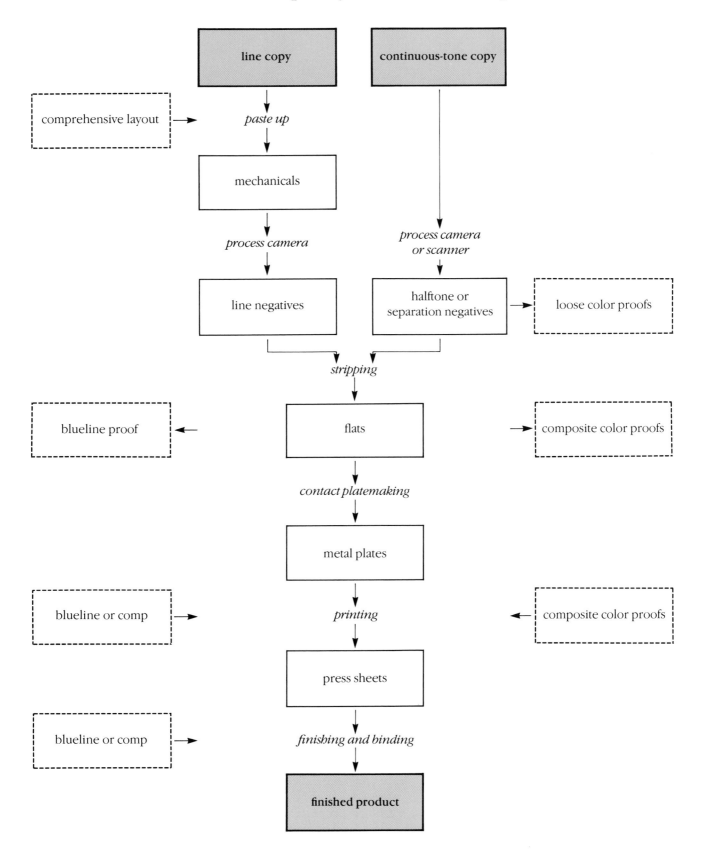

Personal photography is based on a chemical process in which the intensity of light determines the density of emulsion on film. In printing, however, ink is applied to paper on an all or nothing principle. An area of paper either receives ink from the press or it doesn't.

Line negatives transmit light on the all or nothing principle required by the printing process. The clear, image areas of graphic arts negatives correspond to the areas of paper that will receive ink when on press.

Graphic arts film responds to the colors red and light blue quite differently from personal film or the human eye. Red records as black, meaning that red copy can substitute for black. Light blue does not record at all. The disappearing act is highly useful because instructions can be written on mechanicals in light blue and will not transfer to the film. Printers and graphic designers write directly on mechanicals with special pens or pencils in nonreproducing blue.

The color of camera-ready copy does not need to relate to ink colors used when the images are printed on presses. The film sees the images as either black or white; if a color isn't strong enough to record as black, it drops out entirely to become white. When the plate made from the film is on press, the images that recorded as black can be printed with ink that is green or brown or any other color.

The size, complexity, and use of a process camera depends on its purpose. Small machines, often called stat cameras, may include processing units and are found at many type and print shops, ad agencies, and graphic design studios. All process cameras can make positive as well as negative images. Photostats and PMTs (Photomechanical Transfers, a trade name of Eastman Kodak Company) are positives.

Quick printers have process cameras that make plates directly from mechanicals. Often called platemakers, process cameras at quick print shops make plates within the camera itself in an automated sequence. The machines can reduce or enlarge an entire mechanical, but not its individual elements.

Trade camera shops and commercial printers use large process cameras to make negatives. The lens may be almost six inches wide

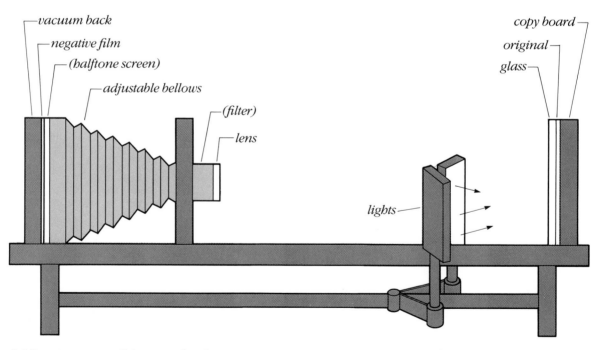

3-3 Process camera. Printers and trade camera services use process cameras to photograph mechanicals and continuous-tone copy. The size of the resulting images is adjusted by changing the distance of the lens and the copy board from the film. Quick printers use process cameras to make plates; commercial printers use them to make negatives. Process cameras use graphic arts film so sensitive that it even records dirt, smudges, and fingerprints. For that reason, mechanicals and art must be clean and without flaws.

and set 100 inches from the film plane. Cameras with such large lenses and focal lengths are necessary to make large negatives.

Commercial printers need to make negatives ranging from 5 x 7 inches to 50 x 77 inches, depending on the size of their presses. The ideal camera holds a piece of film as large as the largest piece of camera-ready copy the printer will typically shoot. The camera must also hold its own lights to illuminate the copyboard and expose the film. Lighting must be intense and continuous (not a flash).

Process camera operators use densitometers to calibrate exposure times. These instruments measure light reflected from opaque material such as continuous-tone prints or transmitted through clear material such as transparencies. Comparing individual density measurements against a standard gray scale, operators adjust exposures to ensure consistency.

Standardization increases precision in printing through accurate prediction of density shifts as a result of exposure changes. Readers familiar with personal photography might think of the printer's gray scale as functioning like the Ansel Adams zone system.

Like personal cameras, process cameras can use colored glass or gelatin filters placed in front of the lens to change light before it strikes the film. Filters may enhance images by shifting colors to more pleasing hues or improve originals that lack adequate contrast. The high contrast nature of graphic arts film means these problems may also be solved by control in exposure and developing.

Enhancing and altering images during process camera work is relatively simple, so costs little more than working with perfect originals. Camera operators, however, are not magicians. If you have problem material, show it to an operator and ask what might be done.

Most commercial printers have their own camera department. Many printers, however, along with many customers, rely on trade camera services. Trade shops typically make both PMTs and negatives of line copy and photographs. Most also do stripping and make plates.

To locate trade camera services, look in classified directories under "lithographic

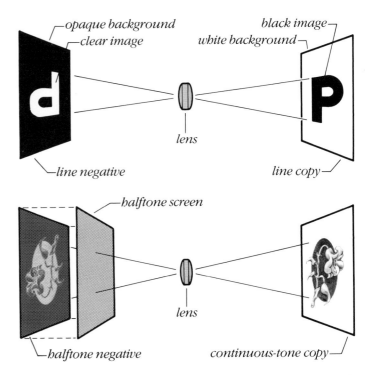

3-4 Line and continuous-tone copy. Line copy, such as type and clip art, is photographed in a process camera to make either a quick printing plate or a line negative for commercial printing. Continuous-tone copy, such as photographs and watercolor illustrations, is exposed through a screen in contact with the film to make halftone negatives.

negative and plate makers." This category will also include color separation services, businesses which have more sophisticated machinery than trade camera shops. PMTs and printing plates are also made by blueprinting companies and engravers. Businesses with either specialty may also be listed in directories in the same classifications as trade camera shops.

Scaling

Frequently a headline, drawing, or photo is the wrong size for a layout. All can easily be reduced or enlarged photographically.

Customers who want copy reduced or enlarged must identify for the printer or camera service the size they need. Scaling determines the new size of the image needed to fit the layout. Changes in size require knowledge of the new size expressed as a percent of the original.

If you want the copy 10% smaller, tell the operator to shoot it at 90%; if you want it 10%

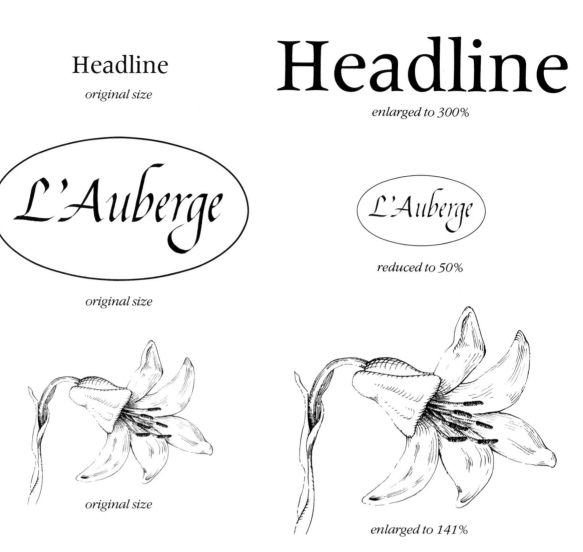

Headline

original size

Headline

enlarged to 300%

L'Auberge

original size

L'Auberge

reduced to 50%

original size

enlarged to 141%

original size

reduced to 83%

3-5. Enlarging and reducing. Both line and continuous-tone copy can be enlarged or reduced to fit layouts. Enlargements over 200% often show deterioration of the image, as can be seen along the edges of several letters of "Headline" at 300%. Reduction can make fine lines almost disappear, as in the case of "L'Auberge" at 50%. Note also that an image reduced to 50% becomes one fourth its original size, not one half. Photographs are reduced or enlarged and converted into halftones all in one shot. (Calligraphy by Katherine McKeown Roush; drawing by Cherry Britton; photo by Kathleen Ryan.)

larger, ask to have it shot at 110%. With no instructions, camera services shoot at 100%. Writing "same size" or "SS" makes it clear that you want copy reproduced without changing size.

Graphic arts professionals scale blocks of type, graphic elements, illustrations, and photographs using a simple device called a proportional scale or wheel. Proportional scales are inexpensive, can be purchased at art and graphics stores, and have operating instructions printed on them.

Customers who don't have a scaling wheel handy can specify changes in size by stating a new dimension and letting the camera operator compute percentages. This procedure, however, has the drawback of not letting you know the second new dimension before the work is done. Scaling wheels allow you to know the new height and width of any reduction or enlargement before ordering the work. With this knowledge, you can know exactly how the image at its new size will fit into your layout.

Because the arithmetic of scaling involves only one dimension (width or height), it's easy to forget that copy shrinks or grows in two directions. A block of type enlarged to 120% may appear much bigger than you expected; a photograph reduced to 50% may lose too many details. Shooting at 200% means the new copy will occupy four times the area of the original.

Enlarging copy magnifies flaws. High quality typesetting and transfer lettering hold their quality up to about 200%, but edges begin to look ragged after that. Reducing copy shrinks its every aspect. Fine lines or dot patterns may end up too thin to print, or disappear altogether.

Process cameras vary widely in their ability to reduce and enlarge. The typical one can reduce to 25% and enlarge to 300%. If your new percentage exceeds the limits of the camera being used, the camera operator must make a second shot. The second generation image will show a slight loss of quality.

When you take delivery of photostats, PMTs, or negatives, check for quality. Look for sharp focus, especially in portions of the image farthest from the center. Be sure stats or PMTs are on pure white paper with no chemical stains. If they must stay camera-ready longer than a few months, ask that they be treated with fixer during development. Measure one or two images to be sure scaling is to your specifications. Finally, be sure that copy is not too fat or too thin from being incorrectly exposed.

Camera services charge by the size of paper or film necessary, not the size of your original copy. You can save money by grouping all images to be done to the same percentage. Grouping, usually called ganging, may come at some loss of quality if originals differ in contrast or density. Ganged images are shot together at a common exposure.

For basic quality printing, a photocopy machine that reduces and enlarges will produce scaled results adequate for camera-ready copy. Process cameras, however, give better quality reductions and enlargements and should be used for good, premium, and showcase work.

Rules

Lines in the graphic arts are called rules and must meet specific quality standards. Straight rules must be straight. Rules drawn by hand or laid from border tapes sometimes look like sagging telephone wires or cutaways of mountain ranges. Curved rules should have uniform arcs. Rules should run only over flat surfaces. Going up and down over layers of paper on a mechanical results in lines that print unevenly.

Like type, rules should have clean edges. Felt tip or ballpoint pens and border tape that has collected dust and lint in the bottom of the desk drawer all give poor results. Rules made by graphic arts and technical pens are good and those made by phototypesetters even better. Ask at a type shop if rules are available. Equipment using digital fonts can add rules of various thicknesses and lengths in position with type.

"The only art I could find for our flier was a clipping from our last year's ad in the yellow pages. My quick printer suggested I show it to a trade camera service. They filtered out the yellow at the same time they made a PMT at 200%. The result wasn't nearly as good as starting with original art, but it was a lot better than nothing and looked better than I expected."

Screen Tints

Graphic arts professionals use screen tints to highlight copy, accent charts and graphs, and simulate changes in the density of ink. The areas of the illustrations in this book that look shaded are screen tints.

Screen tints create the illusion of shading because they are printed in tiny dots instead of solid blocks. In accordance with the all or nothing principle of printing, each dot has the same density as all other ink on the sheet. Paper showing around the dots, however, lightens the overall effect.

Commercial printers create screen tints using negatives that contain rows of clear dots. Light can pass through the dots, but not through the portions of the negative surrounding them. When a screen is placed over photo paper or a printing plate and exposed, it reproduces its pattern of dots on the light-sensitive emulsion.

Dot size determines how dark or light screen tints seem. Lots of paper showing around the dots makes the tint seem light; not much paper showing makes it seem dark. Printers use percentages to describe the amount of ink laid down in a screened area. A 90% screen is close to solid; a 10% screen seems very light.

In addition to percentage of ink in a screen tint, the tint is affected by the number of rows or lines of dots per inch. Screens with relatively few lines per inch are coarse; fine screens have many lines per inch. The number of lines per inch is called the screen's ruling.

If the design for a piece that will be quick printed calls for screen tints, they must be pasted to the mechanicals. Catalogs of transfer lettering materials show standard screen rulings and percentages and offer tips on using the tint material. Most art supply stores carry a wide selection. Press-on tints must be firmly burnished edge to edge. The slightest bubble will put the dots out of focus. Edges must be cut clean with an artist's knife.

Tints from transfer materials are strictly for basic quality printing. If you are using a commercial printer and want good, premium, or showcase work, let the shop add tints when making plates. Simply specify on an overlay where the tints should be and what ruling and percentage you want. You'll get better quality and pay little more than using a press-on tint.

When your design calls for screen tints, keep in mind a few rules of thumb. Some papers, especially those without coatings, absorb more ink than others, so require coarser screens. Coarse screens yield fewer dots per inch so the dots are less likely to spread and run together when printed on absorbent paper.

Tints of less than 10% tend to disappear when printed; tints of more than 70% tend to look solid. Some ink colors look better screened than others. Dark blue becomes light blue, while red becomes pink. To judge how colors will look when screened, consult a tint chart available at most graphic arts stores, commercial printers, and design studios.

Two inks can be screened and overlapped to create the illusion of a third color. Ink colors, paper absorbency, screen rulings and percents, and the way screens align all affect the results. Improper alignment of screens by the printer can cause distracting moire patterns. If you are at all uncertain about the outcome, get advice from your printer.

Charts, Graphs, and Maps

Rules and screen tints combine in hundreds of ways to make charts and graphs. When specifying charts and graphs to a graphic designer, do the arithmetic first. Hire the designer for graphics, not accounting.

Microcomputers equipped with the proper software can do arithmetic and graphic art in the same sequence. To get camera-ready copy suitable for basic quality printing, set adjustable

---

"People come into our place all the time wanting 40% and even 50% screen tints of dark colors under their type. You can hardly see type with tints that dark. I try to talk them into 20% or even 10%. Or maybe they want a whole page of nine point type reversed. I show them our price lists and try to convince them that a little experimental work with our process camera would be a lot cheaper than going ahead and printing something they really won't like when they see it."

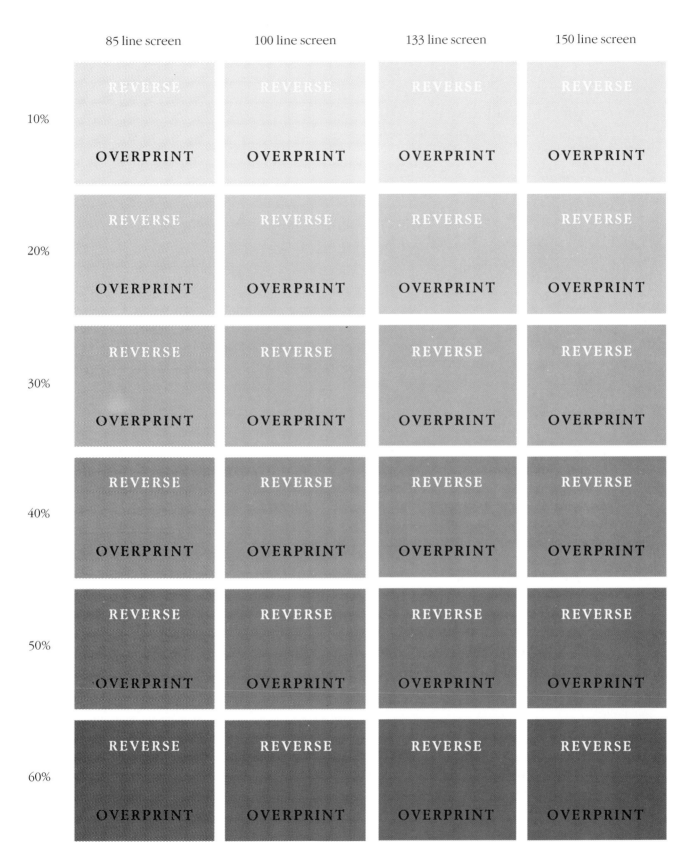

85 line screen   100 line screen   133 line screen   150 line screen

10%   REVERSE   REVERSE   REVERSE   REVERSE
       OVERPRINT OVERPRINT OVERPRINT OVERPRINT

20%   REVERSE   REVERSE   REVERSE   REVERSE
       OVERPRINT OVERPRINT OVERPRINT OVERPRINT

30%   REVERSE   REVERSE   REVERSE   REVERSE
       OVERPRINT OVERPRINT OVERPRINT OVERPRINT

40%   REVERSE   REVERSE   REVERSE   REVERSE
       OVERPRINT OVERPRINT OVERPRINT OVERPRINT

50%   REVERSE   REVERSE   REVERSE   REVERSE
       OVERPRINT OVERPRINT OVERPRINT OVERPRINT

60%   REVERSE   REVERSE   REVERSE   REVERSE
       OVERPRINT OVERPRINT OVERPRINT OVERPRINT

3-6 Screen tints. Tints are described according to how many rows of dots they have per inch and what percent of the area the dots cover. Overprints and reverses must be carefully planned to assure that words stay legible and fine lines do not disappear. Screen ruling for a specific job is dictated by choice of paper, printing method, and quality requirements.

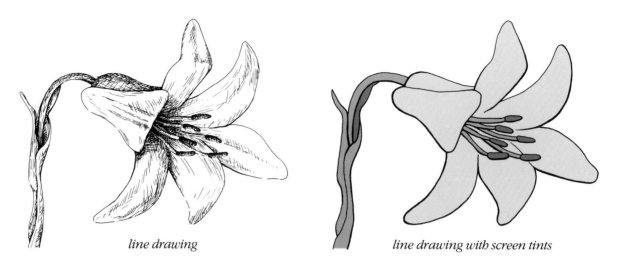

line drawing *line drawing with screen tints*

3-7 Four ways to treat an illustration. These lilies show four ways to add texture and shading to an illustration. One line drawing relies on cross hatching to achieve an effect similar to 19th century steel engravings. A line drawing can also be combined with screen tints. In this example, we used a 150 line screen at 10%, 30%, and 50%. The lilies at the right are each dropout halftones, a good technique for enhancing continuous-tone

dot printers in letter mode instead of graphics mode. For hard copy suitable for good or premium printing, find typesetting equipment that will interface with your computer. For example, both Allied Linotype and Compugraphic Corporation have software that will couple typesetting machines to some computers made by Apple Corporation. Anything on your computer screen can be output with much better quality by a typesetter than by a computer printer.

For ideas about charts and graphs, examine the annual reports of leading corporations. Companies hire the best professional designers for annual reports and insist on outstanding graphics and photography. Annual reports of publicly held companies are public documents available free by writing the company.

Maps and analytical diagrams are more difficult to make than charts and graphs, but still within the abilities of most graphic designers. Computer graphics software often includes

programs for simple maps. Many dot printers do not print the fine lines with sufficient density even for basic quality printing. Pen and ink line plotters interfaced with computers make an attractive alternative, although the machinery is rather specialized and difficult to locate. Complicated and high quality maps require the services of a cartographer.

Illustrations

Illustrations in the form of line copy can come from a variety of sources. Clip art, transfer (press-on) materials, and original pen and ink drawings are most common.

Clip art means preprinted drawings that can be adhered directly to mechanicals. Many ad agencies, design studios, and print shops, and most art and stationery stores, have books or files of clip art arranged by topic such as holiday themes, health care, or family life. Extensive collections come from producers who sell individual sheets and from books offered through stores and by direct mail.

Preprinted art is available either as black images on white paper or as black images on dry-transfer film. Transfer materials are especially popular with architects and others who must execute complicated scenes quickly. Clip

"Each month I lay out a front page for our 27 affiliate newsletters with our logo, a lead story, and a black and white photograph. My camera service strips a halftone of the photo with a negative of the line copy and makes 27 Veloxes. That way I can send every one of the local editors a top quality starting point for each issue."

watercolor halftone   *pencil drawing halftone*

art with no detail in its background. Small halftone dots that would normally show in the white background are dropped out by controlling exposure in the process camera, a procedure no more costly than making a full density halftone. Dropping out small dots may result in losing the finest lines and lightest tones in a drawing, painting, or photograph. (Drawings by Cherry Britton.)

art should meet the same quality standards as typesetting. Art should be in a dense, uniform black without fuzzy or broken lines.

Any dark drawing on light paper will work as a camera-ready illustration. Images printed on white paper can be added directly to mechanicals; images on off-white or colored paper may lack sufficient contrast, but might be enhanced by first making a PMT or photocopy.

When using published material as clip art, be aware of possible copyright infringements. Art published for the specific purpose of illustrating printed products is not copyrighted, but drawings in other publications probably are. If you have any doubts, check with the publisher or artist.

Original hand drawings for line art should have sharp, black lines. Professionals use graphic arts pens with precision tips and ink flow. Hand drawings can also be done via computer using a mouse or electronic screen pencil. For basic quality printing, they should be printed out on a dot printer capable of at least 360 horizontal dots and 180 vertical dots per inch. For good quality printing, dot resolution should be double those figures. Even a computer printer achieving that quality level is producing material only about half as good as that from a digital typesetting machine.

Illustrations in continuous tones made with pencil, felt marker, air brush, ink wash, charcoal, or paint must be screened into halftones or color separations. The processes are identical to those for photographs explained in Chapter Four.

An illustration done originally in full color may be printed in a single color, but requires special attention. If you are uncertain about how an illustration will print, show it to a printer before including it in a design.

Many graphic designers also do illustrations, but the best illustrators tend to specialize in this single aspect of the graphic arts. Illustrators need to know what information drawings must convey and in what style they should be done. When working with an illustrator, the first step is to show some drawings you like and ask if your work can be in the same style.

Clear job definition leads to satisfactory illustrations and means that costs can be closely estimated in advance. A good illustrator will ask

"We needed an image of our hospital, but there are so many power poles that we couldn't get a decent photo. Instead of airbrushing out the poles, we decided to hire an illustrator. We got a line drawing that works extremely well on a variety of our printing jobs."

mounted photo with instructions and crop marks

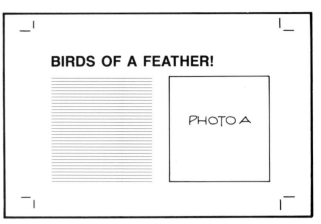

mechanical with keyline

printed piece

3-8 Keying photographs to mechanicals. For best results, photographic prints that will be halftoned in a process camera should be given to printers individually mounted as shown above left. When halftones will be made using a scanner, photos must be unmounted to stay flexible. Above is the mechanical with a keyline showing the correct placement of the cropped and reduced photograph. (Photo by Ken Russon.)

questions, then develop rough sketches for approval before drawing final art.

Fine artists produce work to be enjoyed in its original form; commercial illustrators create work for reproduction by printers. A commercial illustrator's knowledge of printing means jobs should reproduce well on press. In images to be reduced or reversed, there will be no delicate lines which might disappear. Line art will be drawn in black, never green or blue. Drawings will be properly mounted. No colors will be in dyes or pigments which cannot be matched by printing inks. Art will be planned to reduce or enlarge at consistent percentages to assure consistent appearance and economy of camera work.

When soliciting business, illustrators should show examples of their work. To be sure illustrators are sufficiently aware of printing processes, ask to see their work in printed form as well as original art. Check that drawings are reproduced as well as you think they should be.

The work of illustrators falls under the same copyright protections as that of graphic designers and photographers. When hiring an illustrator, be sure to specify what rights you want to buy.

Photographs

Although photographs are continuous-tone copy, not line copy, they may be considered camera-ready for commercial printing. Correctly prepared photographs are ready to be halftoned or separated for making printing plates.

When you deliver your photographs to a commercial printer, each one must be clearly identified, cropped, scaled, and keyed to your mechanical. Identify every photograph with your name, the job name, and a number. For best results, mount each print on a backing sheet. Write all instructions and crop marks on

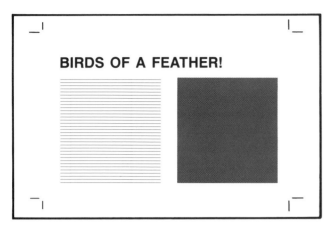

mechanical with Rubylith window

mechanical with position stat inside keyline

3-9 Alternate methods to key photographs to mechanicals. The window-on-mechanical method represented on the left requires precision trimming more conveniently done by a printer than a production artist. The position stat method shown at the right works as well as the keyline method and gives a better idea how the printed piece will look, but costs more time and money to produce.

the mounting sheet or tissue overlay. With un-mounted prints, write in the margin on the image side of the paper.

Avoid writing directly on the back of a print or attaching anything to it with staples or paper clips that may scratch. If you have no margin or mounting sheet on which to put instructions, write on a light weight piece of paper, then tape it to the print as an overlay. If you have no choice but to write on the back of the print itself, apply a peel-off label first. Write on the label, not on the photo paper.

Crop each photograph to indicate the portion you want printed. Ask your printer whether to draw crop marks in black on the white margins, cover each print with a tissue overlay and draw lines on it, or provide scaled photostats. We recommend the latter method because it gives printers the most accurate, complete information and works for transparencies as well as prints. It also allows you to see how the job looks with photographs in position. Photographs can also be photocopied to the proper size and crop marks written on the copies.

Cropped, scaled copies pasted up within keylines are called position stats. Each position stat should have a piece of white tape across it with the number of its corresponding photograph and the words "for position only."

Transparencies given to a printer or color

separation service should be in clear, protective sleeves. Write a numeral or letter on the sleeve, stat of the image, and mechanical so all three are keyed to each other. Crop marks may also be placed on the protective sleeve.

When you scale a photograph, specify dimensions that allow it to overlap the keylines or windows by at least $\frac{1}{16}$ inch on each edge. This gives printers plenty of room to be sure photos fit properly. Photographs designed to bleed should overlap the bleed edge by $\frac{1}{8}$ inch.

Relate photographs to your mechanical using the method that your printer suggests. We recommend the keyline method, not the window method, because printers can usually make windows faster, more accurately, and with higher quality results than production artists. Some print shops even ignore windows on mechanicals, so the time and money spent putting them there are wasted. If in doubt, ask how much money you will save by providing windows yourself. Often it is less than you think.

Whether you indicate photographs with keylines or windows, consider having it done by a typesetter rather than a production artist. Some digital typesetting machines can make keylines and windows faster and just as accurately as artists using technical pens. Ask if your typesetter offers this service and, if so, how to write instructions about placement and scaling.

Mechanicals

Assembling camera-ready elements to be photographed for printing is done with adhesives and mounting boards. The name of the procedure and its end product varies from one part of the country to another. We refer to the procedure as pasteup and to its end product as mechanicals. Some professionals use the terms keylines, artboards, or pasteups instead of mechanicals. People who make mechanicals are sometimes called keyliners or pasteup artists. We call them production artists.

Pasteup requires a knowledge of both technology and art. There are lots of tricks, but few absolute rules; problems often have several solutions. One printer may want pages two-up, another only one-up. One may like masking material used to make windows for photos, another may prefer photo size and position shown with black outlines known as keylines. Variations follow schools of thought among graphic designers and their teachers. Styles vary over time and from one city to another.

Regardless of terminology or fashion, the function of mechanicals is always and everywhere to show a printer precisely how each page should look. The message must be accurate and complete, leaving no doubts about what the customer expects.

Because styles and techniques vary, the only way to know printer's preferences regarding mechanicals is to ask. Find out what fits best with procedures in each particular shop. Following are some specific questions to ask. The meanings of unfamiliar technical terms will become clear in subsequent chapters.

Should each page be separate, or should pages be imposed? If imposed, how? Imposition means correctly positioning the individual pages so they fall in the proper sequence when sheets are folded. Commercial printers consider imposition their responsibility. Mechanicals for quick printing, however, must be imposed by the person preparing them.

Should register and corner marks be inside or outside the trim size? Some commercial printers, especially when using stock already cut to standard sizes, like register marks inside the trim area. When it's time to make plates, markings are simply masked out. When using a printer you haven't worked with before, be sure to ask where on mechanicals the strippers prefer placement of register and corner marks.

Should instructions to the printer be on overlays or on mechanicals? Some printers claim every mechanical should have tissue overlays; others say they tear off tissues before starting the job. Prudence requires writing instructions on the mounting board, but sometimes an overlay is the only place with enough room to write extensive information.

Who will make color breaks? Multicolor printing requires a plate for each ink color.

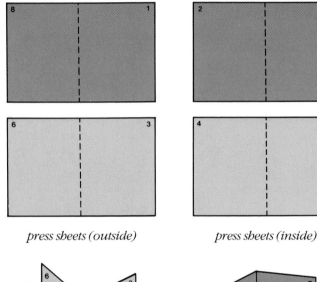

press sheets (outside)   *press sheets (inside)*

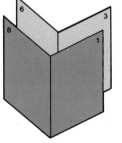 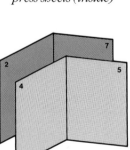

folded sheets (outside)   *folded sheets (inside)*

3-10 Imposition for an eight-page newsletter. Mechanicals or flats must be prepared so that pages fall in proper sequence after printed sheets are collated and folded. In this example, the dark sheet would have pages 8 and 1 on one side and 2 and 7 on the other. The light sheet would have pages 6 and 3 on one side and 4 and 5 on the other. Customers of quick printers must take imposition into account as part of their pasteup. Imposition for commercial printing is the responsibility of the printer.

Sometime before preparation for platemaking, color breaks must be indicated or made.

A color break is an imaginary line dividing copy that will print in one color of ink from adjacent copy that will print in another color. For example, text on one side of the line might be printed in black, while display type on the other side of the line might be in red.

A production artist can indicate color breaks on mechanicals by writing on tissue overlays or actually make color breaks by pasting up acetate overlays. Using tissue, all copy is adhered to the mounting board. The tissue overlay would have handwritten instructions indicating what copy is to print in each color. Using acetate, only copy to be printed in a separate color is adhered to its own overlay. Some printers refer to making color breaks on acetate overlays as making mechanical separations.

We recommend indicating color breaks on tissue overlays and having all copy on the mounting board. Using that method, the printer can make only one negative and simply use masking material to make separate plates from that one negative. This not only speeds pasteup, but also helps to assure precise register.

Process camera operators and strippers have a variety of photographic techniques to make color breaks. Often using one of these techniques is more accurate and less costly than using acetate overlays. When acetate overlays seem necessary, consulting with your printer first will often result in saving time and money.

Should locations for halftones and separations be shown with windows, keylines, or position stats? Many commercial printers want to make their own windows, so recommend keylines. Others follow whatever procedures the

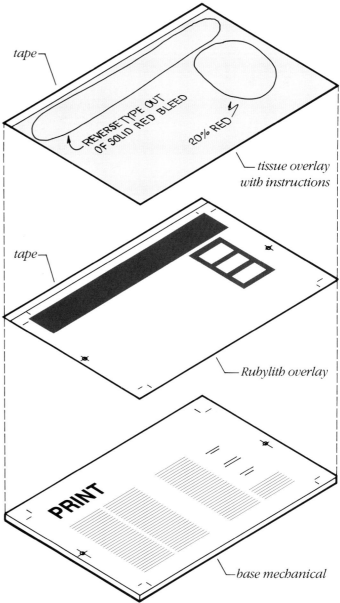

tape

REVERSE TYPE OUT OF SOLID RED BLEED

20% RED

tissue overlay with instructions

tape

Rubylith overlay

PRINT

base mechanical

3-11 Mechanical for a two-color job. The finished printed piece below was printed from plates originating from the mechanical at the right. The plate made from the base mechanical printed the black ink and the plate made from the overlay printed the red ink. Both the overlay and the base mechanical have register and trim marks. Note that the headline "Print" was not pasted up as a reverse and that the production artist used an acetate overlay to make the color break. The printer made the reverse and tint according to instructions on the tissue overlay, but, because of the reverse and the bleed, the production artist decided to make the simple color break.

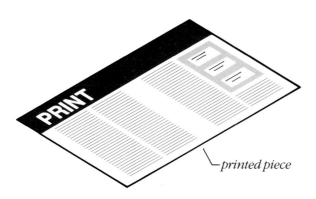

PRINT

printed piece

How to Check Mechanicals

Identification. Make sure that each mechanical and each photograph or illustration is clearly marked with a personal name and the name or number of the job. Information should appear on the front of the board outside the image area.

Correctness. Verify that words say what they are supposed to and that photos and art are what you want.

Completeness. Check that each board and overlay includes all the type, art, and graphics it is supposed to have. All mechanicals, separate art, and dummies should be given to the printer at one time.

Accuracy. Be sure that marks for corners, folding, trimming, scoring, and perforating are the correct distance from each other. Register and trim marks must be correctly positioned and aligned on mounting boards and overlays.

Security. Confirm that all copy is tightly adhered and burnished. Mechanicals should be on strong backings and protected by heavy tissue during handling, transit, and storage.

Cleanliness. Inspect boards, overlays, and tissues to be sure they are free from smudges, fingerprints, bits of glue or wax, and stray guidelines.

Coordination. Examine separate copy such as photos, graphs, maps, and illustrations to be sure they are clean, cropped, scaled, and keyed according to a system agreed on with the printer.

Communication. Look at each board or tissue overlay to assure it includes specifications about ink colors, color breaks, screen rulings and percents, masks, and reverses.

Proofs. When quick printing, make two photocopies of mechanicals so you and the printer each have a proof.

3-12 How to check mechanicals. Because mechanicals are the basis of making negatives and plates, they should be carefully checked to be sure they meet the requirements above.

customer wishes to use. To get the best quality and price from your printer, find out how the shop likes photographs keyed to mechanicals.

Who will cut outline masks for photos or art? Portions of images intended to appear as silhouettes must often be masked. To accomplish the task, opaque masking material is cut to outline the image and block unwanted areas.

As with making color breaks, printers often can make masks more accurately and less expensively than production artists. Printers work directly on the negatives, omitting otherwise necessary work on mechanicals. Production artists can indicate on tissue overlays the outlines of images needing to be masked.

Occasionally a layout calls for a large amount of time-consuming masking that might be done more economically by a production artist than by a printer. Even under those circumstances, consulting with your printer first makes sense because of the inevitable loss of quality during the many steps from overlays to printing plates.

We cannot overemphasize how important these questions are to avoid having a printer ignore or do over something it took a production artist hours to prepare. Discuss the job first to learn how your printer operates.

Printers use process cameras to transfer images from mechanicals to film or plates. When compared to the human eye, however, cameras and films are very unsophisticated. The eye concentrates on details that the brain knows are important, but cameras see everything equally. Dust and smudges get photographed along with type and rules. The eye makes things seem as the brain knows they should be; cameras show them as they actually are. Bubbles, creases, and edges on a surface that should be flat all affect the camera's vision.

Visual 3-12 is a list of features to check to be sure mechanicals are ready for the printer. Also remember an important intangible: mechanicals tell printers how professionally you approach your work. Clean, complete work that is truly camera ready, and is accompanied by clear instructions, gets the respect it deserves.

When you deliver mechanicals, take time for a final check of job specifications. Your printer should agree that mechanicals represent the work described in specifications. If not, determine differences, decide on how they affect production and costs, and write the new information on the specifications sheet. This is the surest way to prevent surprises if you see alteration charges on the invoice when the job is delivered.

Techniques for preparing mechanicals span the entire range of graphic arts technology, from simple hand pasteup to complex electronic assembly. For many jobs requiring basic quality printing, novices can do pasteup. Making mechanicals for printing good, premium, or showcase quality work, however, requires professional skills found at graphic arts businesses.

When hiring a production artist, ask about hourly rates. Pasteup should cost less than either design or typesetting. Also keep in mind that good pasteup requires painstaking work, therefore takes time.

Computer-aided design and electronic page assembly are categories of pasteup. Rates for either may be several hundred dollars per hour. When properly used, however, both can save time and money and may raise quality.

The technology of computer-aided design replaces T-squares and artists' pens and knives with cursors and computer screens. These electronic tools can do the difficult and tedious tasks of making windows, borders, and corners that previously could be done only by hand. Operators work from accurate comps supplied by graphic designers who have indicated coordinates, thicknesses, and shapes. Computer-controlled machines operate within $1/1000$ inch tolerance from one negative to the next, assuring precise and consistent register.

Electronic page assembly lets operators see art and graphics for fully-assembled pages or ads on a screen, often in full color, before producing anything on proofing paper or film. Graphics and art can be changed while visible on the computer screen, stored on a disk, then printed out on demand.

While it is technically possible to digitize type for a computer to assemble along with graphics and art, the cost is usually prohibitive. In most cases, it's much less expensive to add type using standard pasteup techniques.

To locate companies that offer computer-aided design and electronic page assembly, start with color separation services. The software, hardware, and skills are related and many color separators are getting into the computer-aided design business. Look also at ads in national magazines such as *Graphic Arts Monthly*, *Catalog Age*, and *Advertising Age*. ❧

4

Choosing and preparing photographs for reproduction requires a further understanding of the complex relationship between photography and printing. This understanding helps predict how photographs will appear when reproduced and leads to lower costs and fewer missed deadlines.

All original photographs are continuous-tone copy containing many shades and hues from dark to light. Continuous-tone copy must be converted into halftones before it can be reproduced by a printing press.

Photographs that will be reproduced in only one color of ink are converted into one halftone, while those that will be reproduced in two ink colors are made into two halftones and are called duotones. Color photographs that will be reproduced in full color are changed into four halftones called color separations. Full-color reproduction is known as 4-color process printing.

In this chapter, we explain what to look for when examining photographs for printing and show, through use of visuals, differences between images that will print well and those that will not. We define halftones, duotones, and separations and describe how they are made and printed. We discuss working with photographers and other suppliers of photographs.

Photographic terms are so similar to printing terms that precise language is necessary to avoid confusion. We refer to black and white prints, color prints, and transparencies simply

Photographs

as photographs to make clear that these are continuous-tone originals. To identify continuous-tone copy as it is prepared for reproduction on a printing press, we use the standard graphic arts terms halftone, duotone, and separation. These same terms also apply to the printed reproductions themselves.

Although this chapter is about photographs, much of its information also applies to continuous-tone illustrations. They too must be converted into halftones prior to printing.

Black and White Photographs

Printers and trade camera services preparing photographs and illustrations for platemaking should start with the best quality originals that customers can provide. Quality may go down during the many steps between originals and printed pieces, but it is unlikely to go up. To get good halftones, start with good originals.

Visual 4-1 is a checklist to help you evaluate the quality of black and white photographs. When ordering or examining photographs, keep in mind that semigloss photographic paper looks most like the printed piece and gives a better idea of the final outcome. High gloss photographic paper makes blacks look too dense and may have a surface that will crack. Textured photographic paper softens the image and may cause moire patterns. Heavily textured paper has such an uneven surface that its pattern may reproduce along with the image.

Contrast tends to drop during printing, so originals must have good contrast. The original should not look flat (low contrast) or have either highlights or shadow areas without detail (high contrast).

The emulsion on photographic film consists of grains of silver salts that, before being developed, are sensitive to light. Films with rather large grains can capture images using less light than films with smaller grains and are therefore more versatile. Photographers refer to large-grained film as fast and smaller-grained film as slow.

Images made on fast film may not appear as sharp as those made on slower film. Moreover, enlarging photographs makes grains seem bigger. The lack of sharpness carries over into negatives and plates made for printing, detracting from the clarity of the image.

When considering photographs for black and white printing, you will evaluate individual, enlarged prints or contact prints of unenlarged negatives. The groups of unenlarged images on one sheet of paper are proof sheets. Choosing photos from proof sheets (also called contact

---

"Reproducing photos well is harder than doing quality work with line art. When I plan a piece that includes halftones, I know I'll be sending specifications to printers who charge more for the extra attention to detail. I have a memo to myself in my printer file about which shops are capable of the better quality work."

How to Evaluate Black and White Photographs

Focus. Check that important parts of the image are in sharp focus, especially if you plan to enlarge it.

Grain. Be sure that enlargement by the printer will not make the film grain structure so big that it makes the image look fuzzy.

Contrast. Study contrast to be sure you start with strong blacks, clean whites, and a full range of gray tones.

Detail. Inspect shadow areas and highlights for adequate clarity of features.

Flaws. Verify that the photograph is flat and has no scratches, dirt, or blemishes.

Distractions. Examine photographs that will be enlarged to be sure there are no features that may draw unwanted attention.

Photo paper. Make sure that the photograph is on smooth, semigloss paper.

4-1 How to evaluate black and white photographs. The most effective and least expensive way to control the quality of halftones and duotones is to start with good originals. Black and white photographs should meet the above requirements.

sheets) lets you see every image, not just those the photographer wants to present.

Images on proof sheets from 35mm film are too small to inspect with the naked eye. View them through a graphic arts magnifier (sometimes called a loupe or linen tester). Place the magnifier directly on the surface of the print to examine focus and detail. If you prefer, specify the entire proof sheet enlarged to 11 x 14 or even 16 x 20. Many photo services make these sizes for less money than individually enlarging each image.

Remember that all the images on proof sheets were made at once with one exposure. Some may not look as good as they would if exposed individually.

Even using a magnifier, it is difficult to detect on proof sheets distractions such as reflections of strobe flashes that can ruin a picture. If you plan to enlarge an image more than 150% or are uncertain of focus, flaws, or distractions, have a print made to size instead of enlarging it

in the process camera during preparation for printing. The new photograph will reveal whether the image is worth reproducing.

When using proof sheets, specify choices and instructions in black. Use a permanent felt marker or grease pencil to show cropping and areas for the photo service or photographer to lighten or darken during darkroom printing.

Halftones

All photographs must be changed from continuous tones to halftones before they can be faithfully reproduced. Printers make the change by breaking images into thousands of tiny dots. The patterns of dots create an illusion of the original image, tricking the eye into seeing continuous tones. In areas of the image with small dots, more paper shows through, creating highlights; portions of the image with large dots show less paper, thus create shadow areas.

Black and white photographs converted into dot patterns are called halftones; color photographs prepared for printing in color are called color halftone separations. The printing industry refers to color halftone separations simply as separations.

Most halftones for black and white reproduction are made with process cameras; most separations for 4-color process printing are made with scanners. Scanners yield sharper images than process cameras.

When printers convert photographs into halftones using a process camera, they place a screen behind the lens at the focal point of the image. Halftone screens resemble screens used to make tints. Light reflected from the photograph is broken into dots as it passes through the screen.

Process cameras can be loaded with either film or light-sensitive paper. When halftones are made on film, they become halftone negatives; when they are made on paper, they become halftone positives. Halftone positives are for quick printing; halftone negatives are for commercial printing.

Quick printing requires that halftone positives be adhered to mechanicals. Most halftone positives are made quickly and inexpensively

detail dropped out in highlights

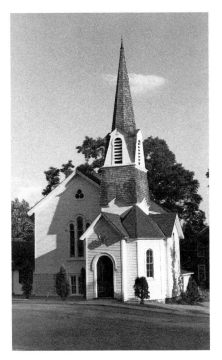

good contrast and detail

detail lost in shadows

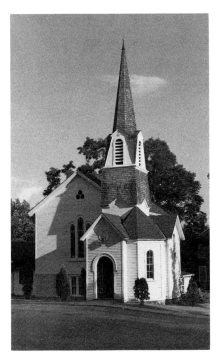

flat contrast

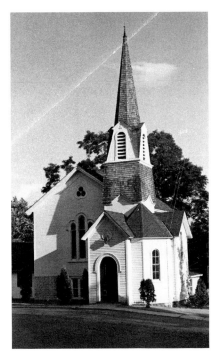

flaws

grain enlargement

4-2 Black and white photographs. Four photos above were poorly exposed or printed by the photographer, so would not look good when reproduced. An original photo that will reproduce well has a full tonal range from white to black that gives it good contrast. Good original prints show details in their lightest and their darkest areas. Low contrast photos reproduce flat and lifeless. Photos with too much contrast lack shadow and highlight details. Images made on fast films with large grains may lose sharpness when enlarged. (Photo by Mark Beach.)

using the PMT process. PMT halftones are suited only for basic quality printing.

Some typesetting machines can be coupled with a simple scanner that converts photographs into halftone positives. The advantage of these machines is that they can scale and place images along with text on fully assembled pages. The quality of the halftone itself, however, is about the same as a PMT.

A halftone positive can also be made by contact printing a halftone negative on light-sensitive paper. Because the paper most often used was once Velox made by Eastman Kodak, the prints are usually called veloxes. When pasted to mechanicals, they produce slightly better results than PMTs but not as good quality as making a plate from a negative.

The velox approach cuts costs for customers who need many prints of the same image, such as for advertisements. It has the added advantage of putting photo cropping and location entirely under the control of production artists.

Be careful that you plan ahead for screen ruling when ordering PMTs or veloxes. Reducing the mechanicals on which the positives appear makes screen rulings finer by moving dots

closer together; enlargement makes screens coarser. A 133 line velox shot at 125% ends up having a 106 line screen and gives no better detail than a less expensive PMT.

Good quality commercial printing may use halftone positives, but usually uses halftone negatives made from photographs given to the printer separately from mechanicals. Premium and showcase quality printing always use halftone negatives, not positives. During platemaking, printers combine the images from halftone negatives with those from the line negatives made by photographing mechanicals.

Quality Considerations

Halftone negatives may be made to a variety of standards depending on whether the job will be printed good, premium, or showcase quality. Some of the quality distinctions come from extra care by process camera operators. Be sure to tell your trade camera service if you plan premium or showcase printing. For showcase printing, you may prefer halftones made by a scanner to those made by a process camera.

Like screens for tints, screens for halftones are measured in lines per inch. Coarse screens such as those used by newspapers and quick printers are 65 to 120 lines; medium screens in news magazines and company publications are 133 or 150 lines; fine screens in premium or showcase quality brochures or annual reports range from 175 to 300 lines.

Printers use technical considerations to decide the right screen ruling for each job. These considerations include quality requirements and the type of press on which the job will run. Sheetfed presses typically reproduce finer screens than most web presses.

Just as with screen tints, the paper on which halftones will be printed affects choice of screen ruling. Uncoated paper absorbs ink quickly: dots may soak in, spread out, become fuzzy at their edges, and touch. A somewhat coarse screen helps shadow areas retain detail on uncoated paper. Coated paper holds ink on its surface, so a finer screen may be used.

With most jobs at commercial printers, 133 or 150 line screens give satisfactory results. As

4-3 Continuous tones to halftones. The ball and background are coarsely screened at 40 lines per inch to make individual dots easy to see. Even these large dots create the illusion of the original continuous-tone image. (Airbrushing by Kathleen Ryan.)

screen ruling gets finer, every step in the process takes more care, so costs more. Contrast and shadow detail are especially hard to reproduce when using fine screens. Showcase quality pieces printed offset might use 300 line screens with 90,000 dots per square inch—nine times the number of a 100 line screen. While yielding extraordinary results, 300 line screens are very difficult to print by offset and only a few printers are capable of reproducing them.

The choice of screen ruling affects quality, cost, and schedule. Consult with your printer. For specialized help, ask your printer or paper distributor for demonstration materials made by paper manufacturers. Paper mills such as S. D. Warren and Hammermill publish booklets showing photographs in many screen rulings and colors, with special effects, and on a variety of papers. These materials are free and make exceptionally good visual aids for learning about halftones, duotones, and separations.

Camera operators can manipulate the way a halftone appears by changing its contrast. For example, you might want a photograph with normal contrast to print flat to achieve a special effect. Some low contrast photographs can also be given more contrast while being made into halftones. Because changing contrast costs almost nothing extra, it pays to tell camera operators how you want photographs to reproduce.

The size of a halftone is limited by the dimensions of both process camera and halftone screen. Screens larger than 16 x 20 are not common; a halftone bigger than that for a poster or mural might have to be shot at a trade camera shop or specialty printer. There is no way to shoot a halftone in two pieces, then fit them together to form one image.

Color photographs may be halftoned for printing black and white, but will not look as good as starting with a black and white photo of

4-4 Halftones in three screen rulings. The halftones at right were made with three screens of different, commonly-used rulings. As the rulings get finer, details in the image become more clear. The choice of screen ruling for a specific job is determined by its paper, printing method, quality requirements, and budget. (Photo by Mark Beach.)

halftone reproduction using an 85 line screen

halftone reproduction using a 120 line screen

halftone reproduction using a 150 line screen

photograph as halftone reproduction

pencil drawing as halftone reproduction

photograph as line reproduction

pencil drawing as line reproduction

4-5 Continuous tones as halftone and line reproductions. The bottom version of the portrait shows what happens when a photograph is printed without being halftoned. The original of the lily is a continuous-tone pencil drawing that reproduces most faithfully as a halftone. Sometimes line reproductions of continuous-tone copy are used for their special effects. (Photo by Kathleen Ryan; drawing by Cherry Britton.)

the same image. If you must start with color originals, remember that graphic arts film sees red the same as black. Red areas of the original photo will lose detail and the resulting halftone may have too much contrast.

Some illustrations require halftoning. Images made with soft pencil lines or brush strokes have continuous tones the same as photographs. Whether to treat a specific illustration as line art or to halftone it is a matter of judgment and often means compromise. When made into halftones, fine lines may drop out

(vanish). On the other hand, the same illustration treated as line copy may lose detail in dark areas. Consult with a printer whenever in doubt about how a specific illustration will reproduce.

Asking a printer to enhance a black and white photograph or to halftone an illustration or color photo may leave you uncertain of the outcome. To check how plates made from halftone negatives will reproduce using white paper, ask for a velox halftone as a proof. The slight extra cost will be repaid with your confidence that the image will satisfy you.

normal halftone with border

outline halftone with border

concentric circle line conversion   *mezzotint line conversion*   *two-color posterization*

4-6 Special effects. Photographs should be examined for how pleasing they will appear when reproduced. The image at the top left lacks interest in the background. It looks better with a printed keyline or with the undesirable area masked out. Some photographs are enhanced when reproduced using a line conversion screen, such as circle or mezzotint, rather than a halftone screen. Posterization may or may not involve a screen. The example above was shot as two line negatives, one for midtones and one for shadows. Plates made from two negatives for a posterization are printed using different ink colors, in this case cyan and black. (Photo by Kristin Finnegan.)

brown impression

black impression

brown and black duotone

4-7 Assembling a duotone. Duotones are combinations of two halftones printed to create a denser image or special coloration. Greater density expands the tonal range, giving the image more contrast. Brown was used here as the second ink color to better simulate the old photograph. (Photo by Thomas Cronise from the Oregon Historical Society.)

Duotones

Two halftone negatives of the same image are used to make two plates that are printed in register to produce a duotone. The two plates can be printed using black ink for both, black for one plus a second color for the other, or a separate color for each.

Good duotones are made from black and white photographs. They should not be made from color photographs.

There are two reasons to use duotones. First, the full tonal range of a good photograph is impossible to capture in a single halftone. A plate made from a single halftone negative cannot be made to print the shadow areas dark enough without sacrificing quality in other parts of the image. Using two negatives, printers can make one to favor highlights and the other to favor shadows. The plate made from each negative can be inked with black or another dark color to produce a rich image.

The second reason to use duotones is to achieve a color effect different from using only black ink. Many effects are possible by combining two colors of ink. An otherwise ordinary photo can be made dramatic by coupling the high contrast of a line shot with its halftone. Duotones can also be created by combining a halftone with a line conversion such as a mezzotint or concentric circle screen.

Because duotones can create such a variety of effects, you must tell your printer or camera service what you want. Use technical language and show printed samples to describe the outcome you seek. To avoid rosettes or moire patterns, your printer may suggest making duotones from screens with different rulings.

To take best advantage of the duotone process, select photographs with long tonal ranges and good shadow detail. Samples of duotones published by paper companies use photos meeting those requirements. Sample books also show duotones in a variety of color combinations that can help you decide whether you want a "normal" duotone with both ink colors about equal or whether letting one color dominate might yield a more pleasing effect.

blue impression

black impression

blue and black duotone

4-8 Duotone effects. Duotones may be printed with halftone negatives that have been exposed for special effects. In the example above, the negative for the blue impression was slightly overexposed, then flashed without a screen to drop out dots in the highlights. The result was a plate that printed blue in the water without putting many blue dots in the sails or sky. (Photo by Mark Beach.)

Duotones cost more than simple two-color printing because they require more precise register and demand excellent stripping and press work. To see how your duotone will look when printed, ask for an overlay color proof.

Printing jobs that call for two colors but lack the budget or quality control for duotones can be done in fake duotones. This technique requires printing a halftone in one color over a light screen tint of the second color. Fake duotones do not demand tight register and look exactly as their name implies.

Color Photographs

Color prints and transparencies must be changed into halftones before they can be reproduced by a printing press. The quality of the resulting separations, like halftone quality, depends on the originals from which they are made. In most cases, the best separations originate from transparencies.

Visuals 4-9 and 4-10 explain and illustrate what to look for when examining color photographs. These visuals cannot, however, convey the importance of using a standardized light source when examining color photographs, proofs, or printing. The kind of light used heavily influences how colors are perceived. Sunlight is not suitable because it varies with the time of day and weather conditions. Artificial lights vary even more.

Examine photographs on a light table or viewer equipped with bulbs rated at 5000 degrees Kelvin. Equipment made to standardized viewing conditions will also have a CRI (color rendering index) of about 90, will cast about 200 footcandles of light on reflective copy, and cast 400 footlamberts through transparencies.

Ad agencies, printers, trade color shops, and design studios that deal with separations should be equipped with proper viewing areas. The area may be as complex as a booth with gray walls and standardized lights or as simple as a light box with appropriate bulbs. Proper viewing equipment is not expensive, especially when compared to the cost of buying and printing separations. If you deal in any way with 4-color process printing, use correct lighting.

How to Evaluate Color Photographs

Focus. Confirm that important parts of the image are in sharp focus, especially if you plan to enlarge it.

Color density. Study colors to be sure they appear strong and fully saturated.

Color balance. Check that colors seem true to their real-life counterparts (original scenes or objects).

Color cast. Look to see that there is no overall color that seems untrue to the original scene or object.

Grain. Be sure that enlargement by the printer will not make the film grain structure so big that it makes the image look fuzzy.

Detail. Inspect shadow areas and highlights for adequate clarity of features.

Flaws. Verify that the photograph has no scratches, dirt, or blemishes.

Distractions. Examine photographs that will be enlarged to be sure there are no features that may draw unwanted attention.

Patterns. Make sure there are no patterns such as checked clothing that may cause moires when printed.

4-9 How to evaluate color photographs. The most effective and least expensive way to control the quality of separations is to start with good originals. Examine transparencies or prints to be sure they meet the above requirements.

Reproductions of color photographs can be made starting with either transparencies or photographic prints. Transparencies give the best results because they are sharper and their colors are more intense.

When projecting transparencies or viewing them on a light box, be cautious. Looking at sharpness and studying key elements under backlit conditions is fine, but the intense brilliance may deceive you about how bright images will appear when printed. Backlighting also shows more shadow detail than can ever be reproduced by a press.

Transparencies are viewed properly with emulsion side away to assure that you see the scene the same way the photographer did. The emulsion side should be down on a light table or toward the screen during projection. The printing on cardboard slide mounts appears on the same side as the film emulsion.

The emulsion on a transparency is easily damaged. Fine particles of dirt can make scratches, and acids in perspiration can etch the emulsion. Be very careful not to touch the image area of a transparency.

Many customers are familiar with transparencies only in the form of 35mm slides. The 35mm format is popular because of the convenient size of its cameras and accessories. Larger format cameras, however, produce photos better suited to many printing jobs.

There is a direct relationship between size of photograph and sharpness of the image when enlarged for printing. A 35mm slide enlarged to 8 x 10 grows by 700%. If the image is cropped even slightly, enlargement can be over 1000%. Enlarging decreases sharpness because the grain structure of the film is magnified. Keeping enlargement to a minimum guarantees the sharpest printed image.

All printing should begin with the best possible photographs in the format allowed by the photographic situation. Ideally, showcase and most premium printing should begin with large format transparencies. In the language of photography, 35mm is small format, 2¼ x 2¼ is medium format, and 4 x 5 and 8 x 10 are large format. It is not likely that you will get 8 x 10 photos under conditions of candid or wildlife photography, but you should expect large format images from studio work.

Color films are made to be exposed under specific lighting conditions. If the light wasn't right, photographs may have an overall color cast that was obviously not part of the original scene. Photographs made with outdoor film, for example, will have a gold cast if exposed under tungsten light and a green cast if shot under fluorescent light.

Color photographic prints made for reproduction are known as C-prints and are made from negatives. Because they come from negatives, C-prints are already second generation images before being prepared for platemaking. Transparencies are first generation images. Prints made from transparencies require an internegative, so are third generation images.

Separations

The technique of reproducing full color photographs is called 4-color process printing. It is also used for the reproduction of continuous-tone color illustrations.

Because 4-color process printing uses four ink colors, original images must be divided into four negatives so the printer can make four plates. The act of dividing a color photograph or illustration into four negatives is called color separating. The negatives themselves as well as the reproductions made from them are referred to as separations.

Technically speaking, color separations are halftones. Plates made from each separation

normal exposure, good detail

blue color cast

overexposure, poor highlight detail

underexposure, poor shadow detail

4-10 Color transparencies or prints. Color films exposed under improper lighting conditions may have an overall color cast. Underexposure or overexposure can also lead to loss of shadow or highlight details. Color separation services may be able to correct color casts when making separations, but cannot put details into separations where none exist in originals. To keep separations consistent, provide photographs all made from the same film and under the same lighting conditions. (Photo by Kathleen Ryan.)

multicolor printing   *4-color process printing*

multicolor enlarged to 600%   *4-color dots enlarged to 600%*

4-11 Multicolor and 4-color process printing. Multicolor printing can use any colors of ink, but 4-color process printing must use only the process colors. Only 4-color process printing can simulate the full color of originals, but it normally costs more than multicolor printing because of the expense of making separations. The multicolor image is printed in black plus two colors of ink. (Painting and drawing by Cherry Britton.)

could be printed with black ink or ink of any other color. It is only because the four halftones are printed in register with each other using specific colors of ink that they simulate the original full color image.

The four standard colors used to print separations are yellow, magenta (red), cyan (blue), and black. These are called the process colors. Using combinations of them, printers create the illusion of full color. The combinations simulate hues in color photographs and art.

Printing color separations is much more difficult than printing single halftones. The dots of each color must align correctly with the dots of the other three colors.

Because 4-color process printing requires precise alignment of four separate images, it is not suitable for quick printing. Basic quality jobs, even when printed by commercial printers, should not involve 4-color process printing. The technique is suitable only for jobs in the good, premium, and showcase categories.

Some customers confuse 4-color process printing with multicolor printing. Process color printing is for reproducing continuous-tone copy. Printers must use all four standard ink colors and only these four. Other ink colors won't work. Multicolor printing, on the other hand, can be used to add color for a variety of effects. Any colors are technically suitable.

Color separations are made by photographing originals four times through different filters to create four negatives. Each filter allows light of a specific color to strike the film and blocks out light of all other colors.

The four separation negatives are used to make printing plates. On press, each plate must print with the appropriate color of ink: one with yellow, one with magenta, one with cyan, and one with black. Printing the dots from the four plates in proper register puts the separation back together to give the illusion of full color.

To understand better the concept of separations, it may be helpful to know that transparencies consist of the process colors. If you could peel layers of emulsion from a transparency, the top layer would be yellow, the middle layer magenta, and the bottom layer cyan.

Color separations can be made with a process camera, but most are made by scanners, which work faster and give better results.

Color scanners are machines that project pinpoints of light onto images to be separated. The light is transmitted from the image, through filters that separate the colors, and back into the machine as it creates a halftone separation. Scanners are usually coupled with computers that can digitize images, store them in electronic memory, and present them on a screen for color correcting.

The current technology of most color scanners requires that images be wrapped around a cylinder, not flat on a copyboard as with a process camera. During scanning, the cylinder rotates as light moves across the image. Photographs, art, and products for scanning must be flexible enough to wrap evenly around the cylinder. When separations are made from 35mm slides, the cardboard mounts are removed before taping the transparencies to the cylinder.

Separations can be made from transparent or reflective (opaque) images. Transparencies give the best results because they are vivid and sharp. Light transmitted through them is far more intense than reflected light. Color prints lack the brilliance of transparencies.

Air brush art, oil and watercolor paintings, and color pencil drawings are all reflective, so they can be separated. The color of many artist pigments and dyes, however, cannot be matched by printing inks. If in doubt, consult your printer. You might also consider making test separations of artists' samples.

Colors in flat products such as wood paneling and fabric can be separated when the products are placed directly on a process camera or scanner. Results may be superior to using a photograph of the same product.

Dot size and screen ruling work the same in separations as they do in halftones for black and white photos. Separations can be made using coarse, medium, or fine screens identical to those used to make halftones.

When planning separations, your printer will have rather strict criteria about screen ruling. Ruling can only be decided as part of the decisions about specific papers and presses and is subject to the same quality considerations as ruling for halftones. If you want to use screens finer than 150 line, discuss your wishes with a printer before ordering separations.

Evaluating Color

Customers who do not understand the limitations of 4-color process printing are frequently disappointed that printed colors don't match originals. Printers work with inks in dot patterns, not with dyes or pigments in continuous tones. Printed images are themselves reflective art influenced by inks, coatings, and especially paper. Working with only four colors of ink, printers try to create the illusion of all colors.

Consider the matter of brightness. A good transparency appears twenty times brighter than ink on gloss paper. There is no way that even the best color printer can come close to reproducing its vivid tones. The mechanical process of printing is no match for the chemistry of photography.

"After two days shooting on location, my client decided to reverse titles out of the sky. If I had known that, I could have framed for more sky. Fortunately, the color separation service could use its computer to add some sky, but it cost the client much more than having me do it right when I was shooting the photographs."

yellow printing negative

original transparency

magenta printing negative

4-12 Color separations. When a color transparency or print is separated, it is photographed four times through four filters to create four halftone negatives. Light from the image passes through a blue filter to create the negative whose plate will print with yellow ink; a red filter makes the cyan printing negative; a green filter yields the negative for the magenta plate. Because an image reproduced with these three colors would lack sufficient contrast, a fourth halftone negative is made to add black ink.

The four ink colors yellow, magenta, cyan, and black are the four process colors. When these four colors are printed in register, they combine to simulate colors in the original photograph. In practice, printers are limited in what they can accomplish with process inks, so reproductions cannot be expected to match original photos and scenes. (Photo by Kathleen Ryan.)

cyan printing negative

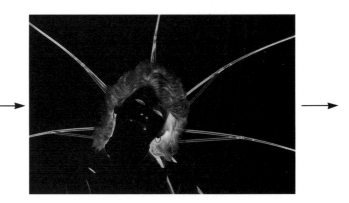

black printing negative

impression from the yellow plate

yellow impression

impression from the magenta plate

yellow and magenta impressions

impression from the cyan plate

yellow, magenta, and cyan impressions

impression from the black plate

yellow, magenta, cyan, and black impressions

Customers need to understand that the process of separating and printing compresses the color spectrum at a loss of detail and contrast. A good color photographic print looks better than most color press work. Color prints are about twice as bright as 4-color process printing on glossy paper.

To get an idea of how the image on a transparency will appear after separating and printing, make a photographic print first. The print will look much more like the printed piece than the transparency.

Color is a matter of taste. What is vivid to one person seems flat to another; a little more red for the designer may seem like a lot more red to the printer; the photographer might see a blue cast which no one else can detect.

Because color is subjective, buyers must speak to separators and printers in language everyone understands. The language is based partly on standards and partly on experience. Colors in ink swatch books and process color guidebooks provide the standards. Printers also speak plain English. You can tell them that you think there is too much orange or that the greens aren't bright enough and let them worry about adjusting magenta or cyan.

Some colors can be made brighter or more vibrant in the printing process by adding a fifth color of ink. For example, red areas already printed magenta become much brighter when printed again with rubine or rhodamine. This technique, of course, requires a separate halftone negative, plate, and press run or inking station for the fifth color.

4-13 Moire pattern. Negatives for tints, duotones, and color separations must be screened at correct angles and assembled properly when reproduced. If they are not, they can cause a moire pattern such as the one above. The possibility of moires is why it is sometimes difficult to make a new halftone of an image already reproduced as a halftone.

Color separators can make the printed product look quite different from the original. When they make changes deliberately according to your instructions, it's called color correcting. An overall change, such as eliminating a green cast, is easy and inexpensive. More precise correcting, such as improving skin tones, takes more attention, thus costs more.

Sophisticated scanner systems use computers to correct color in separations. Color images on a computer screen are adjusted visually using electronic instructions. Separations made with process cameras must be color corrected with chemicals (dot etching) or exposed again through filters (masking).

Electronic correcting is not appropriate for every image that needs improvement. Air brushing and retouching on photographs before they are halftoned or separated may be more convenient and less costly than scanner work. For maximum control over quality and cost, give trade services good originals.

Color looks most vivid when printed on coated, white paper. Coatings prevent ink from absorbing, thus give sharp images. White paper provides a background that assures ink colors will not interact with paper colors to affect the outcome. Like color, whiteness is subjective. If in doubt about the whiteness of a particular paper, ask for comparative samples. Your printer or paper distributor will be happy to give you samples and discuss each in detail.

Most printing jobs that include separations involve reviewing color proofs in two stages. The first stage is when you see one proof for each separation. These individual proofs are called loose proofs because they have not been assembled with type and other copy. Loose proofs are often referred to by brand names such as Cromalin or Matchprint. Examining them is somewhat similar to studying prints of color photographs.

The first batch of loose proofs shows how the color separation service interpreted your photographs and instructions. Critical evaluation of color should be done using that first batch. In most cases, the separation service or printer expects you to ask for color correcting some of the images. Don't hesitate to criticize

4-color process printing in register   *4-color process printing out of register*

4-14 Correct and poor register of 4-color process printing. Register is affected by the accuracy of stripping, the quality of the press and its operator, the quality and condition of paper, and conditions in the pressroom. Effective printing buyers learn to recognize printing that is poorly registered. (Photo by Kathleen Ryan.)

color and ask to evaluate a second batch. Final cropping instructions can also be placed directly on the loose proofs.

After you have approved loose proofs, separations can be assembled with the rest of the job. The proofs made at this stage are referred to as composite or full proofs because they show color images in position with type and other copy. Composite proofs are made from the same proofing material as loose proofs.

In addition to showing separations in position, composite proofs let you check the accuracy of register, color tints, overprints, and other features that do not show well on bluelines. Once composite proofs are made changes become very expensive. If a problem does show up at this stage, be sure to identify who is responsible to pay for correcting it.

Color Separation Services

Color separating is a craft requiring sophisticated equipment and technical skill. Most printers are not equipped to make separations, even those who do a lot of 4-color process printing. Separations are usually purchased from a color separation service.

Although separations are usually purchased by printers, printing buyers can work directly with separation services. Direct dealing requires experience, but results in more consistent quality and may save money.

To locate color separation services, look under "color separations" or "lithographic negatives and plates" in a classified directory, read ads in trade magazines, or ask your printer or graphic designer.

Inquiries about color separation services may reveal sources in distant cities. If you feel nervous about sending valuable transparencies and unsure how you will deal with proofs, ask for references to local customers. Also compare local prices. You may find the savings are not as great out of town as you thought at first, especially after local shops learn that you know about nationally competitive prices.

If you prefer to have your printer buy separations for you, you should still have some direct dealings with staff at the separation service. Whenever possible, you should evaluate proofs on the premises of the separation service. Being at the separator's place of business lets you use its superior viewing conditions while speaking directly with people who will make changes.

When you order separations, tell your printer or color service what you want to achieve. Discuss overall color and note any photos you believe need improving. Point out the areas of each image that you consider most important for holding detail or color fidelity. Try to express your ideal of how the image will look when reproduced. As part of the ordering procedure, double-check scaling and cropping and verify screen rulings.

Ordering color separations involves deciding what quality you want. Color separation services typically offer three quality levels:

Pleasing color. This means you like the reproduction, but it doesn't necessarily correspond to the original photograph. Sky is blue and grass is green, but there's no fine tuning. Pleasing color separations are appropriate to good quality printing.

Match transparency. Tones and hues are balanced and the separation looks much like the original photograph. Match transparency separations should go with premium quality printing jobs.

"When my graphic designer ordered separations to 'match product,' I wish I had known how expensive that would turn out to be. We paid for color correcting just to make an ordinary catalog for selling tools. Who cares if the brown in the picture isn't quite the same as the brown in the hammer handle?"

Match product. The color is adjusted and proofs are examined until you're satisfied that separations are as close as possible to original scenes or objects shown in the photo. Showcase quality printing calls for the additional care that goes into match product separations.

Although graphic arts professionals use the terms "match transparency" and "match product," they know that literally duplicating the colors in a photograph, scene, or product is impossible. Customers who use these universally accepted terms must keep in mind the limits of reality when imagining how separations will appear when printed. The colors, vividness, and sharpness of originals cannot be matched by a printing press.

When thinking about the quality you need or when viewing proofs, keep in mind the reasons why you want 4-color photographs in your printed piece. Unless you are in the photography business, you probably don't care whether separations come close to originals. Think of photographs as media for getting information into print, then evaluate separations and proofs based on the extent to which they will communicate your message effectively.

The order a printer places for separations includes specifications for screen ruling, types of screens and proofs, color correcting and cropping, type of paper, and deadlines. If you buy directly from a separation service, you write the specifications. Unless you're very experienced, it is best to consult with your printer before proceeding.

Staff at color separation services need to know the name and phone number of printers using their separations. Close communication is imperative. For premium and showcase quality printing, the service needs to know what paper will be used and on what press your job will run. Send a sample of the paper.

Separations for advertisements must be made to the specifications of the publication in which they will appear. If you don't know those requirements, tell the separation service the name of the publication. Color separation services own guidebooks in which they can look up specifications for thousands of newspapers and magazines.

Size, quality, turnaround time, and the kind of originals you submit determine the cost of separations. Transparencies cost the least to separate, followed by color prints and other reflective art. Rigid art that cannot be scanned costs the most.

Color separation services can do much more than make separations. They can make halftones, duotones, tints, and reverses, then completely strip and proof the job. Negatives completely prepared are called plate-ready and must be made according to the technical requirements of specific printers and presses. If you order plate-ready negatives that turn out to have problems on press, you are responsible for extra costs to the printer.

Many separation services can do electronic retouching such as that shown in Visual 4-15.

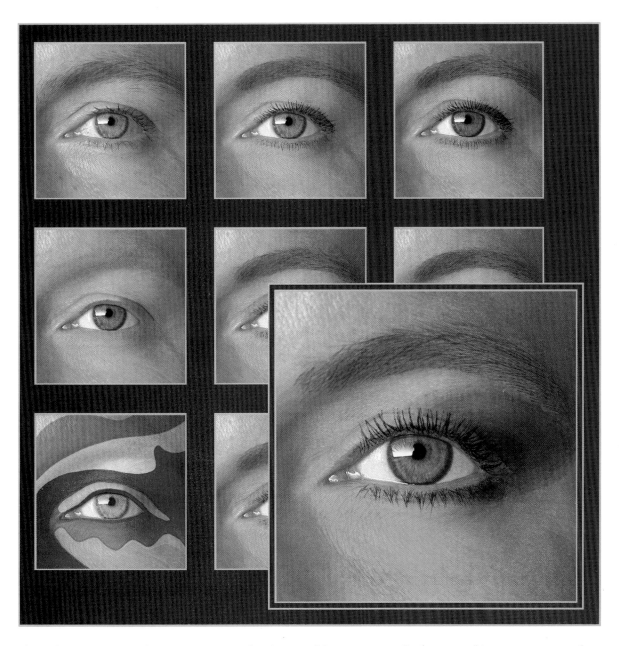

4-15 Electronic retouching. Computer technology enables operators of color retouching computers to alter images electronically after making scanner separations. The computer can eliminate tiny flaws or make bold changes, depending on customer needs and ability to communicate clearly with the operator. Working with only one original image, a computer operator created the variety seen here. (Courtesy of Color Imaging.)

electronically assembled image

unmanipulated images

Electronic retouching involves using a computer to manipulate an image that has been scanned and recorded as digital information. The image appears in color on the computer screen and is enhanced or corrected in response to keyboard commands by the operator.

Separation services that can do electronic retouching can also create new images from several original photographs. Electronic image assembly involves selecting portions of photos that have been scanned and digitally recorded, then combining those portions into a new image. After the new image has been created, it can be electronically retouched.

Taking best advantage of computer capabilities at separation services requires that you give precise instructions. As with ordering any separations, you must tell the service exactly how you want the retouched image to look or what portions of images you want combined. Instructions for image assembly are best given by providing the service with color prints or photocopies of transparencies on which you have circled and described important features.

Separation services capable of electronic image assembly can assemble full pages of color images. Carried out at design terminals, the procedure requires very sophisticated equipment, highly trained operators, and immense capacities for storing digital information. The service is expensive, but can save hundreds of hours of pasteup time and stripping for complex advertisements and pages in consumer catalogs and newspaper inserts.

From a technical standpoint, electronic image and page assembly can include type as well as photographs. From a business standpoint, however, including type is usually not practical for two reasons. First, scanning type or media conversion from one digital format to another is expensive. Equally important, you are more likely to change type at the last minute than photographs or illustrations. Using traditional pasteup methods for type keeps costs down and flexibility up.

Most trade camera shops and color separation services do not use the trade customs giving them ownership of all materials made in the course of preparing jobs. If you buy separations, you own them; if a printer buys separations for you, the printer will probably claim title. To avoid dispute, establish ownership in writing before authorizing work to begin.

Ganging

When several photographs have been halftoned or separated at once to save time and materials, they have been ganged. Getting the best possible quality requires careful planning. Even with the best planning, however, ganging cannot result in quality as good as giving each original individual attention.

Photographs for ganging must be scaled to the same percentage. No camera or scanner can reproduce one original at 100% and another at 75% in the same shot.

To gang photographs at different sizes, order duplicate transparencies or prints to the desired size, then gang the duplicates. Color separation services sometimes have the facilities to duplicate transparencies. If not, ask them to recommend a professional photo lab.

A poorly exposed photograph can often be improved when duplicated. Duplication, however, tends to reduce the sharpness of the image that will be halftoned or separated. Ganging duplicated photographs can cut costs substantially, but is not appropriate for premium or showcase quality printing.

Successful ganging depends on selecting photographs with certain characteristics in common. All must have similar contrasts. Transparencies for ganged separations should all have equal color balance and density and must come from the same type of film.

4-16 **Electronic image assembly**. Operators of graphic arts computers can select portions of several scanned photographs, store them in digital memory, then combine them into a new image. In this example, the starting point was a photo of a gas station called The Bomber. The computer operator removed genuine vehicles from the image and substituted studio shots of toys. Electronic image assembly is costly, but much less expensive than building miniature gas stations or life-sized toy cars and trucks. (Courtesy of Color Imaging.)

Varnishing

Halftones, duotones, and separations can often be enhanced during printing by overprinting with varnish. In addition to adding sheen, varnish protects the surface of the image.

Varnish is applied by a press in the same fashion as ink. Flood varnishing covers the entire press sheet; spot varnishing covers selected areas. Both flood and spot varnishing require a printing plate and spot varnishing has the same register requirements as printing with ink.

Usually a gloss varnish is used to add sheen. Matte varnish, however, is available for situations that call for making an image less glossy. For details about varnish, see the last section of Chapter Six.

Working with Photographers

Photographs by commercial photographers to be used in publications are categorized as advertising, publicity, corporate, or editorial. These categories are very general. For example, corporate photos include those of workers, equipment, buildings, and even products when the purpose is publication in a newsletter or technical manual. Corporate photography includes work for associations, agencies, schools, and institutions, as well as private industry.

The market value of a photograph is determined by its use, not its subject or style. An image reproduced on the cover of an annual report is worth far more than the same image inside a brochure. The measure of value is the client's potential profit or benefit, not the quality of the photo or how difficult it was to make.

Commercial photographers tend to specialize in one of the four market categories. Within each category, they concentrate on styles such as studio work or action. Printed products requiring a variety of photographs may need images from more than one photographer.

Before commissioning work, try to anticipate all your needs. The photographer can work most efficiently if one lighting setup, modeling session, or visit to a site can be made to produce all the images necessary from that situation. Moreover, the photographer might well

unvarnished

portions of photograph spot varnished

entire photograph spot varnished

4-17. Varnishing. Because printing inks often don't seem glossy enough, even when printed on a gloss paper, using gloss varnish can add sheen. Varnish also makes colors seem richer and protects the inked surface. Spot gloss varnishing can add sheen to an entire photo or to portions of it. Varnish, like ink, is applied by a press and requires a plate. (Photo by Gene Ahrens.)

organize the work differently from how you would do it. Professionals should also ask at what size and quality level photos will be reproduced and when you need them.

Some photographers charge by the hour or day, others by the job. The American Society of Magazine Photographers (ASMP) publishes price guidelines, but most photographers charge what the traffic will bear.

A photographer may be represented by an agent. If so, the agent will handle business details so you and the photographer can concentrate on the assignment. Agents are paid by photographers, not clients, and typically get 25% of their fee.

Commercial photographers have large supplies of previously-made images, known as stock photos. Also, stock photo services advertise in magazines serving advertising and public relations agencies and are listed in classified directories under "photographic prints and transparencies." The *Stock Photography Handbook*, published by ASMP, includes details about almost 150 stock photo agencies.

In most localities, there are many non-commercial sources of stock photos. Museums, historical societies, university archives, and government agencies often have large collections and minimum reproduction charges. Serious amateur photographers have collections they may share for expenses and credits. Photos by amateurs, however, usually have not met the same legal requirements as those taken for commercial purposes.

Stock photo services and commercial photographers generally sell rights, not ownership. You will be asked about how you plan to use an image and may be asked to sign a form limiting use. For example, if you buy rights to reproduce a photo in a magazine, you would pay an additional fee to use the same photo later for the cover of a brochure.

Photographers work under the same copyright laws that apply to graphic designers and illustrators as explained in Chapter One. Unless a different contract is made, photographers expect to keep negatives and provide clients with prints. When providing transparencies, they expect to get them back in the same condition as when furnished.

If you want to own copyrights to photographs, have exclusive use, or have access to the images for future jobs without additional fees, negotiate the arrangement before work begins.

In addition to copyright regulations, photographs for publications are affected by laws about privacy and libel. Under certain conditions, your photographer or stock photo service should assure you that you can legally use a photo. Those conditions occur when the image has recognizable people and will be used in a paid advertisement, as public relations, or in any situation that might prove embarrassing to the people.

For an image to be legally used under one of the above conditions, the photographer must have a model release signed by the recognizable people in it. A model release is a contract granting the photographer and the photographer's clients the right to license, sell, and/or reproduce the image. It is the photographer's responsibility to obtain and keep files of model releases. When buying rights to a photograph, a client may ask for copies of releases.

When you receive photos from either a photographer or a stock agency, they will be sent on approval and be accompanied by a delivery memo. A delivery memo is a form verifying receipt of the photos and agreement to contract terms. Even though you keep the photos a week or two, you should sign and return the memo at once.

Photos should always be treated carefully, especially when they don't belong to you. Make sure transparencies stay in their protective sleeves and prints are handled only in their margins. Never leave photos exposed to light for longer than it takes to examine them. Daylight and fluorescent light, including the tubes in a light table, can fade color in a few hours.

While doing design and layout, it's handy to have duplicates of all the images you might use in your printed piece. The duplicates do not have to be made to the same quality standards as the photographs you will give the printer and may even be photocopies. 🍂

5

The transition from mechanical to plate is based on principles of optics and chemistry common throughout the printing industry. With quick printing, image transfer happens in just a few seconds. At a commercial printer, making negatives, flats, and plates may take several days.

The work done in a print shop to get images ready for printing is called preparation. Some printers refer to their prep department or say that a job is in prep. Preparation includes using a process camera to photograph mechanicals, inspecting and, if necessary, touching up the resulting negatives, assembling the negatives ready for platemaking, and making plates.

Understanding how commercial printers make negatives and plates is just as crucial to controlling quality and cost as preparing correct mechanicals. Negatives and plates are the links between design and production. No amount of adjustment on press can improve the quality of images coming off bad plates.

Frequent alterations and poor planning for efficient assembly of negatives can lead to preparation costs that are unnecessarily high. Controlling quality and costs also requires knowing how to read proofs and understanding how much work is involved in making various types of changes.

This chapter is about the processes of transferring images from mechanicals to negatives, then to plates. We describe how negatives made from line copy are combined with those from continuous-tone copy during stripping or

Transmitting the Job

Camera Work

Stripping

Proofs

Alterations

Plates

Saving Negatives

Preparation and Proofs

platemaking and tell how lithographic plates carry images. We explain several types of proofs and discuss ownership, storage, and insurance of mechanicals, negatives, and plates.

In this chapter, we include a checklist about how to inspect proofs of all kinds. Using the list should help assure that you get from your printer the results you planned for.

Transmitting the Job

When mechanicals and loose art such as photographs are given to a printer, they become part of a transient collection of jobs from many customers. Your materials should be submitted all at once, not piecemeal, and should, if possible, all be in one large envelope or box. Your name and the name of the job should appear on the outside and also on each item inside.

At the time that you hand copy to your printer or sales rep, both of you should examine it to make sure everything is there and is ready for camera work or scanning. The inspection should include a review of specifications and instructions.

The materials you give your printer along with camera-ready copy should include dummies and proofs. The specifications you wrote may not accompany the job, so dummies and proofs become key links between you and your printer's staff.

Before your job starts on its path through the printing company, a supervisor prepares its work order. The work order, sometimes known as a job ticket, is a form that travels with the job and helps people keep track of activities and materials related to it. Your specifications are translated onto the work order telling how the job should be handled within the shop. The work order also shows dates on which the job should clear each department and the date of expected delivery.

Work orders are intended for internal record keeping, not for inspection by customers. Because they include entries from various workers as the job progresses, work orders may become the only written record of the time, supplies, and materials required to complete each stage. If your invoice shows a charge for alterations, your printer could have relied exclusively on the work order when computing those charges.

"There's no such thing as proofreading too long, too often, or too carefully. Once I saw a glitch on a blueline that looked just like a squashed bug. I figured it was a flaw in the proofing paper, and didn't hesitate to sign the approval ticket. When I saw the same bug on my 50,000 booklets, I checked my mechanicals. Sure enough, there it was—a camera-ready fly. Now I circle every ding, flaw, and hole for correction, no matter how silly or insignificant it looks. And I don't accept phone calls while I am proofing. Even then, I often feel so nervous that I'm willing to pay for a second blueline just to be absolutely sure all my changes got made."

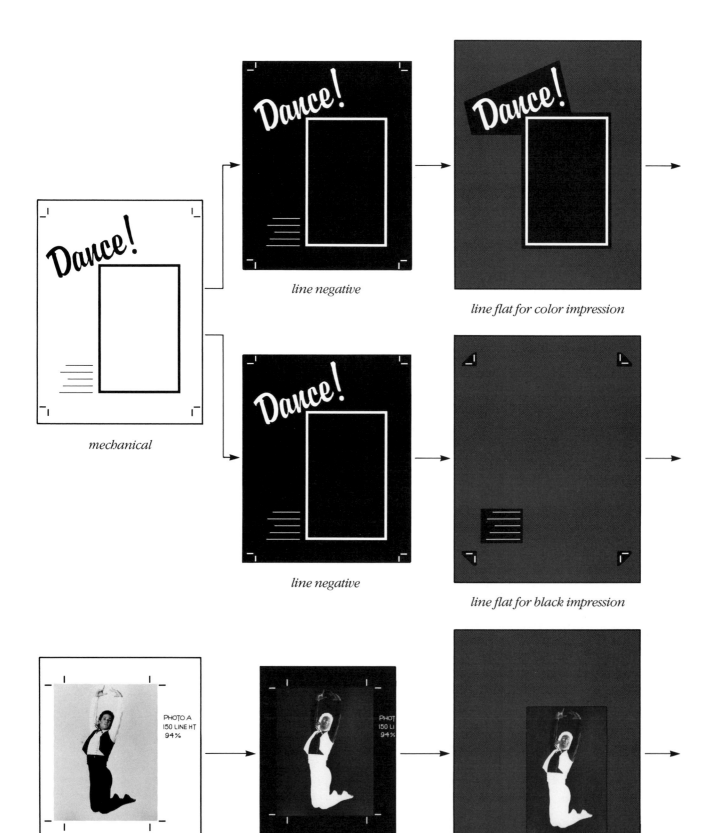

mechanical

line negative

line flat for color impression

line negative

line flat for black impression

mounted photograph

halftone negative

halftone flat for black impression

PHOTO A
150 LINE HT
94%

PHOT
150 LI
94%

plate for color impression

press sheet

finished piece

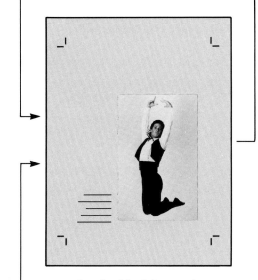

plate for black impression

5-1 From camera-ready copy to printed piece. This schematic presents steps in the production sequence of commercial printing for a two-color job with one halftone. The mechanical has elements for both colors pasted up on the mounting board and would have color breaks indicated on a tissue overlay.

In this example, the printer makes one line negative of the mechanical for the elements that print in color, a second line negative for the elements that print black, and a halftone negative for the photograph. The three negatives are then stripped into three flats. The plate that will print color is made from the flat holding the line negative for the color image. The plate that will print black is made by exposing it first with the black line flat and then with the black halftone flat.

Press sheets are usually larger than finished pieces to ensure there is enough paper outside the image area for grippers to hold. Outside edges are trimmed away in the bindery. In this example, trimming will cut slightly into the word "Dance" and its exclamation mark, thus creating bleeds off the left and top edges of the finished poster. (Photo courtesy of Keith Martin Ballet Company.)

Camera Work

After its work order is prepared, a job is ready for photographing with a process camera that operates as explained in Chapter Three. Most printers have their own camera department, although many use a trade camera service. Separations for 4-color process jobs are usually made using a scanner located at a color separation service. Trade camera and color separation services may also strip negatives and make plates, depending on a printer's needs with a specific job.

On reaching the prep department, materials are examined again by workers who will guide their transition from camera-ready copy to printing plates. Camera operators and strippers read the work order and consult with the sales rep, and in rare cases they speak directly with the customer.

Each shot with the process camera yields a piece of film which, after being developed, becomes a negative. A simple job might have only one negative, a complicated job might have hundreds. Every negative corresponds to an element of copy that might be as small as the address on a business card or as large as a poster.

Process camera operators convert both line and continuous-tone copy into negatives. Photographs for reproduction as halftones would be represented by one negative, as duotones by two negatives, and as separations by four negatives.

Stripping

The negatives from process cameras and scanners must be assembled before platemaking. The procedure, called stripping, involves adhering negatives in correct positions on a sheet of masking paper or polyester film.

Working at light tables, strippers tape the negatives to the masking material. They then cut away the mask covering the image area of the negative. The cut-out area is a window. Light can pass through the image area of the negatives and through the windows in the mask, but not through the masking material surrounding them. The final assembly is called a flat.

One flat may contain all the negatives needed to make a specific plate, or only some of them. For example, one flat might contain halftone negatives and a second flat contain negatives for type. Both flats would be required to make the single plate for printing one side of a piece having both type and halftones in the same ink color.

In Chapter Three, we urged that all copy be adhered to mounting boards whenever possible. We suggested that color breaks be indicated on tissue overlays, not made on acetate overlays. In addition to saving time during pasteup, putting all copy on mounting boards keeps the possibility of register errors during stripping to a minimum. In the case of multicolor printing, the printer either masks the mechanical to make multiple negatives or masks the base negative to make multiple plates.

A base negative shows copy on a mounting board. Getting as much copy as possible onto base negatives minimizes the need for film, camera work, and stripping, thus saves time and money as well as enhancing quality.

Negatives made from mechanicals include register and corner marks added during pasteup. Strippers use the marks to position negatives precisely. The stripper's job is to follow instructions and guide marks on mechanicals. If these guide marks are slightly off, the printed images could end up out of register or wrongly positioned on the paper.

The fact that strippers rely on register marks, corner marks, and keylines to position negatives explains why guide marks are crucial

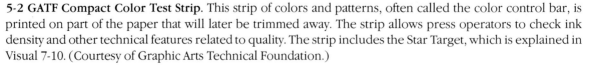

5-2 GATF Compact Color Test Strip. This strip of colors and patterns, often called the color control bar, is printed on part of the paper that will later be trimmed away. The strip allows press operators to check ink density and other technical features related to quality. The strip includes the Star Target, which is explained in Visual 7-10. (Courtesy of Graphic Arts Technical Foundation.)

to quality control. Strippers also refer for guidance to comprehensive layouts or other dummies and to mechanicals. These tools are like roadmaps showing how the job should look.

Printers must know how sheets will fold so they can tell strippers the proper arrangement of negatives on the flats. Consider a simple one-color, 16-page booklet with no halftones, to be folded from one sheet of 23 x 35 paper, printed eight pages on each side. As many as 16 negatives must be stripped into two flats to make two plates, one plate to print each side of the paper. Negatives must be stripped in an arrangement such that, when the sheet is folded, pages appear in proper sequence.

Consider that same 16-page booklet printed black and red and with ten halftones. That product requires 42 negatives: 16 for the black, 16 for the red, and 10 for the halftones. The 42 negatives go into six flats, three for each side of the paper. The three flats are 1) type and line art for printing in black ink, 2) type and line art for printing in red ink, and 3) halftones for printing in black ink.

A large catalog or book such as this one may have 1,000 negatives assembled onto 100 flats. The negatives must be arranged so that pages are in the correct sequence after the printed sheet is folded. Properly arranging the negatives in the flats is called imposition.

Because imposition is complicated, it pays to keep in mind the stripper's job when you make a dummy or write instructions on mechanicals. Make sure that dummies and layouts show accurately and completely how you want the job to appear when finished. Leave nothing for the stripper to guess.

When two ink colors are designed to touch on the printed sheet, it is called a butt fit. The images must be precisely registered. To guarantee butt fits, printers must overlap colors approximately $1/100$ inch. If the overlap isn't planned, variations on press may lead to sheets with a thin, unprinted line between colors.

Overlapping ink is called trapping. Flats and negatives for each color must register for trapping. Halftones and separations designed to print with borders touching them must trap the border lines.

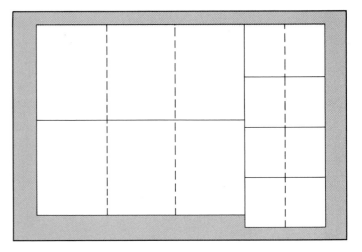

5-3 Ganging. Sometimes several copies of one job, or of different jobs, may be ganged on the same press sheet. In this example, a 26 x 40 sheet yields two menus that will fold to 8½ x 11 and four display cards that will fold to 5 x 6.

While making flats, strippers check negatives for scratches, pin holes, and other flaws. Using either a paint called opaque or red litho tape, they cover defects or unwanted copy. Opaquing or taping a negative is similar to using white correction fluid to cover a typing mistake. Often strippers can repair broken type and lines by scraping the emulsion side of the film to allow light through.

Flaws and mistakes in negatives that need to be changed, not merely opaqued, require additional cutting and stripping. Words, lines, or entire paragraphs as well as graphics and halftones can be cut out and replaced with a piece of film carrying the correct image. Another way to correct mistakes is to mask out the wrong area of the negative and make a flat holding only the correction. The flat holding the correction is double burned onto the plate.

Stripping new material into a negative may save time and cost less than making a whole new negative from a corrected mechanical. On the other hand, correcting the mechanical as well means that both pasteup and film are accurate. In addition, it may be difficult to produce corrections that have the same density as previous material. Shooting an entirely new negative from corrected mechanicals assures consistent density between old and new copy.

Proofs

Every printing job should be proofed before going to press. No matter how good the mechanicals, camera work, and stripping are, there is plenty of room for error.

A proof in the graphic arts is any test sheet made to reveal errors or flaws, predict results on press, and record how a job is intended to appear when finished.

Checking proofs as jobs progress is the only way to verify that mechanicals, negatives, flats, and plates are accurate and complete. Having proofs at press time means that the first printed sheets can be checked efficiently. Proofs also help determine who is responsible for mistakes and should pay for correcting them.

When examining the color in proofs, it is imperative to use proper lighting conditions. Shops that do color printing have special areas for viewing proofs. If standard conditions are not available, use a well-lit place with warm light such as sunlight. Most important, be consistent: don't look at proofs under fluorescent lights and compare them to transparencies held up to sunlight.

After examining a proof, you must decide whether to approve it or ask for another proof. If you approve it by signing your name, you authorize the next step in the production sequence. If you ask for another proof, you will have to wait a day or two to verify changes.

Often customers comment about flaws showing on a proof, but sign it anyway. They feel the flaws are minor and, trusting the printer to repair them, don't want to bother with another proof. Whether a specific situation calls for approving an imperfect proof depends on the nature of the flaws, your confidence in the printer, and your budget and schedule.

Proofs for printing jobs are made in three ways: xerographically (photocopies), photographically (bluelines, overlays, and integrals), and mechanically (press proofs). Each serves specific purposes, depending on the job.

Photocopies. A photocopy of the mechanical is the only kind of prepress proof available with quick printing. We recommend that you make two photocopies of every mechanical, one for you and one for the printer. Stick pages together back to back for two-sided jobs. Collate, fold, trim, staple, or drill just as you expect it to be done in the bindery. Leave nothing to the printer's imagination.

Bluelines. A blueline, sometimes called by the Dupont brand name Dylux, is a photographic contact print of negatives. Bluelines of fully stripped flats are made on paper with the same dimensions as the press sheets for your job. They can be folded and bound so you can check crossovers, backups, and page sequence.

Whether to get a blueline for a routine job depends on how much you trust your printer. If there's only the base negative, probably your

original image   *flopped image*

5-4 Flopping. An image is said to be flopped when it faces opposite from its original. Flopping may be done deliberately to enhance a design or by accident. Photos and illustrations in bluelines should be examined to be sure they are correctly positioned. Type in a flopped image appears backwards, as in the case of the hotel sign above. Flopped images may prove embarrassing when they rearrange urban geography. (Photo by Kristin Finnegan.)

photocopy proof is enough. On the other hand, if there are overlays, halftones, reverses, tints, or anything that will not show on a photocopy, only a blueline will tell you whether everything was stripped correctly.

Because they do not show separate ink colors, bluelines are not suitable for proofing complicated multicolor jobs. With simple two-color jobs, however, color differences can be indicated on a blueline by varying exposure times. Bluelines often have different tones from page to page. They also fade rapidly when exposed to light, especially direct sunlight.

Overlays. Overlay color proofs, also known by the 3M brand name Color Key, are photographic products showing each color of the job on a separate sheet of polyester film. Sheets are laid over each other in register and taped to backing paper. Overlay proofs for 4-color process jobs consist of four pieces of film taped together, one for each process color.

Using overlay proofs helps to visualize what copy is included in each color, a feature especially useful with jobs involving maps, charts, and graphs. Printers using one-color presses need overlay proofs to help analyze ink densities for the separate passes through the press. These proofs are fast and inexpensive to make, but have the disadvantage that the polyester film itself has a slight color cast, either yellow or gray. Looking through three or four layers can distort colors and sharpness.

Available in only a few standard colors, overlay proofs show color breaks, but are not recommended when color matching is critical. They are useful for multicolor printing at all quality levels and for good quality 4-color process work. Overlay proofs are not suitable for evaluating color separations for premium or showcase jobs.

Integrals. Integral color proofs, known by brand names such as Transfer Key, Cromalin, Matchprint, and Gevaproof, are intended primarily for proofing color separations. Integral proofs look quite similar to color photographs or to finished printing done on white, glossy paper. Dyes and toners can be matched to inks, ensuring the best possible parallel between proof and final printed product.

How to Read a Proof

Individual features. Make a list, then check each feature through the entire proof. For example, go through once just counting page numbers then again checking how pages back up each other. Next check borders and rules for alignment and crossovers. Go on to examine headlines and other display type for typos and placement. Finish by studying areas of critical register.

Masking and trimming. Look carefully at each page to be sure no elements have been mistakenly masked out or trimmed off.

Photographs. Check every photograph to be sure the correct image is in the correct space, is scaled and cropped properly, and faces the proper direction.

Flaws. Clearly circle every blemish, flaw, spot, and broken letter, and anything else that seems wrong.

Previous corrections. Confirm that corrections noted on previous proofs were made.

Instructions. Write directly on the proof in a bold, vivid color. Be very clear and explicit.

Finishing. Anticipate problems in the bindery. Measure trims to be sure they are what you want. Check that folds are correct and relate to copy as planned.

Colors. Be sure you know what copy prints in each color when proofing multicolor jobs on bluelines.

Questions. Inquire about anything that seems wrong. Asking questions that may seem foolish is a lot wiser than printing mistakes.

Costs. Discuss the cost of changes and agree about who pays for what.

5-5 **How to read a proof.** When examining a proof, keep the above items in mind. Above all, take your time. Proofs are the last chance to find mistakes before plates are made.

Because they show colors quite close to those of production runs, integral proofs are superior to overlays. The proofs themselves have a gloss finish. A slight disadvantage is that integral proofs sometimes look better than the printed product because they do not suffer from dot gain (explained in Chapter Seven). Integral proofs are useful for all quality levels of 4-color printing and imperative for all premium and showcase work.

Color proofing materials are expensive, so the proofs themselves cost a lot. Integral proofs cost about 15% more than overlay proofs.

Press proofs. Press proofs come from plates put on press, inked, and run on paper specified for the job. Being nearly identical to production sheets, they are the best proof. Only press proofs, for example, show the true effect of dot gain or the way in which the color of paper may affect ink colors when printed. For this reason, some customers regard them as essential to premium and showcase 4-color printing. Press proofs, however, are costly in both time and money and are becoming less necessary as new technology makes overlay and integral proofs increasingly accurate.

Progressives, called progs, are a form of press proof. When they are proofs of 4-color process jobs, all four plates are mounted on press, but some sheets are printed only in a single color or in combinations of the full number. Progs look something like the color separations printed in process colors in Visual 4-12. A full set of progressives shows a press operator precisely what is expected from each plate.

Publications often specify progs of advertising copy. We believe the current high quality of overlay and integral proofs renders expensive progressive proofs obsolete unless you need more than ten complete sets. After about ten sets, the unit cost of progressives will probably be less than that of photographic proofs.

Visual 5-5 tells how to examine a proof. Proofs need every possible set of eyes. Although people at the print shop will look for problems, you cannot assume that they will find them all or, if seeing them, will make repairs. In addition, new mistakes can slip in when old ones are corrected. Everything must be checked and double-checked.

"The art director who retired last year told me the rule of thumb that a change costs $5 on the mechanical, $50 on the blueline, and $500 on the press. I made a poster illustrating that concept and put it where our clients as well as the production people in our agency can see it. Everyone needs constant reminding of how expensive changes become in late stages of a job."

Alterations

Final costs almost always exceed quotes because of changes from the original specifications. Understanding how alterations affect costs helps keep budgets under control. Most alterations take place during film preparation, not press or bindery work.

Printers usually base estimates and quotes on specifications, not final copy. When mechanicals come into the shop, they may include work the specifications sheet didn't mention or the estimator couldn't predict. There may be photographs needing special attention, new copy that needs stripping in, or bleeds the customer forgot to mention.

Alterations also occur when customers change their minds between writing specifications and producing camera-ready copy. A customer may need just a few more photographs or want slightly better paper or decide some headlines should be screened or reversed. New ideas always seem to make jobs cost more, rather than less.

When making or authorizing changes, be sure to put everything in writing. If your photographs turned out beautifully and you decide that you want them printed as duotones instead of halftones, don't just casually mention it to your sales rep over lunch. Write it down.

Printers base quotations and delivery dates on what you promise to provide them. Don't promise complete, camera-ready art, then leave just one or two things for the printer to take care of. If you want more tints, reverses, halftones, or separations than you originally specified, expect to pay extra.

Mistakes fixed after seeing a proof cost someone money. If your printer made the mistake, there should be no charge to you. When you made the error, you pay.

Quotations typically include the cost of one proof. If you or the printer require a second proof to verify changes that you wanted, you pay. If the second proof is necessary because of stripping errors, the printer should pay for making it.

The cost of alterations varies from almost free to very expensive, depending on the nature of the changes and at what stage they occur. We use the rule of thumb that a change that costs $5 at the pasteup stage will cost $50 at the negative stage and $500 on press.

Line art in negatives is easily corrected when designed to print in one color. Changing type that has been screened or reversed is more difficult and costly. Halftones are usually easy to do over. Changing or color correcting separations, however, is always expensive, especially after they have been stripped into flats.

After negatives are stripped, any change in format such as a revised page count, a new trim size, or a different number of colors means major alteration costs. New formats require at least partial restripping and may require refiguring the entire job.

Some complicated jobs require producing flats in two stages. The first involves making negatives and flats called working film. Changes at this stage are relatively easy to make. In stage two, composite film is made from the working film. Composite film is assembled ready for making plates. Even a simple change after the composite film is ready may require a whole new set of negatives.

You can find something wrong with any printing job at any stage of production. The question is whether you want to change it—whether it really matters. Always ask what alterations will cost before deciding to make them. When computing the costs of changes, remember to figure time for you and your staff. All that running around keeps you from getting this job done and the next one started.

Plates

After you have approved photographic proofs, the printer is ready to make plates. A printing plate is the surface carrying an image to be inked and transferred to paper.

To understand how a lithographic plate works, think of a fresh printing plate as you would a fresh piece of photographic paper. Both come from their package with no image and both have light-sensitive coatings. Exposure to light produces an image on the surface of either the paper or the plate.

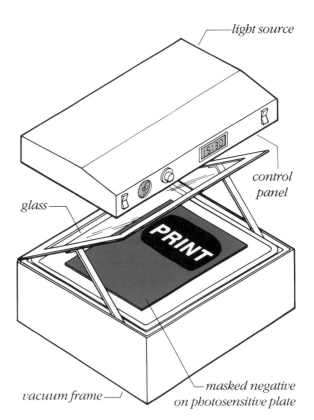

5-6 **Contact platemaker.** Machines for burning plates from negatives vary greatly in size, but function essentially like the one shown here. When the glass cover is closed, the vacuum system assures firm and uniform contact between plate and flat.

Light passing through the clear areas of a negative transfers the image from the negative to the paper (photography) or plate (lithography). When portions of a printing plate are exposed to light, the exposed coating fuses to the metal backing and becomes receptive to ink.

The clear area of the negative through which light passes is the image area. Technically speaking, image areas may be as small as one dot in a halftone or as large as the entire plate. In practice, however, printers refer to the portions of the plates that will carry ink as the image areas. The margins of this book page lie outside its image areas.

Lithographic plates are smooth: both image and non-image areas lie on the same plane. It is only chemistry that attracts ink to image areas and repels ink from non-image areas. Plates for letterpress and gravure printing (explained in Chapter Eight) feel rough and carry ink mechanically, not chemically; image and non-image areas lie on separate planes.

Lithography is based on the incompatibility between ink, which is oily, and water. A plate on press gets a thin coating of water each time the cylinder on which it is mounted revolves. Water adheres to the non-image area, giving it a coating to prevent ink from also adhering. The image area has exactly the opposite reaction: it repels water and accepts ink.

Printers refer to exposing a plate to light as burning it. Making one plate from one flat requires a single burn (one exposure). Using two flats to make one plate requires a double burn (two exposures). Strippers may make separate flats for reverses, tints, or corrections, so some plates might be burned three or four times.

Metal plates are burned by contact printing the plates with negatives stripped into flats. The equipment used is called a platemaker.

To burn a plate, operators put a fresh plate with its emulsion side up in the platemaker. They place the flat with negatives emulsion side down over the plate, then lower a glass cover. A vacuum system in the machine forces the flat into tight and uniform contact with the plate. Once contact is made, the plate is burned (exposed) by very intense light that passes through the glass cover and negatives before striking the emulsion surface of the plate.

Dots for screen tints are burned onto plates by placing a screen between the flat and the plate, then making an exposure. A headline is screened by passing light through its image area on a negative, then through the screen, before the light strikes the plate. The headline may be contained on a separate flat or may be on a

base negative, depending on the printer's style of operating. If the headline is on the base negative, the printer would mask it when burning the body copy, then mask out the body copy for a second burn to screen the headline. This extra work is one reason why screen tints cost more than solid images.

Most platemakers use a pin register system to assure plates and flats are in proper register with each other before burning. The system consists of a row of small metal posts (pins) corresponding to holes at the edges of both plates and flats. When flats and plates are slid over the posts, they lie correctly registered to each other. Because printers use different pin register systems, repinning may be necessary when flats must be used by another printer.

Once exposed, printing plates are developed by wiping chemicals across their surfaces. The chemicals remove portions of coating that were not exposed to light, leaving the image behind. Watching the image emerge as some metal plates develop is much like watching the development of an instant photo.

Camera-direct paper and plastic plates for quick printing are made by a process camera designed to double as an automatic platemaker. The "quick" part of quick printing refers in part to the fact that plates are made directly from mechanicals without the intervening steps of making and stripping negatives. Camera-direct plates are often called masters to distinguish them from metal plates.

Quick print plates work well for jobs not needing fine detail. Designed for short runs, masters typically show signs of wear after about 5,000 impressions. Masters stretch and wiggle on press, making tight register impossible.

Some customers believe metal plates guarantee good results and paper plates yield junk. This isn't true. The difference between quality and junk depends on the job. Quick printing is appropriate for many jobs where commercial printing would be a waste of time and money. Other jobs require results simply not achievable with paper masters.

Shops doing quick printing can mount metal plates on their presses if necessary. The printer would have the plates made at a trade

This is an example of underexposure.
This is an example of correct exposure.
This is an example of overexposure.
This is an example of incorrect focus.

5-7 **Negative and platemaking problems.** Underexposure of negatives or plates reproduces type that is too fat; overexposure makes type too thin. Type that is the correct weight but fuzzy or broken results from the process camera being poorly focused.

camera shop. Using a metal plate, many quick printers could produce good quality work. A quick print press, however, even when using metal plates, is not capable of premium or showcase quality work that calls for more than one ink color.

Saving Negatives

Most printers save flats, but not plates. Plates tend to degenerate quickly during storage. Negatives, however, stay usable almost indefinitely when stored under proper conditions. In addition, negatives can be updated easily, but plates cannot. Although some plates can be used again, most printers prefer to make new plates for reruns. Flats can also be disassembled into loose negatives for stripping into a new job.

Sometimes customers want to leave old flats intact but use some of the same images to create new jobs. While shooting mechanicals and other art, printers can make a second set of negatives to cut apart for other uses. A second set of color separations can be especially valuable, with all of the quality at less than half the cost of the first set.

Flats store easily in horizontal folders and should never be rolled. For jobs frequently reprinted at a shop that you know you will continue to use, ask that print quantities and dates be entered on the folder holding flats for each job or in some other recording system. As the record builds over the years, it helps you plan by telling you how many you printed in what months and years.

Few printers store flats indefinitely. If you think you will ever go back to press, ask about company policy. Some printers routinely throw away flats after storing them for a year or two.

The question of who owns mechanicals, negatives, flats, and plates is different from the question of where they are stored. Trade customs imply that customers own mechanicals and loose art that they furnish and stipulate that printers own negatives, plates, and other materials that they make or provide. Customers have challenged printer ownership from time to time and the issue remains cloudy.

If you want to own materials made by your printer, include your desire for ownership with your specifications or purchase order. Settle the matter as part of the contract, not by worrying about it after the job is delivered.

Ownership of negatives and flats can influence where you take future business. It may be awkward a year later to remove your materials from one shop so you can use the services of another. To avoid this problem, specify with each job that you own negatives but are asking that they be stored at the print shop which, presumably, has proper storage conditions.

Few printers want to store your mechanicals or photos. If you want them stored at the print shop, make special arrangements. If not, be sure the printer returns them promptly, check to be sure they are complete, and sign for them. Mechanicals left at a print shop without instructions may be thrown away after the job is printed and delivered.

Even if you still have mechanicals after a year or two, they may have degenerated to the point that no printer could make new negatives. Degeneration is especially a problem with PMTs and typesetting on photopaper made for temporary use. In addition, waxes and glues used for pasteup may deteriorate to the point that copy falls off mounting boards.

If you store any property at a print shop—artwork, negatives, plates, or finished pieces—examine storage conditions. Some printers simply pile things in a convenient corner of the warehouse. Your materials should be stored so they are reasonably safe from fire, humidity, water damage, and vandalism. Most printers feel responsible for your materials while using them, but not while storing them.

Mechanicals and flats aren't worth much as physical objects, but are priceless because of the effort it would take to replace them. Provisions for insurance on customers' property while in the shop vary among printers. Don't discover too late that mechanicals or photographs waiting for camera work are not insured. Remember to check whether insurance covers the cost of making new flats or the value of your time to furnish new mechanicals. ❧

6

The choice of paper affects every aspect of printed products from design to distribution. Graphic designers often choose paper while products are still in thumbnail stage. Early decisions are imperative for jobs requiring large amounts of paper that must be special ordered. Delivery from a distant warehouse could take weeks; from a mill, months.

The cost of paper represents 30% to 40% of the cost of the typical printing job. Choosing paper should be done carefully. On the other hand, upgrading paper is an easy and often dramatic way to improve an entire publication or project. The cost difference between routine and outstanding paper might be insignificant when compared to the cost of the job as a whole. Upgrading paper adds nothing to the cost of writing, design, or printing.

There may not be a perfect paper for every job. Finding the right combination of finish, color, opacity, bulk, cost, and availability often requires compromise. Creative use of knowledge about paper makes it possible to find paper to suit your needs without lowering quality or raising costs.

Printing papers fall into seven grades: bond, uncoated book, text, coated book, cover, board, and specialty. Each grade has quality levels appropriate to specific applications. You will have greater control over quality and cost when you know the features that distinguish one grade of paper from another and how to coordinate papers from different grades.

Paper and Ink

In this chapter we describe papermaking, define general terms used when talking about paper, explain major types of paper and their uses, describe envelopes and their availability, and discuss the paper business as it relates to printers and customers. There are five charts showing features and uses of various grades of papers. The charts are guides for specifying paper, but the data they contain should be checked locally before ordering. We end the chapter with a similar, though much shorter, discussion of ink and protective coatings.

Throughout this chapter we use "paper" and "stock" as synonyms. Some buyers use more general terms such as "media" or "substrate" to reflect the fact that printing isn't always done on paper.

Making Paper

Mills make paper from cellulose fibers. Wood chips, rags, or other sources of fiber go into huge tanks to mix with sulphite or sulphate and water. Chemical action stimulated by heat separates the mass into individual strands. The result is pulp.

Before sending pulp into the papermaking machine, mills remove impurities and add bleach to increase whiteness. The pulp is beaten to help fibers adhere to each other. Extensive beating yields smooth, translucent paper; minimal beating results in paper that is soft and opaque. During the beating process, mills add internal sizing to pulp for paper to be printed by offset lithography. The sizing agent, usually rosin, makes fibers slightly water resistant so the paper will not act like a blotter during printing. Paper that absorbed moisture during printing would expand, thus making tight register almost impossible.

After pulp is cleaned, beaten, and sized, it is mixed at the rate of one pound of pulp to 100 pounds of water. The resulting blend, called furnish, goes directly into the headbox, shown in Visual 6-1. Immediately below the headbox a fine screen called the Fourdrinier wire forms a wide, endless belt. The wire is mounted on rollers designed to carry furnish forward as well as vibrate it side to side. Furnish flows from the headbox through a slit onto the wire where the combined actions of vibration and gravity withdraw water. As the water drains, fibers settle and interlace to form paper. The movement of the wire aligns fibers roughly parallel to each other, and gives paper its characteristic grain. The amount of furnish released from the headbox

"When I was made responsible for coordinating all the printing jobs for our company, I was also given a budget. The first thing I did was plan how we would use paper. I reduced the quality of paper we used for internal publications like reports that don't need to impress anyone. The money saved by that step let me specify better quality stock for those jobs like brochures that will be seen by our potential customers."

and how fast the wire moves determine how thick the paper will be.

While furnish is still on the wire, it passes under the dandy roll to receive a finish such as laid or wove. As water continues to drain, the side of the furnish touching the wire also takes on a shallow pattern.

Immediately after paper passes under the dandy, the machine trims away excess by passing the edges of the paper under a thin, high-pressure stream of water. A straight stream cuts clean; slight spraying creates a deckle edge.

When furnish reaches the end of the wire, it's still over 90% water. The machine transfers the furnish from the wire belt to one made of felt and draws the emerging paper between pairs of heated rollers. Each pair of rollers gradually removes more water. By the end of its high-speed trip through drying rollers, paper will have travelled almost a mile and its water content will be reduced to about 5%. Proper and consistent water content assures that paper will receive ink correctly when going through a printing press.

During the drying sequence, mills can press in patterns to make textured papers or apply clay to the surface to make coated stock. As paper leaves the drying rollers it may pass through a stack of highly polished calender rollers. Calendering presses the paper to make its surface smoother.

The papermaking machine winds finished paper into rolls weighing as much as four tons. Without stopping the process, workers remove one roll and start another. Later the rolls may be slit for shipping to paper distributors and printers. Paper from rolls may also be cut into sheets and packaged in cartons or on skids. Paper shipped in rolls is ready for web presses; in sheets, for sheetfed presses.

The chemical process described above results in relatively pure paper called a free sheet. Low-grade paper, called groundwood, comes from grinding logs into fibers. Groundwood paper is full of impurities, is not very strong, and yellows quickly. On the other hand, it is inexpensive, very opaque, and works well for newspapers and other short-life products.

Paper Characteristics

Paper has ten characteristics that determine its quality and cost and that also influence whether it is suitable for printing a particular job on a specific press.

Bulk. Printers refer to the thickness of paper as bulk and measure it in thousandths of an inch expressed as point size. Six point paper is .006 inches thick. (Note that the system of points used when referring to paper is not related to the system of points describing type size. Paper points refer to thickness; type points refer to

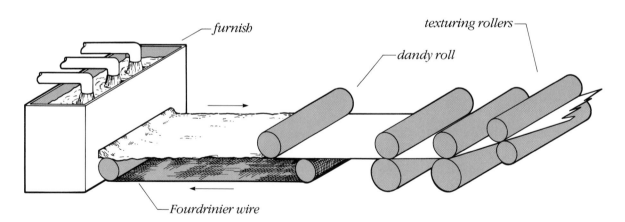

6-1 Papermaking machine. The typical papermaking machine represented by this schematic is 400 feet long and 20 feet wide, and produces about 350 tons of paper per day. Starting at the wet end of the machine, furnish that is 99% water and 1% fiber flows evenly onto the Fourdrinier wire. As the wire passes under the dandy roll, furnish is smoothed and may receive a watermark. After leaving the wire, paper goes between rollers that

height.) Because the instruments used to measure thickness are either micrometers or calipers, printers may talk about a sheet's mike (short for micrometer) size, how it "mikes out," or its caliper. It all means the same thing: stock that mikes at ten points or has a ten point caliper is .010 inches thick.

Book publishers often express bulk in pages per inch (ppi). Knowing ppi is important when specifying type sizes for book spines. Publishers—not ours, of course—sometimes specify high bulk paper to make their products thicker and seem worth more money. Bulk may also add opacity with no increase in weight.

Formation. Ideal printing paper has fibers uniformly distributed across the sheet. When held to the light it shows no clumps or open areas that might result in mottling. Stock with good formation comes from pulp carried on the Fourdrinier wire slowly enough to allow fibers to spread evenly.

Color. Mills add dyes and pigments to pulp to create uncoated paper of virtually any color. Color varies from mill to mill and there is no standard for naming colors. What one mill calls ivory may be called buff or cream at another. Colors from the same mill might show slight variations from one run to the next. Color match may be affected by bulk and finish. Your favorite gray may seem a shade lighter in 24# bond for letterhead than in the 80# cover stock for business cards designed to match.

White is the least expensive paper. Colored paper costs more because it is in less demand. Light colors such as cream and natural cost slightly more than white and costs increase as colors get darker. Most mills will make colored stock to your specifications if you want enough and have plenty of time. Coated stock tends to come exclusively in whites, with a few mills making tones they call cream or natural; uncoated stock comes in white plus light colors; and text papers come in white plus a full range of intense colors. Color in paper increases opacity and decreases brightness.

Acid-free paper resists deterioration and keeps its color for decades. Few customers use acid-free paper, thus paper distributors may not have a ready supply. You'll probably have to order at least one full carton, and perhaps as many as four.

Brightness. The amount of light that paper reflects is expressed as a percentage. Most papers have brightness ratings between 60% and 90%. Fluorescent dyes added to white paper can make its brightness close to 100%. Mills use the brightness scale to assign quality classifications to paper.

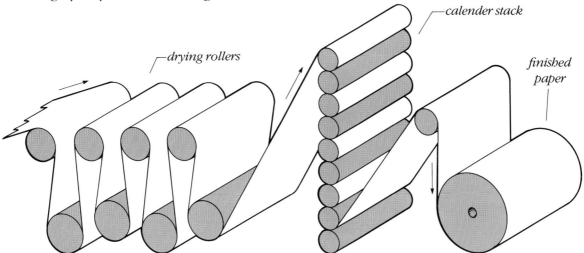

drying rollers

calender stack

finished paper

remove moisture and may also create textures. At this stage, paper might also pass through baths for sizing and coating and between additional rollers for calendering. Although the machine carries paper almost a mile, it operates at such high speeds that furnish becomes paper in less than four minutes. Paper at the end of the process contains about 5% water. Finished paper is shipped as rolls or cut into sheets for shipping in cartons.

6-2 Opacity comparison bars. The opacity of paper determines the extent to which printing on one side interferes with printing on the other. To compare the opacity of two pieces of paper, lay them so that their edges meet at the center line. The one that makes the bars most difficult to see is more opaque.

Opacity. Printing on one side of the paper should not show through to interfere with printing on the other. Opacity increases with basis weight and bulk and is affected by coatings, colors, chemicals, ink color and coverage, and impurities. Mills rate opacity on a scale of 1 to 100, with 100 being completely opaque.

Finish. As mills turn pulp into paper, its surface can be adjusted to affect look, feel, and printability. In addition to texturing by the papermaking machine, other finishes are determined by calendering and embossing as additional steps in the process.

Calendering affects paper in several ways. As the degree of calendering increases, paper becomes smoother and more glossy and has better ink holdout. The heat and pressure of calendering also make paper thinner, less opaque, and often less bright.

Embossing is done off the papermaking machine by steel rollers that press patterns into paper surfaces. Embossed finishes have special names such as stipple and canvas.

A paper's surface determines how easily it accepts ink, how rapidly the printing press can run while maintaining uniform ink coverage, and other elusive factors affecting printability. If a printer grumbles about the printability of a particular sheet, listen.

Grain. During papermaking, fibers tend to align in the direction of pulp flow. The result is grain. Paper on the roll is grain long. When fibers run parallel to the length of a sheet, the stock is grain long; when fibers run crosswise, the sheet is grain short.

Knowing grain direction helps design for folding and strength. Folds in heavy stock are smoother with the grain and stronger against. Folds against the grain may need scoring first. Grain long book pages turn more easily than grain short; grain long letterheads and counter displays are more rigid than grain short.

Grain is usually indicated on paper measurements by underlining the grain direction. On a 23 x <u>35</u> sheet, the grain runs parallel to the 35 inch edge. To check grain direction, uniformly dampen a square sheet on one side. It should curl on an axis parallel to its grain. With

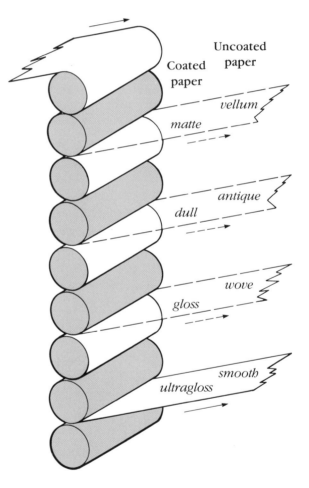

6-3 Calender stack. A calender stack is a set of rollers that smooths paper as it passes between them. The number of rollers used determines how smooth the surface will be. When coated stock exits after going between a few rollers, it has a matte surface; after more, dull; still more, gloss; and all the rollers, ultragloss. Uncoated stock is calendered in this sequence: vellum, antique, wove, and smooth.

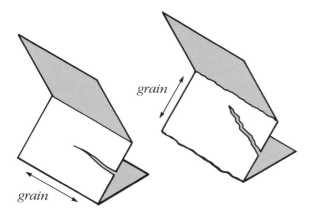

6-4 Grain direction. Paper folds and tears more easily with the grain than against. Thick papers should be scored before folding, especially if against the grain. With any weight paper, folds against the grain will be more durable. Grain direction also determines how paper curls when damp, thus affecting how well paper runs on press.

heavy stocks, simply fold in two directions. The straight, clean fold is with the grain, the rough fold against the grain. If your product has singular needs for smooth folds or stiffness, your printer may have to special order paper.

Weight. Each grade of paper has one basic size used to determine basis weight. Visual 6-11 shows basic sizes for the various grades. (Note that basic size is only one of the many standard sizes for each grade.) Basis weight is expressed in pounds and is figured using one ream (500 sheets) as a standard quantity. To see how this works in practice, take 500 sheets of paper at the basic size for its grade, then weigh the pile. The result is the basis weight of that kind of paper.

Basis weight is designated several ways. Text and book papers are usually referred to simply by the pound, as in "60# book." Written on packages, 60# may also appear as "BS 60." Bond paper is often designated in substance weights; 24# may be expressed as "sub 24." Substance weight and basis weight mean the same thing. Often packages of paper identify both the basis weight and basic size of contents. For example, a ream of 80# text might be marked "80# (25 x 38)."

To help understand the concept of basis weight, consider pulp that yields 80 pounds of paper. The mill could make the pulp into 500 sheets of 25 x 38 book paper or into 500 sheets of 20 x 26 cover grade. Both reams would weigh the same and both would consist of 80# paper. The cover paper would be almost twice as thick as the book paper and its sheets would only be about half the size (520 square inches vs. 950 square inches). In this example, each sheet of book grade and cover grade would weigh the same, therefore each sheet would have the same basis weight.

To become more familiar with basis weights of various kinds of paper, examine paper sample books at a print shop or paper distributor. A few moments of actually feeling the grades and weights of paper will inform you about weight relationships among the grades.

Understanding paper weight increases cost control because paper is sold by the pound. For example, 70# book costs about 15% more per sheet than 60#. If you plan 25,000 copies of an 8½ x 11, 16-page brochure, the cost difference of the paper might be $400. Savings may be even higher when considering postage. If the brochure on 70# stock takes you over a per piece weight limit at the post office, you might pay more to mail than to print.

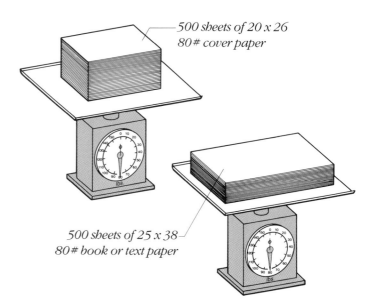

500 sheets of 20 x 26 80# cover paper

500 sheets of 25 x 38 80# book or text paper

6-5 Basis weight. Papers can have different basic sizes but the same basis weight. The scales each hold one ream (500 sheets) of 80# paper, one book grade and one cover grade. The basic size of the cover paper is smaller than the basic size of the book paper. The cover paper, however, is thicker than the book, so the two piles weigh exactly the same.

two 17 x 22 posters

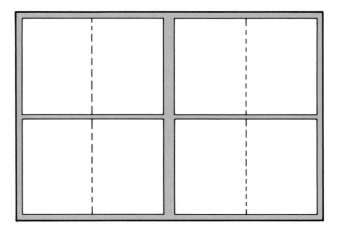
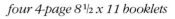

four 4-page 8 1/2 x 11 booklets

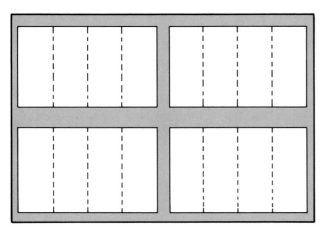

four 8-panel 4 x 9 rack brochures

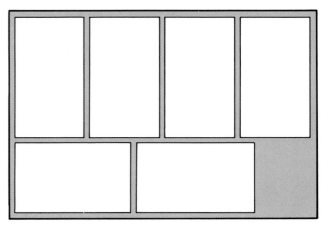

six 8 1/2 x 14 newsletters

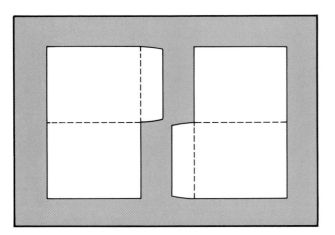

two 9 x 12 pocket folders

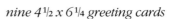

nine 4 1/2 x 6 1/4 greeting cards

6-6 Various ways to use a 23 x 35 sheet. Understanding how paper in standard parent sizes can be cut to yield printed pieces leads to more efficient use of paper. Above, solid lines represent trims and dotted lines represent folds. Shading represents areas of the paper that would be waste because of being trimmed off. Some of the printed pieces depicted are themselves standard sizes and result in very little wasted paper. Pieces that are non-standard sizes can also be ganged on a press sheet to hold waste to a minimum, but must be carefully planned and imposed to take into account procedures in stripping, press operation, and bindery.

Size. The graphic arts industry in the United States measures paper in inches and shows no sign of changing to metric units. A 25 x 38 sheet is 25 inches wide and 38 inches long. Sheets of paper come in the standard sizes shown in Visual 6-11. Mills make special-order paper to nonstandard sizes when the job is large enough. Each mill has it own minimum order and time requirements; at least 5,000 pounds of paper and two months delivery time would be typical on special orders.

Paper mills ship sheets in a variety of sizes. Large pieces, often called parent sheets, are usually printed to fold into smaller pages or to be cut into smaller products. For example, a 17 x 22 sheet could be folded into a 16-page booklet measuring 5½ x 8½ or could be cut into four 8½ x 11 sheets of stationery. Both the booklet and the stationery are standard sizes. Often, however, products are made to a nonstandard size. The 17 x 22 sheet, for example, might be cut into 12 handouts each five inches square.

We cannot overemphasize the economic advantages of familiarity with standard paper sizes. Efficient design coordinates paper and press size to minimize waste. When designing products with unique sizes, knowing how many of them can be cut out of one large sheet of paper increases your control over paper costs and production times.

Quantities. Reams have 500 sheets. Ream-wrapped means sheets are packaged in bundles of 500. Quantities larger than a ream are ream-marked by inserting a colored tab or slip every 500 sheets.

Cartons may contain any number of sheets or reams; there are no standards. Paper distributors use cartons as units of sale. Ordering less than a full carton means increased packing and inventory costs, so the price per ream or pound goes up.

Skids are pallets loaded with ream-marked sheets, then covered to keep out moisture. Paper that is bulk-packed on skids costs slightly less per sheet than paper in cartons. A full skid of paper weighs about 2,000 pounds.

CWT means hundredweight; cost per CWT means dollars per 100 pounds. CWT prices apply to mill orders and stock for web presses.

Paper not bought by the CWT may be purchased by the thousand sheets. Pages from price books, such as the one shown in Visual 6-13, give prices per 1,000 sheets and per CWT.

Carloads weigh about 40,000 pounds and qualify for special freight rates. That sounds like a lot of paper, but a medium-size printer can use it up in a hurry. Because the paper for 20,000 copies of this book will come close to weighing 40,000 pounds, the publisher may order 22,000 books to qualify for the carload price on paper. Incidentally, the "car" in carload refers to a trailer truck, not a railroad boxcar.

Bond

Mills make bond paper for individual correspondence such as letters and forms. Bond lacks the opacity of book and text paper. Because it is designed to carry ink only on one side, show-through may be a problem. Two-sided photocopy on bond works better than two-sided printing on bond because paper absorbs ink, but not toner.

Bond paper is made as either sulphite or cotton. Sulphite refers to chemicals used to create paper from wood fiber.

Sulphite bond comes in five quality levels, although #1 and #4 are most common. The first level, #1 sulphite, is used for routine business stationery. It may be watermarked and textured and certainly will be whiter and more opaque than #4. The everyday stock for typing, mimeo, photocopy, and quick printing is #4 sulphite, which costs about 35% less than #1.

Mills distinguish cotton bond according to percentage of cotton; 25% and 100% are most

---

"I'm a member of our local convention and visitor bureau and I know that they pay high fees for the best designers in town, but they sure wasted their money with last year's membership directory! It looked real artsy with full color photographs on fancy paper and even had gold foil on the cover, but it was too long to fit in a file folder. When I punched it to fit a ring binder, it stuck out an inch over the top. Maybe they thought people would be impressed and use it to decorate their coffee tables. I finally just threw it away."

Type	*Weights*	*Colors*	*Finishes*	*Sheets or Rolls*	*Uses*	*Cost as Percent*
100% Cotton	20, 24, 28	white, off-white, some light colors	cockle, vellum, wove	both	certificates, prestige letterheads	90–100
50% Cotton		white				65–90
25% Cotton	20, 24	white, off-white, some light colors	cockle, laid, linen, smooth, vellum, wove		letterheads, newsletters, resumes	55–70
#1 Sulphite		white, wide range of colors				35–60
#4 Sulphite	16, 20	white, standard colors	vellum		directories, fliers, forms, handbills, photocopy, quick printing	25–37
#5 Sulphite		white				20–28

6-7 Guide to bond papers. Bond papers were early known for their superior performance in written correspondence. Today they are also used extensively for the printed word. This chart shows the common features and relative costs of various types of bond papers. The last column shows the cost of the most expensive sheet as 100% and the cost of other papers in relation to it. These cost relationships are approximate, depending on brand, weight, color, and finish.

common. Both percentages are usually watermarked and available in the same variety of finishes as #1 sulphite. Cotton bonds are for prestige stationery or materials that must be extremely durable. The U.S. government prints currency on 100% cotton.

Bonds come in a variety of finishes and textures. Finishes vary from mill to mill. A laid pattern at one mill may appear quite different from another mill's laid. Laid bond has a handmade look and dates back to Chinese methods of making paper in bamboo molds.

Some mills make a kind of bond called "writing." Writing bond has shorter fibers than standard bond, making the sheets slightly softer and more able to accept ink from pens. Certificates traditionally are made from standard bond whose long fibers give the crisp feel of a formal document.

Mills make linen finishes by embossing dry paper. Because embossing compresses fibers, linen bond seems slightly calendered and has

better ink holdout than laid. Bond with a visible finish should be printed on its pattern side.

Bond often comes with a watermark impressed by dandy rolls while paper is still mostly water. Shallow dies attached to the rolls slightly spread the fibers to leave the watermarked image. Watermarks certify the cotton content and brand name of premium paper and can be seen on most prestige letterhead by holding a sheet in front of a light. Be sure that watermarked bond is printed to read from the same side of the sheet as the watermark.

Mills will add a custom, true watermark at low cost on orders upwards of several thousand pounds of paper. Watermarks can also be made chemically by a process that leaves a translucent design. Some mills will custom watermark paper chemically on orders as small as twenty reams. In addition to enhancing image, custom watermarks guarantee stationery is from a particular author or organization, an important feature for legal and financial documents.

If paper is part of a package including letterhead, cards, envelopes, and other coordinated materials, it's important to choose a paper with matched characteristics in several grades. Many mills make grades, such as text and cover, in colors and weights to complement their bond, although slight color variations may occur between paper batches. If you want a perfect match and are buying in very large quantities, have envelopes made from the same mill run as letterhead. Remember that colors and finishes on cover grades for business cards may seem different from their matching bonds. For example, a laid finish business card may feel smooth on one side and rough on the other, while the side to side difference of its matching letterhead may be more subtle.

Paper for business forms is known as manifold, register, or forms bond. The stock is generally a #4 sulphite, although mills often mix in some groundwood pulp because of the short life of most forms. Forms bond comes in substance weights ranging from 10# to 20#, with 12# and 15# being most popular.

Forms bond must be light and strong, handle writing whether from pens or computer printers, and make a good carbon copy—all while standing up to the rigors of web printing and a wide combination of finishing steps. The stock must be especially resistant to moisture so individual sheets do not expand or shrink to distort the entire form. Forms bond comes in a variety of colors to make easily distinguishable snap-out sheets.

Uncoated Book

Often called offset paper, uncoated book is for general printing of all types. This paper generally comes in several shades of white plus six or eight standard colors, depending upon the mill. Some sheets are more opaque than others, and mills may add the word "opaque" to the name of their product to indicate opacity.

Printers often refer to offset as #1 or #3. The first is brightest, most opaque, comes in the greatest variety of colors and finishes, and is most costly. One mill makes #1 offset in 20 colors and seven finishes. In contrast, #3 offset

offers fewer choices, lacks the high grade feel of the premium version, and costs less.

Light weight versions of uncoated book paper run well on web presses and are popular for large books, catalogs, and direct mail items. Although this stock tends to cost more per pound than medium weight, the extra money might be saved several times over at the post office. Mills make light weight papers with good bulk and opacity. Most of these papers come only in rolls because the long print runs required by high volume direct mail and catalogs typically go on web presses. Finding a printer who can do your job on light weight stock might save you thousands of dollars.

Light weight papers are often hard to run through sheetfed presses and folding machines. Both set-up time and paper waste may be higher than with medium weight stocks.

Text

An uncoated stock, text (short for textured) paper looks impressive even in the unprinted areas of a brochure or announcement. Light striking textured surfaces gives added depth. Specific finishes have special characteristics.

Felt text is made by rollers applying patterns to paper that is still wet. The process requires little pressure, and yields stock with high bulk and stiffness. Because fibers have not been compressed, felt text is ideal for embossing.

Laid text is made the same way as laid bond. Mills occasionally put both laid and felt patterns on the same sheet, yielding a very distinctive surface.

Vellum text has passed through calender rollers just enough to make its surface uniform, but not smooth. The result is good bulk and stiffness with a somewhat dull surface well suited to printing soft illustrations.

"I specified a real toothy paper for our convention program and thought it would be fun to give delegates note pads made from the same stock. I put a pad and pen in everyone's folder. Well, the surface of the paper was great for printing, but it ruined every felt tip pen in the meeting room within three hours."

Guide to Uncoated Book and Text Papers

Type	Weights	Colors	Finishes	Sheets or Rolls	Uses	Cost as Percent
Premium Text	80, 100	white, off-white, wide range of colors	antique, canvas, felt, linen, smooth, vellum, wove	sheets	annual reports, announcements, art reproductions, books, brochures, calendars, posters, self-mailers	86–100
Text	70, 75, 80					70–85
#1 Book	60, 70		antique, smooth, vellum, wove	both	books, brochures, calendars, catalogs, fliers, manuals, newsletters, programs	40–60
#1 Book	30, 32, 35, 40, 45, 50	white, off-white				
#3 Book	50, 60, 70	white, off-white, standard colors			catalogs, direct mail, manuals, rate books	30–35
Groundwood Book	30, 32, 35, 40, 45, 50	white, off-white	wove	rolls		25–30
Light Weight Book	19, 20, 22, 24, 26, 28	white	smooth		Bibles, dictionaries, large reference books	50–65

6-8 Guide to uncoated book and text papers. Although text and uncoated book are different grades of paper, they have many similar applications to printed pieces. This chart shows the common features and relative costs of various types of these two grades. The last column shows the cost of the most expensive sheet as 100% and the cost of other papers in relation to it. These cost relationships are approximate, depending on brand, weight, color, and finish.

Rollers create embossed text finishes after the stock has dried, yielding paper with good ink holdout due to slight calendering. Linen and canvas are common names for embossed finishes on text.

Text comes in a wider range of colors than other grades. Moreover, mills make a good selection of cover stocks in the same shades as their text so, for example, invitations made from cover will match envelopes made from text. Whether white or colored, text often looks brighter than book or bond papers because mills add more fluorescent dyes to the pulp.

Because of its high quality, text runs well on press and handles easily in the bindery. It works well in operations such as die cutting, foil stamping, and folding.

Text papers bring combinations of color and finish to jobs that otherwise might seem flat. Illustrations that feature high or wide objects look more vivid when printed on a text surface with pattern lines running the same direction as the art. Text makes a good choice for products such as quarterly reports, programs, posters, invitations, greeting cards, and menus.

Coated Book

Paper that is coated offers several advantages over uncoated book and text for specific jobs. Coated paper gives better ink holdout than uncoated. Ink holdout is the extent to which ink dries on the surface of paper instead of soaking in. It is especially important when printing photographs: dots stay sharp at their edges, giving the image contrast and good detail. In comparison, ink on uncoated paper absorbs and dries quickly, leaving images fuzzy.

Type	Weights	Colors	Finishes	Sheets or Rolls	Uses	Cost as Percent
Premium Ultragloss	80, 90, 100	white	gloss	sheets	annual reports, books, calendars, catalogs, brochures, magazines, posters	90–100
Premium #1	70, 80, 100		dull, gloss, embossed	both		85–90
#1						80–87
#2	60, 70, 80, 100					70–75
#3					brochures, catalogs, company directories, direct mail, magazines, newsletters	65–72
#3 Matte	50, 60, 70, 80, 100		matte			60–70
#4	40, 50, 60, 70		dull, gloss	rolls	directories, direct mail, magazines, newspaper inserts	50–60
#5	35, 40, 45, 50		gloss			40–50

6-9 Guide to coated book papers. Coated book papers were developed for the faithful reproduction of photographs, but have a wide range of applications. This chart shows the common features and relative costs of various types of coated book papers. Most coated book is available only in white, although some also comes in off-whites which may be called natural, cream, or ivory. The last column shows the cost of the most expensive sheet as 100% and the cost of other papers in relation to it. These cost relationships are approximate, depending on brand, weight, color, and finish.

Coated paper enhances ink gloss. Ink includes varnish and other chemicals to make it glossy. The sheen stays on the surface of coated stock better than uncoated. Coating gives a flat, smooth surface ready for uniform ink coverage. As with uncoated stock, mills rate coated papers by numbers according to brightness.

Mills apply coatings in a range of thicknesses. Wash, or film, coating gives just enough coating to yield a decent photograph. Wash coating is something like priming raw wood—enough to seal, but that's all. Wash coated papers are good for publications such as club directories that include pictures of members.

Matte coat has more coating than wash coat and offers good bulk. It works well with body copy and multicolor printing. Matte coat often appears mottled in areas of heavy ink coverage.

Dull coat, also known as suede or velvet, is heavily coated and moderately calendered, yielding good contrast between paper and high gloss ink or varnish. Like matte, dull is well suited to materials with extensive type because its low glare minimizes eye fatigue.

Gloss coat has the same amount of clay as dull, but sheets are more highly calendered and polished. Colors reflect well and dull ink and varnish give good contrast. Color photographs look crisp. Gloss paper costs slightly less than dull and tends to run a little less white than a dull of the same name. The heat required to polish gloss stock also slightly browns it.

Type	Weights or Calipers	Colors	Finishes	Sheets or Rolls	Uses	Cost as Percent
C2S Cast Coated	.006, .007, .008, .010, .012	white	gloss	sheets	business cards, calendars, covers for annual reports, books, catalogs, and directories, folders, greeting cards, invitations, menus, point of purchase displays, post cards, posters, table tents, tickets	90–100
C1S Cast Coated						70–90
C1S and C2S Bristol	.008, .010, .012, .015					40–60
Colored Cast Coated, Metallic, and Plastic	.010, .015	rich colors, metallic colors	embossed, gloss, matte			125–195
Premium Ultragloss	70, 80	white	gloss			80–95
#1 Coated	65, 80, 100	white, off-white	dull, gloss, matte	both		70–80
#3 Coated						60–70
Premium Text	65, 80, 88 100, 130	white, off-white, rich colors	antique, canvas, felt, linen, smooth, vellum, wove			70–100
Text	65, 80					55–70
#1 Uncoated	50, 65	white, off-white, assorted colors	antique, smooth, vellum, wove			

6-10 Guide to cover papers. The variety of cover papers means they can be used for many products in addition to covers. This chart shows the common features and relative costs of various types of cover papers. The last column shows the cost of the most expensive sheet as 100% and the cost of other papers in relation to it. These cost relationships are approximate, depending on brand, weight, color, and finish.

Coated paper comes in shades of white identified by terms such as balanced, warm, and cold. Be sure to view samples of each before specifying. Cream and natural tones are also popular. Stronger colors are rare because coated stock is often used to show off color printing and doesn't need to have color itself.

Calendering coated stock increases gloss, but reduces bulk and opacity. Using coated stock may result in a product that seems surprisingly heavy. For example, 60# uncoated has about the same bulk and opacity as 70# matte coat. A book printed on the 60# premium uncoated may look just as good, but will weigh 15% less than one printed on 70# matte coat.

Two recent developments affect the choice of coated stock. First, high postage costs have led some mills to make a bulkier product. A high bulk, 80# gloss coat might be as thick as another mill's 100#, but weigh less. Second, ultragloss paper has appeared which, although costly, gives wonderful results. Using ultragloss may also mean you don't have to varnish unless you need the extra protection.

Cover

Cover sheets are simply extra heavy book or text papers. Printers use cover stock to cover books and catalogs, make folders, and run brochures and cards.

Mills make some cover stock without coating to match uncoated book and text papers, some coated cover to match coated book, and some, such as cast coat, unique to the grade. C1S, meaning coated one side, is for the typical book cover or folder that will print only on the coated side. Stock coated on two sides is termed C2S. For additional protection and gloss, printers often coat again with varnish, plastic, or laminating film after printing.

Cast coated paper has a very thick clay coating dried slowly over a chrome drum to achieve almost a mirror finish. Kromekote is a common brand name for this type of paper. The cast coating process is slow and expensive, resulting in stock that may cost more than double a #1 coated sheet of equivalent weight. Cast coated stock comes in several colors and is ideal for fine postcards, presentation folders, and covers of prestige annual reports.

Mills identify some cover stock by caliper rather than basis weight. The most common thicknesses are eight, ten, and twelve point. Small paperback books typically have eight point C1S covers: the stock measures .008 inch thick, with clay on the printed side only.

Board

The paper industry refers to heavy weight, bulky cover stock as board. The material tends to be rigid, strong, hard, and durable. Names such as index, bristol, and tag are common. Sometimes an additional name gives a clue to intended use. For example, weatherproof bristol makes good lawn signs; plate bristol has a hard surface for business cards; vellum bristol is soft with good bulk for business reply cards.

Because there is no consensus about basic sizes for board stock, basis weights can vary greatly. Furthermore, some boards are described in caliper and others in ply. Ten ply board, for example, consists of ten sheets of

paper laminated like plywood. Ply board, also called railroad or poster board, comes in many colors and may be weatherized for outdoor use.

Mills make chipboard from mill waste without concern for strength or printability. This inexpensive material is used for light-duty boxes and backings on notepads. Chipboard may be designated by caliper or by number of sheets in a 50-pound bundle.

Board stock is printed in a variety of ways depending on its thickness. Thinner board runs satisfactorily on sheetfed offset presses; board over 20 point is generally printed letterpress or screen printed.

Bristols come in various finishes. Vellum bristol is used for business reply cards and self-mailers. Bulky and very porous, it runs well on quick print presses. Index bristol is used for file and index cards as well as direct mail pieces. Its hard surface gives good ink holdout. Tag is a heavily calendered, dense, hard paper for products that must be durable and strong.

Specialty Papers

Carbonless papers have chemical coatings that duplicate writing or typing on an undersheet. The stock is used primarily for multiple-part business forms. Sheets come in three types: CF (coated front), CB (coated back), and CFB (coated front and back). A four-part, carbonless form would have a CB first sheet, CFB second and third sheets, and a CF fourth sheet. Special glues adhere to the coatings, but not to the papers. Glue applied along the edge of a large stack of carbonless sheets assembled in proper sequence will pad them into forms, each having the correct number of sheets.

"Why are people always so fussy about having exactly the right color or finish of paper? With some jobs I'm real particular, but with others I'll use almost anything the printer has gathering dust on a shelf. Like our newsletter. Each member of our club only gets one copy, so who cares if the whole batch was printed on three different papers? My printer is always happy to get rid of odd quantities of paper left over from other jobs and gives me a great price when I use it."

Guide to Printing Paper Grades

Grade and Basic Size	Common Names	Features	Surfaces
Bond 17 x 22	bond, ditto, erasable, forms, ledger, mimeo, onionskin, photocopy, rag, writing	light weight, matching envelopes, pastels and light colors, watermarked	cockle, laid, linen, parchment, ripple, wove
Uncoated Book 25 x 38	book, offset, opaque	easy folding, wide range of colors	antique, smooth, vellum, wove
Text 25 x 38	text	deckle edged, textured, wide range of colors	antique, embossed, felt, laid, linen, vellum
Coated Book 25 x 38	coated offset, dull, enamel, gloss, matte, slick	good ink holdout, ink gloss, smooth surfaces, usually white only	cast, dull, embossed, gloss, matte
Cover 20 x 26	bristol, C1S, C2S, cast coat, cover, text cover	durable, stiff, strong	*uncoated:* antique, embossed, felt, laid, linen, smooth, vellum, wove; *coated:* cast, dull, embossed, gloss, matte
Board	blanks, bristol, board, card, chip, index, plate railroad, sulphite, tag	stiff, strong, thick, variety of colors and surfaces	coated, embossed, plate, vellum, water resistant
Specialty	carbonless	standard colors	wove
	kraft	brown or manila, opaque, strong	vellum
	gummed, label, pressure sensitive, self-adhesive	variety of colors, glues, and surfaces	*uncoated:* English finish, vellum; *coated:* dull, gloss; *synthetic:* acetate, mylar, vinyl
	newsprint	inexpensive, light weight	vellum
	synthetic	durable, tearproof, water resistant	smooth, textured

6-11 Guide to printing paper grades. This chart is a broad guide to various characteristics and uses of all grades of printing papers. Not all paper in a grade, however, comes in every combination of size, weight, color, and finish listed. Because surfaces are named by the mill that makes the paper, there can be many different names for them. Most paper

Standard Sizes	Weights	Thickness Range	Uses
8½ x 11, 8½ x 14, 11 x 17, 17 x 22, 17 x 28, 19 x 24, 19 x 28, 22 x 34, rolls	9, 12, 16, 20, 24, 28	.002–.006	certificates, directories, fliers, forms, handbills, letterheads, newsletters, photocopy, quick printing, resumes
17½ x 22½, 23 x 29, 23 x 35, 25 x 38, 35 x 45, 38 x 50, rolls	30, 32, 35, 40, 45, 50, 60, 70, 80	.003–.006	books, brochures, calendars, catalogs, direct mail, fliers, manuals, newsletters, programs, rate books
17½ x 22½, 23 x 35, 25 x 38, 26 x 40	70, 75, 80, 100	.005–.008	annual reports, announcements, art reproductions, books, brochures, calendars, posters, self-mailers
19 x 25, 23 x 29, 23 x 35, 25 x 38, 35 x 45, 38 x 50, rolls	*sheets:* 60, 70, 80, 100; *rolls:* 40, 45, 50, 60, 70, 80, 100	.003–.007	annual reports, books, brochures, calendars, catalogs, directories, direct mail, magazines, newsletters, newspaper inserts, posters
20 x 26, 23 x 35, 25 x 38, 26 x 40	65, 80, 100; *calipers:* .007, .008, .010, .012, .015	.006–.015	business cards, calendars, covers for annual reports, books, catalogs, and directories, folders, greeting cards, invitations, menus, point of purchase displays, post cards, posters, table tents, tickets
22 x 28, 22½ x 28½, 23 x 29, 23 x 35, 24 x 36, 25½ x 30½, 28 x 44	67, 90, 100, 110, 125, 140, 150, 175; *ply:* 4, 6, 8, 10, 14	.006–.050	business reply cards, covers, displays, file folders, paper boxes, signs, screen printed posters, tags, tickets
bond sizes	12½–38	.003–.007	forms
rolls	30, 40, 50	.003–.006	bags, envelopes, fliers
17 x 22, 20 x 26, 24 x 30, rolls	60, 70	various	labels, signs, stickers
rolls	30	.003	directories, fliers, newspapers, tabloids
23 x 35, 25 x 38, 35 x 45, rolls	various	.003–.010	banners, games, maps, tags

distributors can supply paper of each grade in the common sizes, weights, and thicknesses shown in columns five, six, and seven. Use this chart to stimulate ideas and inquiries, not as an exclusive guide to ordering paper. Visuals 6-7 through 6-10 provide further guides and cost comparisons for bond, uncoated book and text, coated book, and cover papers.

Kraft paper is a cousin to newsprint made for wrappings and bags. It costs very little, may be hard to find for commercial printing, prints slowly, and comes only in the familiar brown and manila. Kraft's distinctive color and feel give an old-fashioned look to mailings, newspaper inserts, and menus.

Dry gum paper has glue on the back ready to activate with either moisture or heat. Mills apply water-soluble glues to stock for stamps, shipping labels, and sealing tape. Heat-sensitive glues are used for labels in retail applications such as meat packing.

Pressure-sensitive papers, often called self-adhesive, are printed to make the popular peel-off label. Adhesives can be either temporary or permanent. Almost any kind of paper is available with a self-adhesive backing.

Newsprint comes from groundwood pulp and usually runs on open web presses. It can be sheetfed, but runs slowly due to impurities that lead to frequent cleanings of plates and blankets. The impurities make this very inexpensive stock opaque, but likely to yellow with age.

Synthetic papers are petroleum products with smooth, durable surfaces. They are very strong, as anyone knows who has tried to tear a synthetic envelope. Synthetics make fine maps, covers for field guides, game boards, and other products that must withstand weather, water, and hard use. Synthetics cost about three times more than premium coated book papers.

Because synthetics are relatively new, some printers have no experience with them. Manufacturers help by providing paper distributors with instruction materials and samples to hand their printer customers. If a synthetic seems right for your job, encourage your printer to try it.

"We designed a fantastic calendar that all our outlets could imprint and mail to their customers, then went crazy trying to find square envelopes the right color to match. Finally we gave up and had to have the envelopes custom made. It cost us two fortunes—one for the custom making and one for being in a super big hurry. Next time we'll design envelopes at the same time we design the job, not as an afterthought."

Envelopes

Paper distributors sell envelopes made from a wide variety of paper. Quality ranges from uncoated book and kraft to fine bond and text. Terms used to describe the color, weight, and finish of envelopes are identical to those for the paper from which they are made.

Commercial, or business, envelopes come in the standard white made from a special bond paper just for envelopes and in higher quality versions made from finer bond, book, or text paper to match the letterhead inside. Commercial envelopes usually have the familiar V-shaped flap, but some are also available with square, oversized flaps for business reply and remittance use.

Standard white envelopes as well as some business reply envelopes are available with frosted or clear windows. Windows on stock envelopes come in standard sizes and positions; information designed to show through windows must be placed with window size and location in mind.

Social envelopes, often called announcements, are for invitations and greetings and are most readily available in text paper to match the card, letter, or note inside. Social envelopes are more square than commercial envelopes and have a square flap which, in more costly versions, may have a deckle edge. Most social envelopes come in A-sizes. There is also a series of social envelopes called Baronial which have V-shaped flaps and standard dimensions that are slightly different from those of the A-sizes.

Catalog (open-end) and booklet (open-side) envelopes are made of kraft, synthetic, or other sturdy paper for shipping catalogs, brochures, and similar large or bulky items. The booklet format has flaps at the side suitable for sealing by automatic inserting equipment.

The cost and availability of envelopes correspond to the paper from which they are made and to consumer demand. Commercial envelopes come in the greatest range of prices and colors; social envelopes have higher prices and a smaller choice of colors; catalog envelopes come in white or manila and, size for size, cost about the same as commercial envelopes.

Envelopes come in boxes that are used as units of sale. Commercial envelopes come in boxes of 500; social envelopes in boxes of 250. Boxes of larger envelopes contain fewer units as the size of envelope increases.

Paper distributors usually represent several envelope manufacturers and can order custom-made envelopes either printed or unprinted. As with all special orders, allow plenty of time for delivery and order enough to justify the price. If you need custom envelopes, you might save money buying them directly from an envelope wholesaler rather than from a paper distributor. Find outlets under "envelopes" in classified directories.

The Paper Business

With few exceptions, paper mills sell to distributors, not directly to printers or the public. Mills supply distributors with swatch books, printed samples, training materials, and other sales aids. Larger mills have regional sales coordinators who help distributors' salespeople handle major accounts and understand new products.

Classified directories list distributors under the heading "paper dealers and distributors." Paper distributors, also known as paper wholesalers or paper merchants, can be anything from one-person sales offices to huge companies with inventory in several states. Many sell paper towels and plates, office products, and graphic arts supplies in addition to printing paper. Several wholesalers in a region may each carry the same brand of paper from a specific mill. Shopping pays.

Paper distributors live by a variety of rules. Some sell only to printers, while others will do business with anyone. Most have minimum purchase amounts, but a few operate retail as well as wholesale outlets. Quick and in-plant printers who rely mainly on cut stock often use the retail branches virtually as their warehouses.

Most distributors have staff who work with mills, handle complaints, make dummies and samples, and keep track of inventory. Many employ a graphic arts or specifications consultant. Paper consultants know graphic processes thoroughly and can be as helpful as a good printer

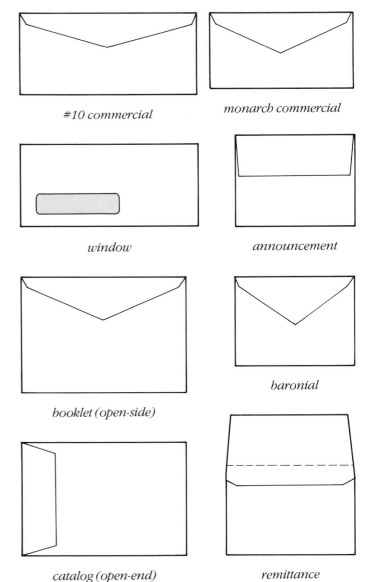

#10 commercial
monarch commercial
window
announcement
booklet (open-side)
baronial
catalog (open-end)
remittance

6-12 Common envelope styles. Envelopes can be bought in several standard styles and, within each style, a large variety of standard sizes. Paper distributors and their retail outlets stock #10 and announcement envelopes that match many of the printing papers they also sell.

in solving problems. They can tell you about new products, colors, and finishes. They can help you choose the right paper for your job as well as suggest alternate sheets or combinations. Most important, a paper consultant should tactfully speak up when you're about to choose stock wrong for the job.

Distributors usually stock a wide selection of sheets, but only a small inventory of rolls. Printers using web presses must buy and store large quantities of several types of paper in rolls, and customers depend almost exclusively on their selections. Unless a web job calls for at least 40,000 pounds of paper, using a printer's selection will be cheaper than specifying an alternative, custom stock.

When printers buy paper for a specific job, they mark up the price 15% to 40%. The markup reflects the fact that the paper is sold against the printer's credit and that the printer is taking responsibility for having enough of the correct stock for the job. Paper must also carry its share of the printer's overhead and profit.

Commercial printers usually have two or three types of paper, called house sheets, such as an uncoated and a coated book. They buy this stock in large quantities for routine jobs to keep costs down. Using the house sheet may mean printing on paper that isn't quite what you had in mind. On the other hand, often the house sheet is perfectly adequate and less costly than paper you originally specified.

When you specify paper for a job, your printer checks with one or two distributors to be sure it's readily available. If the stock is locally warehoused, printers may not even order until a few days before press time. Never assume, however, that printers can get any paper you want in a matter of days. Stock that must come from a distant warehouse or directly from the mill may take several weeks to arrive.

Occasionally customers order paper and have it delivered to a printer. This may prove economical on large amounts of paper, but may also prove disastrous. If sheet size or grain direction is wrong, the job may not print or fold properly. Not every customer knows exactly how to buy paper. Some make mistakes which, although the printer isn't responsible, still end up costing the printer time and money.

"I had one customer who wanted to supply paper instead of having me buy it and, as if that wasn't enough, wanted me to store it six weeks until mechanicals were ready. I laughed and told him it was a bad idea because some press operator might run another job on the paper by mistake. What I really should have said is that I'm running a print shop here, not a warehouse."

Customers who buy their own paper often overlook spoilage factors. Makeready, sheets consumed while setting up presses and bindery machines, may use as much as 10% of the stock. How much waste occurs depends on the number of ink colors and passes through the press, quality standards, press conditions, and even humidity in the pressroom. Printers anticipate spoilage taking these factors into account. If you buy bad paper or do not buy enough, your printer isn't responsible.

Paper is sold in price brackets expressed in either weight or number of sheets. A typical page from a price book shows cost per CWT for less than one carton, one carton, and perhaps four and sixteen cartons. With larger orders the price brackets will be something like 5,000, 10,000, and 40,000 pounds. Unit costs drop as quantities increase. For example, if cartons of a certain stock hold 1,000 sheets, then a 4,000 sheet order (four full cartons) may cost less than one for 3,600 sheets (three full and one partial carton).

Like other businesses, paper distributors have sales. Orders get cancelled, specifications change, color and weights go out of style, discontinued items are closed out. If you have a job where precise color or weight and availability for reruns aren't crucial factors, check for bargains on specials or close-out lists or have your printer check for you.

In the highly competitive paper business, distributors have various ways to cut prices to customers. To avoid additional handling costs, some will order stock shipped from the mill directly to printers. In some states, distributors can save customers sales tax by shipping direct from an out-of-state mill. Distributors may discount 20% or even 30% for large quantities. Think about your paper needs for a year or the possibility of cooperative buying with someone else. Savings might be substantial, but you must plan ahead to take advantage of them.

Distributors provide samples in a variety of forms easy to use and handy to have on hand. Get samples from distributors or ask your printer to get them for you. When requesting directly from distributors, ask to speak with someone in the sample department.

OFFSET OPAQUE BOOK
Plain edge, vellum finish
Approximate caliper: Basis 50, .0041; Basis 60, .0049; Basis 70, .0057
Matching cover also stocked

	Price per CWT			
	Broken Carton	1 Carton	4 Carton	16 Carton
White—Basis 50	156.25	106.25	98.15	91.90
White—Basis 60 and 70	151.55	103.05	95.20	89.15
Cream White	155.05	105.20	97.15	90.95
Regular Colors	174.90	123.70	114.20	106.95
Dark Colors	185.95	133.25	123.05	115.20

				Price per 1000 Sheets			
25 x 38 Basis	Size	M Sheet Weight	Sheets to Carton	Broken Carton	1 Carton	4 Carton	16 Carton
White							
50 Lb.	17½ x 22½	41	3000	64.06	43.56	40.24	37.68
	23 x 35	85	1500	132.81	87.59	83.43	78.12
	25 x 38	100	1500	156.25	106.25	98.15	91.90
60 Lb.	17½ x 22½	50	3000	75.78	51.53	47.60	44.58
	23 x 35	102	1500	154.58	105.11	97.10	92.77
	25 x 38	120	1000	181.86	123.66	114.24	106.98
70 Lb.	23 x 35	119	1000	180.34	122.63	113.29	106.09
	25 x 38	140	1000	212.17	144.27	133.28	124.81
Cream White							
70 Lb.	23 x 35	119	1000	184.51	125.19	115.61	108.23
	25 x 38	140	1000	217.07	147.28	136.01	108.23
Regular Colors (Blue, Canary, Gray, Green, Ivory, Pink, Tan)							
70 Lb.	23 x 35	119	1000	208.13	147.20	135.90	127.27
Dark Colors (Bronze, Charcoal, Indigo, Purple, Scarlet)							
70 Lb.	23 x 35	119	1000	221.28	158.57	146.43	137.09

6-13 Facsimile page from a paper price book. The typical page in a paper distributor's price book shows the manufacturer and grade of paper and the sizes, weights, colors, and finishes carried by the distributor. The page shows prices per CWT (100 pounds) and prices per M (1,000 sheets) in four brackets. Note that buying less than a full carton means paying substantially more per sheet. Prices are subject to change without notice and are usually confirmed at the time an order is actually placed. All prices are negotiable, depending on the market, size of order, and likelihood of future business.

Mill swatch books show samples of actual sheets and give information about what the mill makes in sizes, weights, colors, and finishes. Mills give swatch books to distributors. The books don't show prices or specific sizes distributors carry. Unless you have time to wait for delivery of a special order, verify that your distributor keeps the sheet in inventory before ordering paper shown in mill swatch books.

Blank sheets are samples in the actual size anticipated for the press and are especially useful for making dummies of jobs requiring special folds. They also help you think about ganging jobs because you can visualize two or three pieces printed on one large sheet.

Paper dummies are blank sheets folded and bound to look like the product you have in mind. They are important to any job involving binding because they let you see, feel, and weigh the final outcome. Most paper distributors will supply dummies bound like books.

Printed samples are useful to check opacity and how stock will receive certain ink colors. Printers and distributors each have samples of various papers with printing on them, although samples of printing on paper of uncommon weight, finish, or color may be hard to obtain.

Samples and dummies are free, but should be requested with discretion and courtesy. Ask for only what you are seriously considering and be sure to be clear about all specifications, including trim size and binding. If you can, describe whether the job will be printed by a sheetfed or web press and any other aspects of the printing you can think of.

Although the cost of paper represents about 40% of the average invoice for printing, it is a lower percentage of the total cost of the job. Total costs include research, writing, design, and distribution as well as printing and binding. Viewed from this standpoint, paper is a much smaller percentage of the overall budget.

Specifying Paper

After deciding what paper you want, you must describe it clearly to your printer or paper distributor. The description will be short, but must be accurate and complete to prevent confusion.

Good paper specifications deal with eight characteristics. If you are buying paper yourself, you must handle all eight; if your printer is buying for you, you need only deal with the last five. Visual 6-14 shows proper paper specifications using all eight characteristics.

Quantity. Specify the number of sheets or pounds needed.

Size. Describe sheets or rolls in inches.

Grain direction. Show grain direction by underlining the correct numeral. A sheet 25 x 38 is grain long: the grain runs parallel to the 38 inch edge.

Weight. Use the basis or sub weight from the sample book or price page.

Color. Write the exact name that the mill uses for the color.

Brand name. Usually this will be the name for a line of paper made by a specific mill.

Texture or finish. If it isn't part of the brand name, specify the finish.

Grade. State whether you want bond, book, text, or cover, or use the name of a specialty paper.

Sample Paper Specifications

62,500 sheets, 23 x 35, 100# white, Lustro dull book

5,000 sheets, 26 x 40, 65# Del Monte Red, Beau Brilliant cover

78,525 lbs, 35 inch, 80#, Lustro dull web book

14,400 sheets, 25 x 38, 7pt., WarrenFlo cover

5,000 sheets (10 reams), 8½ x 11, 24# Chiaro grey, Filare script bond

2,500 sets, 4 part 8½ x 11, precollated sets NCR, black print bond

1000 sheets, 20 x 26, 60# white, Fasson satin litho Crack 'n Peel Plus label

1 skid (approximately 16,000 sheets), 25 x 38, 80# white, Shasta gloss book

6-14 **Sample paper specifications.** These eight orders for paper show how paper specifications should be written to show quantity, size, grain, weight, color, name, surface, and grade. Sometimes the grade is omitted when the name is so specific that confusion is impossible.

Ink

Of all the factors to consider when managing printing jobs, ink seems the least complicated. After choosing a color, most customers give it little thought. Choosing ink that performs well on press is the printer's responsibility. Your printer does, however, need to know if you are considering paper with an unusual surface or have a special need such as fade resistance.

Printing ink is normally made to be transparent. Swatch books for color matching systems and other samples are printed with normal ink. With transparent ink, the underlying paper color affects the final outcome.

Ink manufacturers also make opaque ink that blocks out paper color, but 100% opacity is impossible to achieve with only one impression. Truly opaque coverage may require a second pass through the press to apply a second coating of ink. Even that technique, sometimes called double bumping, seldom yields a clean image when using light ink on dark paper. Another standard technique is to print the first pass in opaque white and the second in the appropriate transparent color. Either technique costs less than two-color printing because there's no second negative or plate.

Ink is normally made to look glossy when dry. Darker colors look more glossy than lighter ones; heavy layers of ink increase gloss. Paper, however, has more effect on ink gloss than does the ink itself. Uncoated stock absorbs ink rapidly, making it appear dull. Coated and heavily calendered sheets absorb ink more slowly, allowing more of it to dry on the surface and bringing out its luster. Presses with heaters (heat-set webs) also enhance ink gloss. After heat quickly evaporates solvents, the printed paper runs through chill rollers which set the glossy ink surface.

Matte images are easy to achieve—in fact, hard to avoid—with ordinary ink on uncoated stock. If you want a matte look on coated stock, specify dull or matte ink or varnish. They cost a bit more and may be harder to run on press. Dull ink also shows fingerprints and scuffs more readily than gloss. Coating with dull varnish may help.

Printing ink has the consistency of thick honey. To change colors, presses must be thoroughly cleaned of one color before a new color goes on. Press operators use rags soaked in solvent to wipe every trace of ink from the fountain, blanket, and rollers. Washup may take ten minutes on a small press or as much as an hour on a large one.

The customer whose job requires changing colors pays for washup. Because black is the basic color for printing, presses have black ink on them most of the time. Almost every time you use a color that's not black, you pay for at least one press washup.

Ink is a relatively small part of the cost of most printing jobs, especially large ones, but special ink or mixes for short runs may drive up costs. Printers buy and charge for ink by the pound, which is far more than needed for a few hundred letterheads or fliers. The price of a pound of special ink for the letterhead job may represent 10% of the total invoice, while the same pound of ink entirely used up printing a 48-page magazine may represent only 1% of the total cost.

After black, the most common and least costly ink colors are the basic ones used in color matching systems and the three process colors cyan, magenta, and yellow. Printers prefer certain brands and plan press chemistry to conform. Basic and process colors are standard mixes; every printer doing color work has a supply on hand.

You can order almost any ink color you want, but must be able to specify it to your printer. Use a color matching system such as the one developed by Pantone, Inc. Ink color matching

---

"Some people are fanatics about color. One customer even wants the orange in the annual reports we print to match the orange of her company trucks. Sales reps at the color separation service they use say that her marketing people can spend whatever it takes on photography and color correcting. We know she will take twice as long as other customers for a press check, so we figure the cost of idle press time into quotations. Our people do the best they can, but there's no way to make ink on paper look the same as paint on metal."

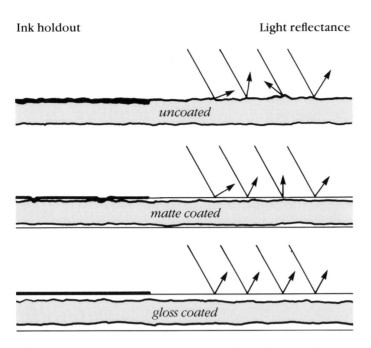

uncoated

matte coated

gloss coated

6-15 Ink holdout and light reflectance. This side view of paper illustrates the effects of coating on ink absorption and brightness. The left side of each sheet shows the amount of ink it will absorb, the right side the way in which it reflects light. Uncoated paper absorbs ink and has a rough surface that scatters reflected light, thus minimizing ink gloss. Matte coated paper holds more ink on its surface and is smoother and brighter. Gloss coated paper has superior ink holdout and is very smooth and bright.

systems are languages for selecting, specifying, and controlling colors in the graphic arts. They help customers and printers communicate. Instead of asking for bright red printing, specify color by using the number printed in a swatch book next to the color you want.

Color matching systems are communication tools, not limits on creativity. You can specify or try to match any color that you find attractive. Matching systems help everything go smoothly and quickly by assuring that everyone is talking about the same color.

The system developed by Pantone Inc. is built around eight basic colors plus black and white. Printers who keep the basic colors in stock can mix ink to match the 500 colors shown in guides and swatch books published by Pantone, Inc. These books show colors printed on a variety of papers such as uncoated and coated book, newsprint, and forms bond. All editions tell the precise amounts of basic colors required to mix hues to match individual

swatches. Keep in mind, however, that colors shown in ink swatch books may appear more or less vibrant when printed on different paper.

In addition to ink formulas, color matching systems include marking pens, paper, and transparent overlays. Using these materials, designers can create dummies with colors that match inks. Swatch books and artists' materials are available for purchase at most stores that sell art and graphic supplies. Printers, ad agencies, and designers should have copies of the basic books and often have the more specialized guides as well.

You can specify an ink color to match a sample, but remember that printers have a hard time matching colors made from pigments not found in printing inks. Matching an ink color to a sample of paint, dye, colored paper, or fabric may require extensive consultation between printer and ink manufacturer. The customer pays for that extra attention.

If color is critical to your job, ask for a draw down. Your printer applies the exact ink specified to the exact paper chosen for the job. Draw downs are the only way to see how ink and paper interact on press. Printers and ink manufacturers make draw downs at your request and usually at no charge.

Special Inks

Many kinds of special ink are available for a variety of purposes. Metallic ink in gold, silver, and bronze hues comes from a mixture of varnish and metal dust or flakes. It tends to tarnish and scuff when dry, so should have a coating of varnish or plastic. Metallic ink shows off best on coated paper. Even stock with good ink holdout, however, may require two layers of metallic ink for satisfactory coverage of large solids. Although metallic ink cannot be mixed from basic colors, swatch books often show standard metallic colors.

Fluorescent ink comes in many colors and seems extra bright because it absorbs ultraviolet light. It must be printed on white paper to achieve full effect. Because fluorescent has more opacity than standard ink, it overprints other colors effectively.

Fade-resistant and sunfast inks are useful for window displays and other materials often exposed to strong sunlight. Formulas are easy to make and print, but cost a bit more than standard ink. Cool colors such as blues and greens resist fading better than reds and yellows. Even these special inks, however, are likely to fade in a few weeks when subjected to direct sunlight.

Use scuff-resistant ink for packaging, book covers, and other products exposed to a lot of handling. It works best when coated with scuff-resistant varnish or plastic. Scuff-resistant ink must pass rub tests by a machine that rubs printed surfaces against each other at a pressure of three pounds per square inch. Normal ink shows significant scuffing after a few rubs, while scuff-resistant ink should stand up to 100 or more rubs.

Yet other specialty inks are available. The U.S. Food and Drug Administration approves nontoxic ink for printing items that contact foods. Scented ink can be made to smell like just about anything: strawberries, chocolate, roses, or sweat socks. It works best when printed on highly absorbent, uncoated paper. Scratch-off ink is used for contest forms and lottery tickets. Few printers are familiar with these inks, so be sure to do some test runs or review their samples before committing to the entire job. Magnetic ink allows machines to read numbers on checks and other documents. Sublimated ink is heat sensitive so it will transfer from printed paper to polyester items such as T-shirts when heat is applied.

Special ink costs more than normal transparent ink, may take extra time to obtain, and may require special handling on press. Consult with your printer well beforehand whenever considering special ink for a job.

Protective Coatings

All dried ink is subject to fingerprints, scuffing, and other blemishes from normal handling. Smudging is especially a problem with dark solids. A beautiful brochure or report cover can be ruined in only a few minutes. The answer is some form of protective coating.

Varnish goes on like ink, costs about the same as another ink color, and comes in either a glossy or dull (matte) finish. It can also be lightly tinted with pigment, thereby achieving both color and protection for the cost of only one. For a deeply matte effect, print dull varnish over dull ink on glossy stock. Varnish works best on coated paper and, in fact, may absorb so completely into uncoated stock that it will neither protect nor beautify.

Printers either flood or spot varnish. Flood varnishing means covering the entire sheet; spot varnishing refers to hitting only certain areas, such as photographs, so requires another negative as well as plate. Varnish adds sheen to beautify, accent, and protect. Spot varnished photos on glossy paper can appear as lustrous as original continuous-tone prints.

Varnish tends to deepen the color of the underlying ink, slightly discolor white paper, and yellow with age. Printers not skilled with varnish may use too much anti-offset powder, resulting in sheets that feel like fine sandpaper. The coarseness comes from powder trapped in the varnish.

Pens and rubber stamps don't work very well on varnish. If you plan to write or rubber stamp on a product like a catalog, leave an unvarnished window to accept the individual message. Foils stamped over varnish may bubble from trapped gas. Varnishing should be the final step on press.

For even more protection and sheen than varnish, some printers can coat with lacquer or plastics. These products give very tough surfaces for book covers, record jackets, and table tents. Film laminate, stronger yet, works well to protect menus and tags. Some of these tougher coatings involve bindery work and are discussed in detail in Chapter Nine.

From the standpoint of the customer, ink and coatings are the least troublesome aspects of specifying printing. Understanding how they interact with paper and presses, however, can help control costs and assure appropriate quality. Coatings promote good looks while helping your product have a long life—surely worth the expense after all the time and effort required to make it. ❧

7

Offset lithography is the most popular commercial printing method because printers using it can produce quality results relatively quickly and inexpensively. Other processes are better in specific situations, but lithography is best for most jobs.

Lithography yields excellent results because plates carry sharp images and precise dots. It's fast because plates are relatively easy to make and, once on press, allow for long runs at high speeds. Easy platemaking and fast press speeds mean lower costs. Unless you need less than 100 copies or more than 500,000, offset is probably the cost-effective way to print.

Knowing how offset presses work means you can plan jobs to take full advantage of different machines and avoid expensive problems. Understanding presses leads to sound decisions about quality categories and how they relate to costs. Finally, familiarity with presses makes you a better judge of service and whether you are likely to stay on schedule.

Printers vary greatly in the types, sizes, and abilities of the presses in their shops. Customers who understand the limitations and advantages of various presses make better choices among printers to assure economy and quality.

In this chapter we describe offset press components, types of presses, and the influence of press operators on printing. We explain what quality levels can reasonably be expected from printers using presses of different sizes and complexity. Using concepts such as register and

Offset Lithography

Press Components

Press Types and Sizes

Quality Considerations

Register

Ink Density

Miscellaneous Quality Problems

Press Checks

Offset Printing

ink density, we spell out what you should expect of jobs in the four categories of printing quality introduced in Chapter One. Finally, we describe when and how to make press checks.

This chapter includes a chart showing what features should characterize printing in each of the quality categories. Information on the chart is organized to be consistent with concepts also used in the text. We developed the chart to help readers select the quality category appropriate for specific jobs and evaluate printing that is claimed to be within one of the categories.

Offset Lithography

"Lithography" literally means "writing with stone." The technique began as a way of making art prints. Artisans inscribed images on flat stone, then used the stone as a printing plate.

Lithography is based on the chemical principle that water and oil repel each other. Ink is oily. In early lithography, images were carried on the stones by keeping water on the non-image area, thereby forcing ink to stay only on the image area. Modern lithographic plates function on the same chemical principle. The ink-receptive coating on plates is activated only in the image area.

The original lithographers printed images by pressing paper directly against the inked surface of the stone. Modern lithographic presses transfer images from an inked plate to a rubber blanket. It's the blanket, not the plate, that comes in contact with the paper and actually prints the image. The image is offset from plate to blanket, then offset from blanket to paper. Because all modern lithographic presses use the offset principle, the method is simply called offset printing.

Offset printing produces a sharper image than printing directly plate-to-paper because the rubber blanket conforms to the tiny surface variations of paper. In addition, offset printing is convenient because plates are right reading. If images went directly from plate to paper, they would have to be backwards on the plate. You could read them in a mirror, but not on the plate itself. Right reading plates are easy to work with because the image reads exactly as it will on the printed product.

"I've been running presses in this town for over twenty years. The whole process of printing boils down to making an enormous number of little corrections to an enormous number of little things that are always going wrong. You wouldn't believe all the things that can go wrong with a printing job on press. Lots of customers don't appreciate that. Some of them think that all it takes to run a press is enough sense to keep my fingers out from between the rollers. Sure there are sloppy printers, but often the fault lies with the customer who provides dirty mechanicals and blah photos and then expects us to work miracles. Given how tough the work is and how fast it has to be done, the real miracle is how much good printing comes out."

Press Components

All offset presses have six basic components. Feeding units deliver paper into the machine. Register units assure paper is placed under the printing units in the same place each time an image is made. Ink and water units convey liquids to plates. Printing units transfer images to the paper. Delivery units remove and stack the printed paper.

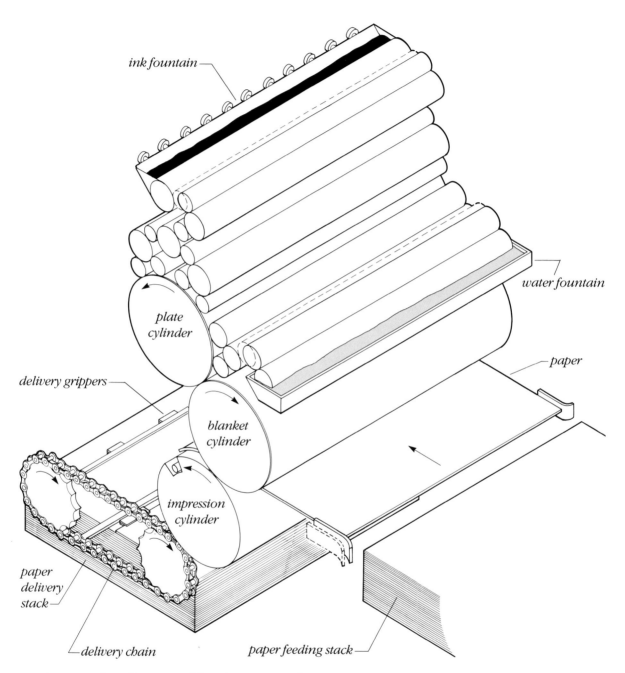

7-1 Concept of an offset press. Although a press may have many printing units, all presses function similarly to the one shown here. Rollers carry ink and water from their respective fountains to the printing plate mounted on the plate cylinder. The inked plate transfers the image to the blanket which then transfers it to the paper. The impression cylinder presses the paper against the blanket to assure complete ink transfer.

The visual above illustrates a sheetfed press. On a web press, the fountains, rollers, and cylinders are similar. The two kinds of presses differ primarily in how they feed the paper into the printing unit. That difference is significant because it affects the speed at which the press can operate.

The feeding and register units of a sheetfed press take one sheet of paper at a time and position it ready for printing. Good register requires that each sheet enter the printing unit from precisely the same position. Guides on one side and at the leading edge hold the sheet in place while it waits for grippers to draw it under the rotating cylinder holding the blanket.

The feeding and register units of small, inexpensive presses may vary the position of each sheet by as much as 1/16 inch. Large, costly presses may have register tolerances close to 1/1000 inch. Perfect register is a difficult task for a machine that may be running as fast as two sheets per second.

After the sheet is in position, metal fingers called grippers pull it into the printing unit. There the impression cylinder presses it against the blanket cylinder, transferring ink from blanket to paper. While printing is actually taking place, register is affected by adjustments to blanket and impression cylinders.

When printers talk about the gripper edge of paper, they mean the leading edge that enters

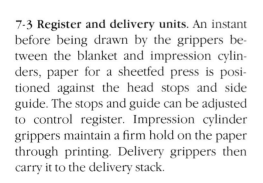

ink unit

water unit

printing unit

7-2 **Ink, water, and printing units.** Proper ink coverage requires precise control over the amounts of ink and water that reach the plate. Ink flow is controlled by adjustable screws across the fountain, and rollers help distribute the ink correctly. Computer-controlled presses with densitometers on each printing unit continually monitor and regulate ink and water flow to assure uniformity through the run.

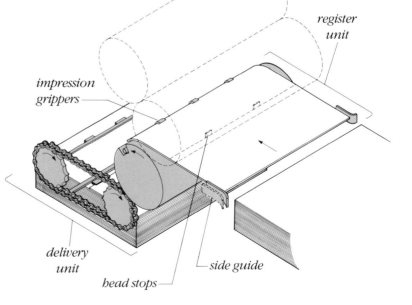

register unit

impression grippers

7-3 **Register and delivery units.** An instant before being drawn by the grippers between the blanket and impression cylinders, paper for a sheetfed press is positioned against the head stops and side guide. The stops and guide can be adjusted to control register. Impression cylinder grippers maintain a firm hold on the paper through printing. Delivery grippers then carry it to the delivery stack.

delivery unit

head stops

side guide

the printing unit first. Paper for small presses goes in shortest dimension first. On an 8½ x 11 sheet, 8½ is the gripper edge. Large presses take paper the wide way. A 35 inch press takes a 23 x 35 sheet, with the 35 inch side being the gripper edge.

Grippers hold tightly to about ⅜ inch of paper, forming a strip that cannot receive ink. With large presses, the gripper edge is usually no problem because paper is almost always trimmed or cut up after being printed. Small presses, however, usually run stock cut exactly to 8½ x 11 or 11 x 17.

Be careful when planning jobs that will run on stock already cut to final trim size. Grippers can actually run into the image area if inking is planned too close to the leading edge of the sheet. Designs for pieces to be printed on small presses should avoid image areas within ⅜ inch of the leading edge of the sheet.

Grippers also affect planning for bleeds. A bleed is any image that goes directly to the edge of the paper, seeming to run off (bleed) from the sheet. Presses cannot print up to the edges of paper. Designs calling for bleeds always require the use of larger paper and sometimes mean using a larger press, both of which may increase costs.

Inking units are also important to understand. Ink is a pasty liquid transferred from can to fountain with an ink knife that looks like a spatula. The fountain itself is actually a trough serving as a reservoir. By adjusting screws,

known as keys, press operators control ink flowing from the bottom of the fountain onto the first in a series of rollers. Using the keys, operators can increase or decrease the flow to control the amount of ink applied to specific sections of the plate.

A small press has only one ink fountain with 10 or 12 keys. A very large press may have eight ink fountains, each having 50 or 60 keys.

Ink rollers transfer ink from fountain to plate. The number of rollers varies with press size. Small presses have four or five rollers per plate while large presses have 18 or 20. These rollers work together to smooth the ink and spread it evenly across the plate in order to achieve uniform density.

Simultaneously with ink from the ink fountain, water must get onto the plate from the water fountain. The water usually contains additional ingredients such as acid, gum arabic, and alcohol. Press operators call the mixture the dampening solution.

Plates must receive just enough dampening solution to prevent ink from adhering to non-image areas, but not enough to transfer to either blanket or paper. The craft of offset printing depends heavily on maintaining proper balance between ink and dampeners.

A printing unit consists of the series of rollers and cylinders that transfers the inked image to paper. Presses may have one or more printing units. Printers describe the number of printing units a press has by referring to how many colors it will print. A press with four printing units is known as a four-color press.

Once a sheet has been printed, the delivery unit carefully removes it from the last printing unit and deposits it in a pile. This seemingly simple task becomes complicated as the amount of ink on a newly printed sheet increases. Areas of heavy coverage must not be marked by exit wheels and guides. Sheets with heavy coverage all the way across may not be delivered unmarked.

Delivery units normally include a system for spraying fine powder over the sheets to inhibit wet ink from transferring from the front of one sheet to the back of another. Some presses also include a heater or oven to hasten drying.

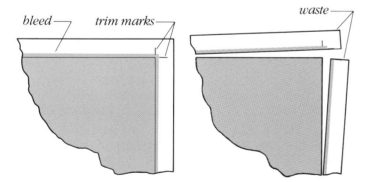

7-4 Bleeds. A printer creates bleeds by printing on sheets larger than the trim size of the final piece, then cutting away edges. The trims actually cut into the inked area to create the illusion that the press transferred ink right up to the edge of the sheet.

Press Types and Sizes

We have described the components and principles of a typical offset lithographic press. In practice, there are presses of two basic types. Each type comes in a variety of sizes and can have many special features.

The printing industry categorizes offset presses as either sheetfed or web. Visuals 7-1 through 7-3 illustrate a typical sheetfed press. The printing process on a web press is the same as on a sheetfed press, except that paper feeding into a web press comes off a roll and is cut into sheets after printing. Paper feeding into a sheetfed press has already been cut.

A closer look at each type of press reveals they are further divided by size. Press size is identified according to the largest sheet or roll of paper the machine can handle.

Small sheetfed presses print sheets 12 x 18 or less. That size category includes most presses at quick and in-plant shops, whose maximum is typically 11 x 17. Those printers use machines with brand names such as Multilith, A. B. Dick, Chief, and Davidson.

The printing industry refers to inexpensive small presses as duplicators. The term seems to imply that the machines and their operators cannot attain the quality of large presses. The implication is often true and always irrelevant. Small presses are made for printing small jobs efficiently. Criticism because of their limitations is pointless.

Small presses run black ink on uncoated paper most of the time, but many are capable of much more. Look for shops that display samples of multicolor printing or pieces on coated stock. Printers anxious to push a small press up to good quality standards like to show off their work and deserve your business.

Large sheetfed presses can run stock anywhere from 12 x 18 up to 55 x 78. A 35 inch press could run sheets smaller than 35 inches wide, but not larger.

Most commercial printers consider 19 x 25 and 25 x 38 press sizes versatile enough to handle almost any job. Machines in these sizes come with brand names such as Harris, Miehle, Heidelberg, Miller, Solna, Maruka, Komori, and Royal Zenith. Large presses prove highly efficient for many jobs because they gang images. An 8½ x 11 flier prints eight up (eight copies of the flier) on one 23 x 35 sheet, so a press able to run 8,000 sheets an hour can print 64,000 fliers in 60 minutes.

Many large sheetfed presses and some small ones can print more than one color at once. Sheets pass under two, four, or as many as eight blanket cylinders, each adding a different ink or varnish. When medium or long runs justify the added set-up time, multicolor presses save time and money. Multicolor presses register well and, unlike single-color presses, allow everyone to see the finished job as the first sheets are printed.

Perfecting presses print both sides of the paper during the same pass through the machine. Some sheetfed and all web presses are perfectors. Some perfecting presses print both sides simultaneously as paper goes between two blankets; others automatically turn paper over to print the other side.

Presses that print more than one color on both sides during one pass through the press are multicolor perfectors. A large web press, for example, might have eight printing units for each side of the paper.

Web presses come in three general sizes. Forms webs for business forms and direct mail pieces run paper from rolls less than 17 inches wide. Half webs, sometimes called 8-page webs, run rolls up to 26 inches wide. After printing, a sheet cut from a 26-inch roll can be folded to create an 8-page, 8½ x 11 booklet. Full-size commercial webs take rolls so wide that they can print 16-page booklets folded from one sheet cut from the roll after printing.

"When I was only doing small printing jobs, I could miss a press date and the printer would always work me in a day or two later. I figured that I was a regular customer and that's how everyone in the printing industry scheduled time. When I started having clients with jobs involving long runs on web presses, I had to learn that a missed press date might cost me several weeks in rescheduling. Printing time on those huge presses is tied up that far in advance."

Printers refer to paper going through a web press simply as the web. If the paper tears coming off the roll or while passing through the press, it's called a web break. The press must be shut down and the paper rethreaded.

The circumference of the impression cylinder on a web press is its cutoff and determines the maximum length of the image area. A web press with a 23-inch cutoff and running a roll 35 inches wide would print images imposed similarly to a sheetfed press running 23 x 35 stock. Cutoff is not adjustable.

Knowing cutoffs for specific presses helps plan for efficient use of paper. A 9-inch rack brochure, for example, will produce efficiently on a press with an 18-inch cutoff, but a press with a 23-inch cutoff would waste five inches of paper on every impression.

Web presses are categorized not only by size but according to their ability to dry ink. Open webs allow the ink to dry on its own. Heat-set webs pass the printed paper through drying ovens before cutting it into sheets.

To achieve high ink gloss on coated stock, heat-set webs also have chill rollers that harden ink. In contrast, open web presses can only print uncoated stock, which dries ink primarily through absorption. Open webs work economically for products such as newspapers, telephone directories, and direct mail inserts. Forms presses are usually open webs.

Some web presses have a huge advantage over sheetfed presses because they can fold and bind in sequence with printing. Paper enters the first folding unit immediately after being printed and before being cut into sheets. Of course, not every web can make every fold you might design, but you can save a lot of money by designing to take advantage of the folding abilities of specific presses. In addition to folding, some web presses can perforate, punch, number, and even bind.

Generally speaking, web presses print long runs more economically than sheetfed presses. The point at which one type of press becomes more economical than the other varies greatly from job to job and shop to shop. If a job requires more than 20,000 press sheets, it might pay to get prices from a web printer. More than 100,000 press sheets almost always calls for using a web press.

Note that the measure of quantity with regard to presses is press sheets, not finished products. One sheet of paper or one web cutoff equals one press sheet regardless of how many products it yields after being cut into pieces.

Web and sheetfed presses can perform equally well for basic, good, and premium printing. Only a few of the most sophisticated web presses, however, are capable of showcase quality. When you want showcase quality, evaluate web printers very carefully.

Quality Considerations

Customers make the most important decisions about quality when they plan jobs and select printers. They signify to printers what quality they want by the appearance and content of specification sheets, layouts, and mechanicals, by how expertly they examine samples and proofs, and by the questions they ask as their job moves toward completion. Printers use these signs to decide how much quality an individual customer recognizes and demands.

Many printers refer to a job in terms of the effort they believe it will require. Some jobs are considered routine while others call for the shop's best effort. Your task as a customer is to know the difference between routine and superior work at an individual shop and to tell the printer which you want. When the printer knows which level of effort you want, your job should be priced accordingly.

"When I first learned about web presses, I started specifying web or sheetfed for each job. I thought I was being very sophisticated, but really I didn't know what I was doing. One time I'm sure I paid much more for a rerun because everything had to be restripped when I said I wanted a web press. Now with most jobs I just pay attention to how much the job will cost, how it will look, and when it will be ready. Sure, there are some jobs where it's obvious that web work will be much less expensive, but mostly I just let the printer worry about what kind of press to use while I worry about preparing proper mechanicals on time."

The different levels of effort within a shop may or may not correspond to the four quality categories of printing that we introduced in Chapter One. For example, routine work at some quick printers is simply not good enough to meet even the standards of basic quality. In those situations, basic quality requires the best the shop has to offer.

An individual print shop may be capable of different printing categories for different kinds of jobs. For example, a shop might be capable of showcase single-color work, but only good 4-color process printing.

Basic quality printing doesn't receive a great deal of attention at any stage of the job. The emphasis is usually on speed and legibility. Many customers don't even proofread basic work. Good quality jobs get more attention to preparation and proofs, and more care in press operation. With good quality, there is more concern for pleasing and consistent appearance.

The amount of attention given jobs increases significantly with premium quality printing. Pressroom and bindery operators are especially trained in quality control. Customers buying premium quality printing are often more sophisticated and more likely to be graphic arts professionals than those buying basic and good quality. With showcase quality jobs, everybody involved strives for perfection.

Quality-conscious printers regard printing as a craft, not merely a manufacturing process. The press operators they employ must be constantly and simultaneously alert to dozens of variables and make frequent adjustments, often while machines are running at high speeds. Mistakes can cost the print shop thousands of dollars in wasted paper and time.

As quality expectations increase, the demands on press operators become intense. Operators at all quality levels, but especially for jobs printing premium and showcase, must have a distinctive mix of physical and mental attributes. They must be able to perceive tiny variations in register and subtle changes in ink density and color. They must feel confident controlling complicated machinery and pay meticulous attention to detail.

We cannot overemphasize that controlling

How to Cut Production Time

Copyfit. Write and edit with character counts in mind so that type fits layout the first time.

Simplify. Specify fewer type styles, reduce ink colors, eliminate photographs, use standard folds and formats.

Standardize. Rely on clip art, stock photos, standing dies, and predrawn layout sheets.

Avoid alterations. Get copy and art right the first time, then resist the temptation to make improvements.

Exploit technology. Use a word processor instead of a typewriter, a modem instead of the mail.

Reduce buyouts. Keep the job under one roof and in the production sequence of one business.

Lower quality. Give up the goals of inspired prose, error-free type, perfect pasteup, flawless tints, consistent colors, and precise trims.

Expedite approvals. Reduce the number of people who must review copy and proofs.

Be clear. Use correct terms and symbols. Avoid making people call you with questions.

Cut dead time. Eliminate days that the job is on a desk waiting for approval, a shelf waiting for typesetting, a table waiting for stripping, a pallet waiting for binding, or a dock waiting for delivery.

Speed up delivery. Pick up the job today instead of waiting for tomorrow's delivery; pay for partial shipment via fast carrier and the rest via standard conveyance.

Shop for speed. Find typesetters, designers, and printers whose schedules can accommodate your rush work.

Ask for speed. Tell your regular printer and other services that the schedule is tight and you need their help.

Pay for speed. Let everyone know that you need rush service and will pay for it.

7-5 **How to cut production time.** When there isn't enough time to complete a job using normal scheduling, examine the above list for ways to meet the tight deadline. Using any of these methods may cost money, reduce quality, or both.

printing costs demands matching jobs and printers. Too many customers take good and even basic quality jobs to premium and showcase quality printers. They are wasting time and money on quality control they don't need.

Register

Whether a piece is printed well can be judged mainly by register and inking. Register means that printed images appear where they were planned to appear.

Properly registered images are correctly placed in relationship to each other and to the edges of the paper. If a mechanical shows a headline to begin one inch from the left edge of the paper, but the finished product has the headline only $^{15}/_{16}$ inch from the edge, the headline is not registered correctly.

The concept of register includes backups and crossovers. A backup occurs when images on both sides of a sheet align with each other. The line at the foot of this page should back up the corresponding line on the previous page.

Crossovers are type, rules, art, or photographs planned to line up across the gutter after sheets are folded, trimmed, and bound. Crossovers require precision stripping, printing, and folding. Even keeping a line of headline type properly aligned across the gutter can be difficult and expensive. Perfect crossovers are very difficult to achieve and should be expected only with showcase printing.

Register on one-color jobs simply requires getting the image onto the sheet correctly positioned and aligned with the edges. Two-color jobs are more difficult to register because two images must be properly aligned with each other as well as with the edges of the paper. Each color requires paper to pass under a separate blanket inked by a separate plate. Variations of no more than $^1/_{64}$ inch can ruin the job.

"For 15 years I've been buying printing and for 15 years I've been hearing about hairline register. When I was young, I didn't want to seem ignorant, so I never asked anybody else if they knew how wide a hairline is. Finally the question just popped out. My printer didn't know, but guessed it might be the width of one dot on whatever screen we were using at the time. I said that would mean that a 'hairline' could vary from $^1/_{100}th$ inch to $^1/_{200}th$ inch and asked if her printing could vary by 100%. We finally settled on $^1/_{100}th$ of an inch as the definition. Someone should put that in a book."

7-6 Crossovers. No matter how carefully you plan nor what quality of printing you are paying for, you can never be quite sure how crossovers will align

With multicolor work, and especially with 4-color process printing, register becomes critical. Good quality 4-color process work calls for register tolerances of $^1/_{100}$ inch; premium and showcase separations must be registered with no apparent variation.

Presses vary greatly in their ability to register. Equipment at quick printers should get one-color jobs properly aligned with the edges of the paper with variation of no more than $^1/_{16}$ inch. Those machines can handle two-color register where the colors need not align precisely. Presses found at most commercial printers should handle tight, multicolor register easily. A good operator should be able to get pleasing 4-color process work from most medium and large presses.

Every good press operator checks constantly for register, setting adjustments carefully when the run starts and checking periodically to assure consistency. But press quality and adjustments are not the only influence on register. Paper which does not lie flat or has absorbed moisture can cause problems.

Too much moisture in paper comes primarily from high air humidity, although it can also result from excess dampening solution. As its moisture content doubles, paper can expand across the grain by as much as .5%. That much expansion would hardly affect simple jobs on small sheets, but could cause major problems with 4-color process jobs on large sheets intended to print premium or showcase quality.

You should expect the best register that equipment at the print shop can provide. Your printer has a corresponding expectation that you design jobs appropriate to the machinery in that specific shop. You and your printer should agree before the job is contracted that the shop is capable of the register you want.

until you see the printed piece. This crossover is within a signature, so its chances of good alignment are better than one lying where two signatures join.

Ink Density

In addition to registering images accurately, printers must control ink flow. Improper flow can result in paper getting either too much or too little ink.

Printers refer to getting the right amount of ink onto paper as controlling ink density. Proper density means that line copy is vivid and has sharp edges. Halftones should have contrast without losing shadow detail.

When not enough ink is transferred to the paper, images are washed out. Type looks thin and pale; large solids and photographs seem weak. When the small dots in highlights of halftones and separations do not print because of insufficient ink, they are said to be dropped out.

Too much ink makes type appear fat and fuzzy. When large dots in screens and halftones receive too much ink, they run into each other. The effect is called plugging up. Plugged up halftones lose shadow detail.

Proper ink density is a fundamental requirement of even the most simple printing jobs. And it's more than a matter of aesthetics. Legibility requires good contrast between type and paper. Washed out type lowers contrast and makes messages more difficult to read.

Problems with ink density are most common with jobs printed in the basic and good quality categories, especially those run on small presses. Small presses deliver ink less efficiently than larger presses. They easily go out of adjustment and may be run by unskilled operators.

Press operators are responsible for achieving the right ink/water balance, then maintaining it. In quick print shops, operators are often hurried and typically judge density only by watching sheets as they are delivered. In commercial shops, operators usually have more time to set up and control jobs and should use a densitometer to measure density.

Most commercial print shops assure proper ink density by running jobs on paper large enough to accommodate quality control strips. The strips, known as color control bars and reproduced as Visual 5-2, are printed along the edge of the paper.

Color control bars are meaningful to press operators using densitometers. Evaluating them is not the responsibility of a customer. Customers should inspect jobs for satisfactory results and let printers worry about how to achieve them.

Ink density should be uniform across the sheet. All presses have ink and water fountain controls that can be adjusted to assure uniform density from side to side. Whether the sheet measures 8½ x 11 or 38 x 50, ink everywhere on the sheet should have the desired density.

Occasionally a job will show a portion of the sheet with a density problem that will repeat sheet after sheet. Low spots in blankets cause areas that print too light. A worn gear or ink roller can cause a light streak running perpendicular to the direction in which the paper moved through the press. If these density problems make your message less effective, don't accept the sheets on which they appear.

Small rollers or wheels on the delivery units of some sheetfed presses can cause narrow streaks parallel to the direction the paper moved through the press. When the exit wheels pick up ink, tracking shows as a light streak of the ink color. When the exit wheels go over freshly printed solids, tracking shows as streaks

"Once I went to a press check that seemed to go OK, but it really was the beginning of disaster. None of the ink colors on the finished job matched the sheet I had approved. The press operators must have been taking turns to see who could get the most variation into a thousand impressions. When I complained, I asked the printer to match random samples from the job to the press sheet I had approved. The printer ended up running the job again, but then tried to bill me for extra paper and press time. No way! If a job isn't done right the first time, that's not my problem."

lighter than the surrounding image. Neither form of tracking is acceptable, even with basic quality work.

Conscientious press operators check every 50th or 100th sheet throughout a run to be sure the press is consistently delivering its best work. Basic quality print shops let more marginal sheets remain than do other shops. The refuse containers at premium and showcase quality printers are full of sheets which, at first glance, may seem acceptable. Good press operators and supervisors instantly see flaws that come to the attention of most customers only after careful inspection.

Basic quality jobs should have at least 75% of the sheets printed with uniform density, good quality should have at least 95%, premium and showcase quality should have 100%.

Consistency from one press run to the next is harder to achieve than consistency during one run. Brochures printed in March may look different from those reprinted in July; logos on envelopes may look different from those on letterhead. Big jobs such as magazines, books, and catalogs often have consistency problems from page to page because one signature may print today, another tomorrow, or the front of one sheet today and the back tomorrow.

Differences in papers, inks, and presses make some variation in density inevitable. Nevertheless, customers can minimize the problem by letting printers know that consistency from run to run is very important. It's also a good idea to require a press check for critical jobs.

"Sometimes the little details can ruin a job. I remember the first time that I ran for city council, my campaign manager persuaded the owner of a chain of supermarkets to donate printing by their in-plant print shop. We could get 15,000 announcements produced very fast for nothing more than the price of the paper. My constituency was very pro-labor, so we double-checked to be sure that the print shop employees were union. The shop manager, who had been there at least ten years, assured us that they were. When my announcements were ready, I noticed they had no union bug, and called the manager to ask about it. 'Oh,' she said, 'we're members of the grocers union, not the printers union.'"

Presses whose ink flow is controlled by computer reduce problems with consistency throughout the run and from one run to the next. Operators adjust flows until achieving satisfactory results, then make a densitometer reading of the color control bars. Data about densities are fed into a computer directly from the densitometer. From that point on, the computer controls ink flow to assure consistency.

Large solids often look washed out when printed on small presses. As a rule of thumb, small presses have problems with solids larger than about 3 x 3 inches square and with type larger than 72 point. Large presses can easily handle solids 9 x 9 inches, but bigger solids than that may require special attention. On very large solids, especially with metallic or opaque inks, the printer may need to print two layers of ink to eliminate streaks and spots.

Large screen tint areas, like large solids, are tougher to print than small ones, as the slightest ink imbalance will make the tint seem uneven. Producing tints that are consistent from page to page is very difficult, even for printers operating large presses.

Small presses often have a problem with scumming. It may appear as a streak or tinge of ink running the length of the sheet or show up as fat or fuzzy type. Scumming occurs when the plate is receiving too much ink or too little water, leading ink to stray into non-image areas. Often scumming is so faint it can hardly be seen. Scummed sheets, however, show poor press work and don't belong in your job.

Mottled images are blotchy and uneven. The problem stems from either press conditions or paper. Poor ink transfer caused by improperly adjusted cylinders or worn blankets can lead to mottled images. Inadequate paper coating, formation, calendering, or sizing can also cause mottling when ink absorbs unevenly. Paper with coarse fibers tends to mottle more readily than stock with more delicate strands. Uncoated or lightly coated sheets mottle more easily than fully coated stock.

Mottling is especially noticeable in large solids, halftones, and screen tints printed in dark colors. All require high quality presswork and materials to assure uniform coverage.

If you see what appears to be mottling in a duotone, color separation, or overlapped tint, double-check that it's not a moire pattern. Moire patterns are caused by overlapping screens and are consistent; mottling is random.

Trapping refers to printing one ink over another. If the second color adheres to the first, drying dense and uniform, it is well-trapped. Poorly trapped second colors look mottled. Trapping is usually not a difficult press operation with good, premium, and showcase printing, so mottled trapping should be considered poor work at those quality levels.

Miscellaneous Quality Problems

Although most quality problems occur with register and ink density, there are several other problems that sometimes develop.

Color mismatch. Press operators and supervisors are responsible for correctly matching ink colors. If you specified a color of ink by its number in a color matching system, people in the pressroom must be sure the right formula gets into the ink fountain. If you requested matching a color sample, operators should control mixtures and flows to make the match as close as possible. Even when you approve a press sheet, press operators must ensure that the color you approved stays consistent throughout the run.

When specifying ink colors, remember that colored paper will make the ink look different from how it appeared in a swatch book printed on white paper. Also keep in mind that printing trade customs allow for "reasonable variations" between colors on proofs or swatch books and colors during the press run. The amount of variation that is reasonable depends on the proofing system, paper, press, and quality control of the shop. Premium and showcase printing should result in nearly perfect ink matches at every stage of the job.

Ghosting. When an unplanned image appears within areas of heavy ink coverage, it's called a ghost. The phantom image is always a pattern of something else on the plate. As the name implies, the image is faint and elusive.

Ghosts begin with layouts that have not taken the potential problem into consideration. Customers need to recognize these layouts. Printing salespeople and production planners should also help spot layouts with potential ghosts, but often they don't. The job may get past the preparation department and pressroom supervisor before the problem finally becomes apparent on press.

Ink starvation leads to ghosts of two kinds: a light pattern within a solid or a dark pattern within a lightly screened area (such as a 20% tint). Eliminating either kind requires running the job on a larger press or changing the layout.

7-7 Ghosts. Ghosting is usually the result of inadequate ink coverage of a solid, tint, or halftone that is preceded by a heavily-inked image as the paper travels through the press. The solution is to change the layout or pay for printing on a larger press with greater ink distribution capacity.

	Register: 1 color
Basic	May vary $\pm$ $\frac{1}{16}$ inch
Good	May vary $\pm$ $\frac{1}{100}$ inch (hairline)
Premium	No apparent variation
Showcase	No variation
	Register: multicolor and 4-color process
Basic	Every color could vary $\pm$ $\frac{1}{16}$ inch
Good	Every color could vary $\pm$ $\frac{1}{100}$ inch
Premium	No apparent variation
Showcase	No variation
	Register: crossovers and backups
Basic	May vary $\pm$ $\frac{1}{8}$ inch
Good	May vary $\pm$ $\frac{1}{16}$ inch
Premium	May vary $\pm$ $\frac{1}{32}$ inch
Showcase	Nearly perfect alignment
	Appropriate ink density
Basic	Some variation
Good	Slight variation
Premium	Precise
Showcase	Precise
	Ink density: across the sheet
Basic	Some variation
Good	Slight variation
Premium	Uniform
Showcase	Uniform
	Ink density: sheet to sheet and throughout the run
Basic	Some variation
Good	Slight variation
Premium	No apparent variation
Showcase	No variation
	Large solids, tints, and halftones
Basic	May be thin, uneven, mottled, and ghosted
Good	Dense, even, occasional mottling and ghosts
Premium	Dense, even, no mottling or ghosts
Showcase	Dense, even, no mottling or ghosts

7-8 Guide to four categories of printing quality. This chart identifies 14 features of products and spells out standards they should meet to be within a quality category. The quality features of halftone, duotone, and 4-color process reproductions require comparison with original

	Flaws: scumming, setoff, hickies, smudges, and wrinkles
Basic	Frequent scumming and setoff, other occasional flaws
Good	Occasional hickies, no wrinkles, other flaws rare
Premium	Rare hicky, no other flaws
Showcase	Rare hicky, no other flaws

	Photographs: halftones
Basic	Diminished contrast, detail, and sharpness
Good	Good contrast, some shadow detail, sharp image
Premium	Excellent contrast and shadow details, very sharp image
Showcase	Almost match original prints

	Photographs: duotones
Basic	Not applicable
Good	Moderate contrast, sharpness, and detail
Premium	Excellent contrast and sharpness, good detail
Showcase	Excellent contrast and sharpness, good detail

	Photographs: 4-color process
Basic	Not applicable
Good	Pleasing color, moderate detail and sharpness
Premium	Almost match original transparency or print
Showcase	Almost match original product or scene

	Trimming
Basic	Trims square, dimensions vary $\pm$ 1/16 inch
Good	Trims square, dimensions vary $\pm$ 1/32 inch
Premium	Trims square, occasional $\pm$ 1/64 inch variation
Showcase	Trims square, occasional $\pm$ 1/64 inch variation

	Folding: accuracy
Basic	Single folds vary $\pm$ 1/8 inch
Good	Single folds vary $\pm$ 1/16 inch
Premium	Single folds vary $\pm$ 1/32 inch
Showcase	Single folds vary $\pm$ 1/64 inch

	Folding: alignment
Basic	Inconsistent alignment
Good	Occasionally crooked
Premium	Rarely crooked
Showcase	No variation

photographs. To be considered acceptable within a given category, a piece should meet or exceed the quality definition for all the applicable features. Keep in mind that reasonable performance at every quality level depends in part on giving the printer enough time.

Ghosts are most likely to appear with layouts having large solids. Large, bold headlines, clusters of halftones, large tints, and reverses are all possible problems. Whenever you plan large solids and want premium or showcase quality printing, consult with your printer to ensure that your job is not haunted.

Setoff. As printed sheets are delivered into a pile, the accumulating weight of sheets falling on top of each other while the ink is wet may transfer the image from the top of one sheet to the bottom of another. Printers call the phenomenon setoff, or offsetting, and prevent it by spraying a fine powder over the wet sheet to separate it from the next one falling on top.

Customers sometimes incorrectly identify setoff as show-through. It is rare that a sheet is printed so heavily that ink from one side soaks through to the other.

Freshly printed sheets should sit a few hours or even overnight before handling. Some jobs set off if trimmed too soon because paper cutting machines hold piles of paper under heavy pressure to make sure sheets don't move while being cut. Ink can also set off if sheets are folded too soon. Give your printer plenty of time to allow ink to dry between press runs and before trimming or folding.

Smudges. Sheets showing smudges, dirt, or fingerprints have no place in your job. An occasional bad sheet will slip through the best quality control, but work showing consistent problems should be rejected.

"We worked all weekend to finish printing those posters. There were only 1,000 of them, but they had to be perfect. We ran the press slowly and with extra care and took plenty of time to spot rejects. Even with that expensive paper, we tossed every tenth one, then slip sheeted the rest. Monday morning we shipped them via overnight delivery service in plenty of time for the gallery opening. Two days later the customer called asking where the posters were. The high-priced overnight service had lost them. All their insurance would pay was the cost of paper and ink. Not a penny for our time or, worse, our customer's lost business. We reprinted them, but of course the most likely buyers had been at the opening when there were no posters to sell them."

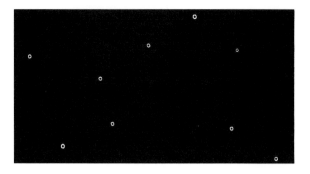

7-9 Hickies. Hickies show up in inked areas as small, white donuts. They can appear anywhere that ink covers paper, although they are most obvious in halftones and solids. Because the dust and impurities that cause hickies can come from many different sources, it is almost impossible to produce a job totally free from this common flaw.

Hickies. Dirt and fibers from paper can lead to hickies and other flaws. Conscientious printers keep their presses clean.

Hickies look like tiny white donuts with a spot of ink as the donut hole. They come from specks of dirt or dust on the plate or blanket that prevent ink from transferring properly. The particles can be dirt from the press itself, imperfections in the ink, or flecks of coating or fiber from the paper. When particles of paper or coating cause the problem, printers refer to it as picking. Good paper resists picking.

Although hickies may appear in type and halftones, they show most commonly in large solids. Because hickies are caused by loose particles, they wander around the sheet and come and go during the run. They are very difficult to prevent. Good printers spot the large hickies, but a few small ones are inevitable on most jobs.

Wrinkles. Occasionally a printing job includes some wrinkled sheets, especially when run on light weight paper. Wrinkled sheets should not be accepted.

Web pull. Heat-set web presses may yield sheets with a slight waviness, especially when there's heavy ink coverage. The theory is that paper going through a web press under tension ripples as it wets with ink. Drying units bake in the distortion. Some presses and papers ripple more than others, but web pull may happen with almost any job.

| normal | dot gain | doubling | slurring |

7-10 GATF Star Target. When printed on part of a sheet that will later be trimmed off, the Star Target helps the printer detect inking problems by magnifying the effects of ink spread. Note that the problems affect not only screened areas, but type as well. (Courtesy of Graphic Arts Technical Foundation.)

Dot gain. Plate and blanket pressures, particularly on web presses, make halftone dots grow larger as blankets transfer ink to paper. Dot gain makes halftones, duotones, and separations lose detail and print darker. The problem is especially critical with middle tones that print with dots in the 40% to 60% range.

Customers buying basic printing should not quibble about dot gain because fidelity of photographs is not critical. When buying halftones, duotones, or separations from a color separation service for good or premium quality jobs, be sure the shop knows the type of press and paper your printer will use and can adjust for dot gain. Adjustments are especially important for printing on uncoated paper or paper with poor ink holdout. For jobs that will print showcase quality, people at the separation service should consult directly with the printer to coordinate separations to specific presses.

Doubling and slurring. Doubling happens when dots or type blur because of a slight second contact between paper and blanket. When dots double, each shows a tiny shadow. Slurring makes dots appear oblong instead of round. The problem shows as smears on trailing edges and comes from poor blanket pressures or ink tack. Slurring is rarely a problem when using uncoated paper.

The Graphic Arts Technical Foundation (GATF) provides printers with quality control images, some of which are shown in Visual 7-10. Printers who add appropriate images to mechanicals, negatives, and plates increase control over register, ink density, dot gain, doubling, and slurring. Quality control images are often part of color control bars.

The problems of dot gain, doubling, and slurring result from the sizes and shapes of dots, not their ink densities, and are difficult to measure. Even using GATF control images, detection and correction require judgment. Some printers use GATF's new Dot Gain Scale II that shows gain in midtone dots in seven increments. As with any new standard, understanding and widespread use will happen gradually.

Press Checks

Photographic proofs, no matter how good, only simulate the printed piece. Nothing substitutes for examining the first sheets off the press. The examination, known as a press check, is your last chance to approve a job or make changes.

When making a press check, you should have the previous proofs to compare to press sheets. Of course, a blueline proof isn't supposed to look like the printed job. Its only function is to show complete content and imposition. Color proofs, on the other hand, should look very close to press sheets. Often they do, but several things affect the approximation.

Color in proofs comes from toner or dye, while color in printing ink comes from pigment and varnish. The two kinds of colorant are optically different and may result in variations.

Printing paper is different from proofing paper. Color proofs come on glossy, white stock. Printing on uncoated paper, off whites, or colored stock looks different from the proof.

Halftones and separations likely to suffer from dot gain may be etched to reduce dot size on the negatives with the expectation that dots will grow on press to their proper size. Dot

"I never assume that a printer shares my expectations about quality. I still remember the one who absolutely insisted the shop could print color photos to my standard but couldn't show me samples of work with separations. At the press check I actually had to shout 'Stop the presses' because dot gain ruined the images. I took my job to a different printer and had to pay a second time for stripping and making plates and setting up the press. I should have demanded to see comparable work from that first printer. What an expensive lesson!"

How to Do a Press Check

Preparation. Bring with you or have the printer provide mechanicals, photos, proofs, and any other materials relating to the job. In addition to proper lighting, the check area should have a graphic arts magnifier.

Overview. Scan the entire sheet. Savor the moment. If you like what you see, say so. Everyone else has worked hard, too, and is entitled to share your satisfaction.

Paper. Confirm that the paper is the brand, color, finish, and weight that you specified.

Ink colors. Verify that ink colors are those you specified or that they match the samples you provided.

Register. Examine copy to be sure that it is properly placed on the sheet and that copy in different ink colors is properly aligned. To check the register of 4-color process printing, look through a magnifier along the edges of color photos or in the white area of type reversed from photos. If you see a line of dots from any of the four process colors, the register is slightly off. Be sure everything is in register before checking for color. Changes in register can affect the color of separations.

Color balance and ink density. Study photos, type, and other crucial elements to be sure they satisfy you.

Other elements. Inspect type, tints, and reverses for pinholes, mottling, hickies, ghosts, and other flaws. Check the photographs one last time. Proof the content of headlines to make sure they read correctly, especially if they were changed after seeing the last proof.

Finishing. Fold the sheet and have it trimmed to be sure backups and crossovers work as planned.

Moderation. Be reasonable. Insist on correcting flaws only if letting them remain would impair the product's ability to reach the goals you set for it. Perfection, or at least your idea of it, may be impossible.

7-11 How to do a press check. When doing a press check, take plenty of time to examine the press sheets. Because the press check is the last chance to make any changes, the person responsible for coordinating and paying for the job should decide whether a press sheet is acceptable.

etched negatives produce proofs that appear weak in comparison to the printed product, so press sheets should appear more vivid than proofs. This is an area where experience and close consultation count for everything.

Ask for a press check whenever quality control is critical or you are dealing with an unfamiliar ink, paper, or printer. Often a printer will ask you to come for a press check just to be sure everything appears as planned. A press check should be part of every premium and showcase quality job and is quite appropriate with good and even basic quality work.

A press check takes place at the print shop or plant as the production run is about to begin. Your printer will ask you to examine a sample sheet from the press and, if you approve, to sign it. Now is the time to examine carefully every aspect of the job.

Some printers do press checks in the press room while others meet with customers in special proofing rooms. Because a press check shows everyone for the first time the job on the paper chosen, the event always generates some excitement. The press operator, pressroom supervisor, and perhaps your sales rep wait for your reactions. Excitement can change to tension; the room may be noisy, you may feel rushed, and responsibility for final approval may make you feel tense.

If you feel pressure at a press check, remember that the printer's job is to produce the piece properly and efficiently, but your job is to make sure the piece accomplishes its goals. You are the customer and must have the last word.

Press operators and supervisors should be alert to poor register and ink density and other possible flaws. Their standards may not, however, be the same as yours. Printers may think that a hairline scratch in a halftone is barely noticeable while you feel it detracts from the message. Moreover, printers may not have the same sensitivity as customers to subjective features such as whether photos are snappy enough or colors match samples well enough.

You should expect the quality that is reasonable for the specific press and for which you are paying. If you are not getting it, you should politely but firmly insist on further effort. That effort might mean simply increasing ink densities by 10% or might mean remaking an entire plate that was improperly exposed. Do not approve a press sheet until you feel satisfied.

Problems with press sheets can be ranked

using the categories for evaluating the job as a whole that we describe in Chapter Ten. Some problems are critical errors, some are major defects, and some are minor flaws.

In many situations, especially those involving 4-color process printing, very slight ink adjustments result in significant color changes. Those adjustments are easy to make. After the third or fourth adjustment, however, things should look as good as they are going to get.

Treat signing a press sheet as you would signing any other proof. If the sheet has a hickie or other minor flaw, circle it, sign the sheet, and leave. When there is a major defect or critical error, however, you should refuse to sign. Whether you sign, wait to inspect a new sheet, or return for another check depends on the nature of the problems and your faith in the printer to solve them.

Theoretically, all subsequent press sheets in the run will match the one you sign. The theory, however, often does not work out in practice. Even the best presses go out of adjustment, especially with regard to ink density, and some press operators do not watch for consistency as diligently as they should. On large sheets with many complex images, it is easy to overlook new flaws or areas where color no longer matches color on the sheet that you approved.

Your best chance of satisfaction with an entire press run comes from staying close to the press until the last sheet is delivered. If that is not possible, tell your printer that you intend to compare samples to the press sheet that you signed. When you examine those samples, do not hesitate to reject sheets with clearly inferior quality and to ask that your invoice be adjusted accordingly.

Press checks are expensive: as much as several hundred dollars an hour while presses run at slow speeds while people discuss the product. Checks should take place only when you and your printer agree that quality considerations justify the cost.

Usually you will know the day when a press check will take place, but will not know the time until your printer calls you with a few hours notice. Your printer should be accurate in telling you when to arrive and not make you feel rushed to approve. You should arrive promptly, pay close attention, and help get the job moving in the least possible time.

Printers build the cost of an average press check into the price of jobs. If you take longer than the average amount of time, you probably will not get charged extra. Customers who take too long at press checks, however, often get quoted higher prices on future jobs.

Most press checks are positive experiences with competent printers being hosts to satisfied customers. Occasionally things go wrong. Press problems force long delays, paper causes quality problems, or the perfect photo prints too dark because of an adjacent solid. These rare situations call for an extra measure of understanding from both printer and customer as each strives to keep quality up, costs down, and schedules intact.

During lengthy press checks, remember that the printer is probably spending more press time than anticipated and may end up losing money on your job. It's especially expensive for the printer if correcting a flaw requires shutting down the press and making new plates. Be kind to your printer when it's clear that every person and machine has already given you the best they have.

Press checks are great times to learn and to build good relations with the staff in print shops. Be sure to praise good work, clean presses, and orderly pressrooms. People who know their efforts are appreciated give their best. 🐚

8

Although offset lithography is the most popular commercial printing method, several others are useful for specific purposes. In this chapter we describe these other kinds of printing and ways to locate printers who use them. Some of the methods are available from printers who focus on a single process.

Some printers using printing methods other than offset specialize in particular products such as labels in rolls, clothing, engraved stationery, or boxes. These products can be purchased through offset printers, but usually at a substantial markup. Going directly to a specialty printer will save money. Knowing about such printers and the special services they offer also increases options in planning and management because certain effects simply cannot be achieved with offset printing.

Some of the printing methods described in this chapter may be available only from printers who work for the trade, meaning they limit their business to other graphic arts professionals. If you are not part of the trade, you may have no choice but to let your offset printer subcontract for those other methods.

Printing is any process that repeatedly transfers an image from a master such as a plate, die, negative, stencil, or electronic memory. All of the methods here fit that definition. Not all, however, are available in every locality. Depending on the method used and your needs for quality and quantity, some may require dealing with a printer that you are unable to visit in

Other Printing Methods

person. In chapter Ten, we give some tips about working with out-of-town printers. The descriptions of printing methods in this chapter conclude with suggestions about how to locate printers locally and in other cities.

In this chapter we do not systematically refer to the four quality categories defined in Chapters One and Seven. Although concepts such as register, density, and consistency remain the same, reasonable quality standards vary considerably from one printing method to the next. Only when discussing a method, such as photocopy, that may be used as a direct alternative to offset lithography do we refer to one of the quality categories.

Letterpress

For centuries, printing was synonymous with letterpress. Chinese artisans invented the process, using movable type made of clay. Gutenberg developed the process in Germany, using characters molded from lead. He assembled these characters in wooden galleys, inked their surface, then pressed paper against them to transfer the image.

Letterpress is a form of relief printing: characters to be printed are higher than the material surrounding them. Rubber stamps work on the same principle. Type printed on a letter press appears sharp and clean, and may feel indented because of the direct contact between type surface and paper.

Modern letter presses are versatile because their printing surfaces can be made in several ways. Some printers still set individual letters by hand. Others use Linotype machines to make solid lines of type out of lead. Plates can be molded from a variety of materials, including plastic, and can be etched photochemically.

Photochemical etching is the modern way to make halftones and art for letterpress work. The etchings are called cuts, a term applied to all letterpress art. The process of etching removes the non-image area from the plate, leaving raised lines, halftone dots, or other matter that will print. Printers mount the cuts on wood, then arrange them in galleys together with lines of type according to the layout for each page. Before the day of camera-ready art, printers maintained a supply of standing cuts to use much like today's clip art.

Letterpress is a relatively simple technology appropriate for the specific tasks of imprinting, crash printing, numbering, scoring, perforating, and die cutting.

Imprinting is the printing of information on items that have been previously printed and

"I became a lot more creative in my work when a sales rep told me about printing techniques available at some binderies. They can do die cutting and foil stamping that I always thought were too expensive for us. Now that I've learned those methods don't cost that much and are easy to design for, we use them often."

8-1 **Letterpress printing**. The raised surface of the metal type used in letterpress printing is inked before being pressed against paper.

stored. Business cards are a typical example. A large company may offset print 20,000 three-color cards on 20 x 26 cover stock, then cut the sheet into individual cards. As employees are hired or job titles change, a letter press imprints new names on a few hundred cards. Letter presses work well for imprinting because they easily handle small items and short runs.

Crash printing is done with a letter press because the image needs to stamp through the top sheet onto additional sheets in a carbon set. For example, a letter press will crash print an association name and address on a three-part business form bought at a stationery store. The form's own carbon paper or carbonless coating transfers the printing to underlying sheets.

Some letter presses can do numbering when set up with numbering machines, automatic units that work similarly to a rubber stamp with changeable dates. Numbers can be imprinted or crash printed. Numbering machines can number forwards or backwards and can be set to print only even or odd numbers. Numbering backwards is useful when forms will be used in numerical order. When the press run starts with the highest number, the lowest number ends up at the top of the pile.

While letter presses are ideal for certain routine jobs, they are also used to print special pieces intended to be appreciated for their artistry. Operators of letter presses using handset type can carefully adjust spacing and leading, and can easily proof the type repeatedly until satisfied with its appearance. In addition, fine letterpress printing is cloaked with five centuries of graphic tradition that, for some people, lends its products an ancient mystique. Fans of letterpress artistry may refer to it as fine printing and regard it as more authentic than offset.

Handcrafted letterpress printing is suited to posters, announcements, and books whose limited editions may be from 50 to 500. Even a single piece of printed art, such as an elegant certificate, could be created on a letter press. Artistic letterpress printing may also be enhanced by the use of handmade or especially beautiful paper.

Many letterpress artists are hobbiests or lithographers who do letterpress work only occasionally. They are not usually listed in classified directories. To find them, ask publishers of limited edition poetry books or owners of commercial art galleries. Fine letterpress printers may also be known to designers, engravers, die cutters, and similar graphic artists.

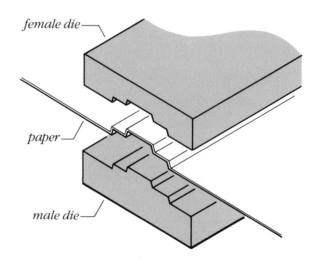

8-2 **Embossing**. Embossing requires two matched dies. The image is transferred when paper is pressed between the two dies, one of which is heated. Because not every paper is suitable for embossing, consult with the printer who will do the work before specifying the paper to be used.

Embossing and Debossing

For prestige printing and special effects, embossing and debossing take printing into a third dimension: depth. Paper is pressed between two molds, called dies, that sculpt its fibers.

Images higher than the rest of the paper are embossed; images lower are debossed. Both are often produced under heat to assure detail in the impressions. Heat also makes the images smooth and shiny.

Embossing and debossing have identical requirements for type and graphics, skills in die making, and press operations, and have similar considerations for paper.

Embossed impressions made without having to register over a previously printed image are said to be blind embossed. Blind impressions cost less than impressions over ink because press operators don't have to register dies precisely.

Dies are made from either magnesium or brass. Magnesium is easy to engrave using chemical processes, so can be made into dies photographically from camera-ready mechanicals. Engravers cut brass embossing dies by hand. Their art deserves the time all artists need to do good work.

Some printers do multilevel embossing. Chemicals etch dies in stages, each deeper than the last, to achieve a layered effect. Die makers also make multilevel dies by hand. The craft is complicated because the design being cut is backwards, yielding a right reading image when embossed or debossed. A complex multilevel die can be very costly.

Regardless of how embossing dies are made, designs should not call for lines so fine that paper will not press into them. Deep dies must have beveled edges to avoid cutting paper.

Die makers need to know what paper you will use. Soft stock takes impressions more easily than hard, and textures may become smooth under pressure. Most customers using heavily textured paper view smoothness as an advantage because of its contrast with the surrounding texture. Ask experienced embossers for their advice before specifying paper and the depth of dies.

Die Cutting

Letter presses can cut paper using thin metal strips embedded in wood. The dies are pressed into the paper to cut the desired shape. Die cutting can make irregular shapes such as pocket flaps on presentation folders and large holes such as in door hangers.

Dies are made from metal strips soft enough to bend into desired shapes. After being shaped and sharpened, strips are pressed into grooves in wooden blocks. The metal strips, called rules, are higher than the wood, creating cutting edges. Dies are heat-tempered to withstand the pressure on press.

Metal rules for scoring and perforating can also be mounted in wood. In fact, the three functions—scoring, perforating, and die cutting—can all take place in one impression.

Letterpress printers may keep a supply of standard dies for common items such as table tents. Custom dies, however, must be made by artisans using special tools and skills.

Because die cutting is a press operation, it may cost about the same as running one ink color. Costs depend on complexity of the die and length of the run. To reduce waste and keep the process simple, avoid intricate shapes.

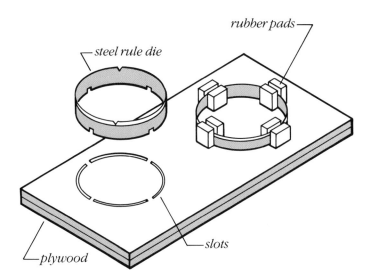

8-3 Die cutting. Dies for cutting are made of thin, sharpened metal mounted onto a plywood base which in turn is mounted onto a letter press. The press forces the steel cutting edge into the paper. After cutting, the rubber pads push the paper away from the die, allowing it to continue through the press.

Labels and decals are usually made by kiss die cutting. Cuts are made through the printed paper, but not through the release paper on which the label is mounted. Kiss die cutting is common with flexographic printing for decals.

Complicated shapes that are impractical or impossible to cut using metal dies may be cut using lasers. Camera-ready art is prepared in the customary way, but there are design requirements available from the laser service.

Lasers can be focused to pinpoints of light that burn away paper, leaving intricately-cut shapes. Because the process involves intense heat, various papers react to it differently. Before proceeding, ask for a test.

To locate a laser die cutting service, ask at a bindery or write Printing Industries of America.

Foil Stamping

In foil stamping, hot dies with raised images press a thin plastic film carrying colored pigments against the paper. The pigments transfer from backing film to paper, bonding under heat and pressure. This process is similar to rubbing the back of a sheet of transfer lettering to make a character go from backing onto a mechanical, except that the press is forming the image at the same time it's transferring it.

Any product that can stand up under heat and pressure can be foil stamped. Designers use it on pencils, toys, and picture frames as well as on paper products.

Foil stamping is done on letter presses. The size of the foil image is limited only by the size of the press and of the roll of foil.

Foil comes in a large variety of colors and sizes of rolls. The most common colors are bright metallics that take advantage of foil's shine, but foil is also available in dull, pastel, clear, matte, and wood grain.

Images that are foil stamped are so opaque that they cover any underlying color. For example, white foil stamped onto dark paper prints sharp and dense, whereas white ink for the same image might require two or even three impressions to attain similar density.

Because most foil is opaque, offset printers don't have to reverse out areas in halftones or solids that the foil will cover. Foil, however, may blister when applied over ink or varnish containing silicone or wax. The blisters come from trapped gas released by heat. Gas trapping can also occur if the foil image area is too large.

When designing for foil stamping, allow adequate space between lines to be stamped or the foil may not pick up from non-image areas. How much space is needed depends on the material being stamped. Check with your printer.

Foil stretches, so foil stamping mixes well with embossing for dramatic results. The process is called foil embossing and looks best on high grade text, cover, and bond papers. Foil embossing is appropriate for portfolio covers and annual reports as well as stationery. Successful foil embossing demands the right blend of paper, design, and printer. Get advice and samples before going ahead.

Several companies make hand-operated foil stampers suitable for offices and small print shops. Use them to stamp initials and logos on portfolios, badges, and certificates. Image size is limited to about two by four inches. Have dies custom-made or use metal type sold through the same sources as the machines.

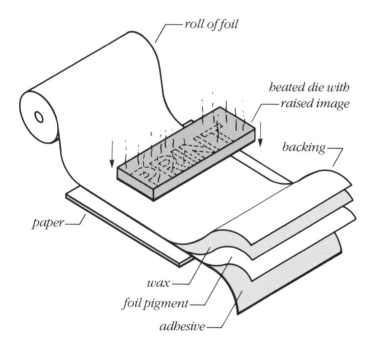

8-4 Foil stamping. Foil is adhered to paper in the shape of the raised image on a heated die. For best results, avoid designs with fine lines and intricate shapes.

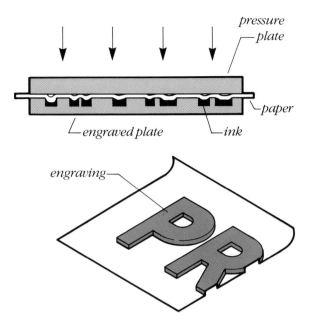

8-5 Engraving. The intense pressure of an engraving press forces paper into recesses etched into the plate. Engraving ink is very thick, making the raised image even more distinct.

Engraving

For years, commercial printers were called "printers and engravers." Printing used letter presses; engraving involved images cut (engraved) into heavy metal plates. Although commercial printing today is usually lithography, engraving remains the method for making fine wedding invitations and prestige stationery.

Engraving yields the sharpest image of any printing method and is used to print currency and certificates with delicate details. Photographs and continuous-tone illustrations, however, cannot be reproduced with engraving.

Images for engraving are cut into the metal plate rather than raised above plate surfaces as in letterpress. The surface of the plate is covered with ink, then wiped clean, leaving the recessed engravings full of ink. The press forces paper into the inked recesses, transferring the image. The thick ink used results in the slightly raised printing characteristic of the process.

Presses for engraving apply high pressures over small areas and tend to be small. To get images at both top and bottom of a letterhead, for example, requires two impressions.

Engraving takes special techniques and presses and costs more than offset. Dies can be cut by hand or chemically etched from camera-ready mechanicals. Hand-cut dies are made of steel and chemically-etched dies of copper.

Whether to use engraving dies cut by hand or photochemistry depends on needs for quality, variety, and quantity. Hand-cut steel dies give the highest quality and the longest press runs, but engravers making them may be limited to only a few typefaces. Copper dies are limited to press runs up to about 5,000 impressions.

People who appreciate engraved printing also recognize fine paper. Anything less than the best reduces engraving's exquisite effect.

Thermography

Also known as raised printing, thermography costs less than engraving, can be produced more quickly, and, to the untrained consumer, looks and feels similar.

Thermography is a five-stage process that begins with printing by any method that can deliver sheets with slow-drying ink. Offset is most common. Printed sheets exit from the press onto a conveyor belt taking them through the next four stages. First, sheets are sprayed with a resin powder that sticks to the wet ink. A vacuum unit then collects all powder not adhering to ink. Next, a heating unit melts the remaining powder into the ink. It swells as it melts, so the printing rises above the surface of the paper. Finally, a fan dries the image to a gloss.

Powder used for thermography may be fine, medium, or coarse. Choice of powder depends on the image being thermographed. Medium powder works well in most situations, but fine lines require fine powder for best results.

How much rise a thermographed image has depends on how much powder adhered to its ink when wet. Very little powder can adhere to the wet ink of fine lines and small dots, but larger type and solids hold powder easily. Control over ink, powder, and heat also determines whether the outcome will be uniformly glossy or have a stippled, orange-peel effect. Consulting with a thermographer will let you know what is possible with a specific job.

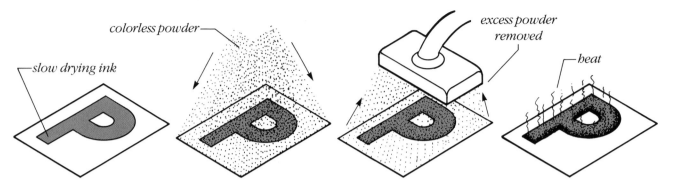

8-6 Thermography. While the slow-drying ink applied by a press is still wet, thermography powder is sprayed over the printed sheet. Powder not adhering to the wet ink is vacuumed away. Heat melts the remaining powder, making it rise. Having no color itself, the melted powder takes on the color of the underlying ink.

Thermographed images may scratch. Abrasion is no problem with lightly handled products such as announcements, but can make images on catalog covers appear dull after heavy use. Thermography also does not stand up very well to warmth. The powder may melt, losing its rise and luster.

Although thermography is used mainly for business cards, invitations, and stationery, the method is applicable to many other products. You could use thermography on the covers of booklets and directories, on greeting cards of all kinds, and on small fliers and posters.

Thermography can be done using several ink colors and even works with screen tints having coarse rulings. The melting powder may, however, plug up finely ruled tints and fine lines in reverses.

Costs and Availability

Embossing, die cutting, foil stamping, engraving, and thermography are all options to dress up products. Four of these processes require dies. Single level dies cost about the same regardless of how they will be used. Dies cost more as they get more complex, but their cost stays about the same regardless of the printing method. Thermography doesn't require a die, thus takes less time and money to get on press.

Despite the virtually equal cost of making dies, engraving costs almost twice as much as embossing and about 75% more than foil stamping. The difference lies in press make-

ready and running times. Engraving presses may run as few as 1,000 impressions an hour.

Presses used for foil stamping set up relatively quickly. Operators simply install the dies and rolls of foil; there's no ink to wash up. Once ready, letter presses with foil run at moderate speeds of about 2,000 impressions an hour—slow compared to other printing methods, but twice as fast as engraving. Embossing goes even faster than stamping once dies are on press. There's no ink to let dry and no foil to keep adjusted. A job that takes two hours engraving and one hour foil stamping might take about 45 minutes embossing.

Many printers with letter presses do embossing, die cutting, and foil stamping. Many trade binderies do die cutting, but the dies themselves are most likely made by independent die makers. Engraving and thermography have in the past each been special services—so special they may have been available only in large cities. Thermography machines, however, are cost effective for some printers to own, so are becoming common.

When die cutting, embossing, engraving, foil stamping, and thermography are coupled with offset printing, they are frequently subcontracted. In many cases, it's easier and may not cost any more simply to let the offset printer buy out the additional work.

Classified directories will help you locate printers able to use most of the methods described in the last few pages. Printers with letter presses may mention that capability in their directory listings. Those shops usually do die cutting, embossing, and foil stamping as well, although these three methods also have separate listings in larger directories. Engravers are listed separately as "engravers—metal" to distinguish them from "engravers—photo" that do process camera work. If you need a thermographer, ask a printer to refer you.

Flexography

The market for high-speed printing on plastics and foils led to the development of flexography, a process using rubber plates on a web press and sometimes called web letterpress. Highly volatile inks dry almost instantly, allowing fast running speeds on nonporous substrates.

Flexography doesn't give the solid ink coverage or close register of offset, but is popular for labeling and packaging because offset cannot print on most nonporous substrates. Plates for flexography are inexpensive and easy to make. The process begins with camera-ready copy made with standard techniques. The copy is photographed and the resulting negative used to burn a master plate of etched metal. The master plate is then used to make a plastic mold from which plastic or rubber plates can be quickly made and put on press.

Presses printing flexography run rolls of plastic for products such as bread wrappers and may print 1,000 feet per minute. Highly absorbent, low-grade paper for grocery bags can run even faster.

Because flexography uses a relatively soft plate and prints plate to surface (not offset), it works for rough materials such as fabric, wallpaper, corrugated cardboard, and panelling where quantity requirements make screen printing prohibitive. It's also useful for printing labels and decals because the same plate that prints can also kiss die cut. One disadvantage of flexography is that plates lay down rather thin layers of ink. Colors may seem weak.

To locate flexographic printers, look in classified directories under "packaging" and under products such as boxes, labels, and bags, or ask for information from the Flexographic Technical Association.

Gravure

In contrast to other printing methods, gravure makes everything, not just photographs, into halftone dots. Plate cylinders carry images consisting of tiny cells filled with ink. The cells vary in depth and width, so some hold more ink than others. Mounted on web presses, the cylinders transfer ink directly to paper.

Gravure presses run wide rolls of paper to produce millions of products quickly. Dense ink coverage yields good colors even on inexpensive papers, and inking remains constant throughout the run.

Paper for gravure must be relatively soft and extremely smooth. Paper with even minor irregularities tends to miss contact with some of the tiny wells carrying ink. But stock doesn't have to be expensive. In fact, gravure is attractive for jobs such as direct mail catalogs because it works well on relatively low-grade paper.

Gravure competes with flexography for printing packaging materials and special products such as floor coverings. It rivals lithography for long run publications such as supplements to Sunday newspapers.

To compare gravure with lithography, examine any copy of *National Geographic* published since 1975. Both text and photographs

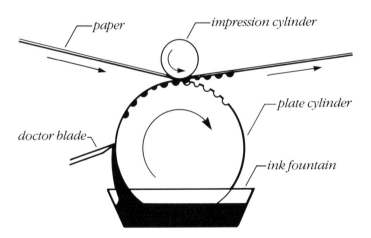

8-7 Gravure printing. The smooth edge of a scraper called a doctor blade removes ink from the surface of a gravure plate, leaving ink only in the millions of tiny cells. Ink transfers from the cells to the paper, reproducing both line and halftone copy as composites of dots. Gravure printing is fast and dependable, but platemaking and setup is more expensive than for offset.

are printed gravure, while the advertising and cover are printed by offset lithography.

Because plates are expensive to make, gravure is usually appropriate only for runs of over a million impressions. With these long runs, the process is capable of delivering work at any quality level at rock bottom prices. Furthermore, new platemaking methods may make gravure competitive with web offset for runs as low as 100,000.

If you choose gravure, be sure to ask about film specifications. Density control in plate making is very tricky, so your printer may ask you for film positives developed to density standards you find unfamiliar.

Only a few cities have commercial gravure printers, who are listed in classified directories under "rotogravure." Many gravure printers advertise in trade journals aimed at printing buyers for catalogs and national magazines, and are known to printing buyers at companies that mail consumer catalogs. The Gravure Technical Association is an additional source of names.

Screen Printing

Silk screen is the most simple of all printing processes. All a printer needs is a screen stencil, ink, and a squeegee. The screen fabric may be nylon, wire, or cotton rather than the traditional silk. Ink forced through the screen with the squeegee prints in the stencil's pattern.

Stencils for screen printing are cut by hand, stamped by machine, or made photographically. Photographic stencils are made by exposing light through a negative onto emulsion spread on the screen. Commercial screen printing may be done by hand using only simple equipment or on automatic presses of varying size and complexity.

Halftones can be screen printed. On smooth surfaces such as bottles, 80 line screens work fine. On fabrics, halftone dots must be large enough to adhere to the mesh of fiber. Ideally, one dot will print at the intersection of at least four threads. Fabric mesh counts should be about four times the line count of halftone screens. Screen printed halftones look better on synthetic rather than natural fibers because monofilament threads give sharper images.

Commercial screen printers make stencils photographically, so copy must be prepared to the same camera-ready standards that apply to

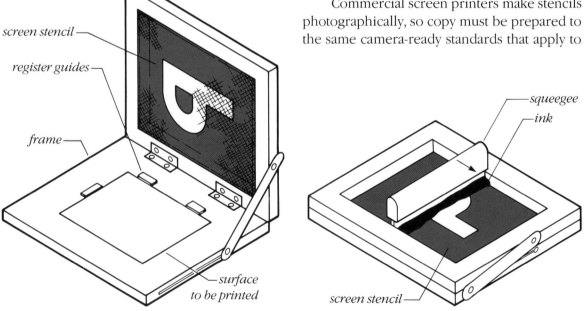

8-8 Screen printing flat surfaces. This illustration represents a hand-operated screen printing press that might be used to make a few hundred posters. After the paper is positioned, the top holding the screen stencil is lowered. Using a squeegee, the operator forces ink through the stencil to transfer the image. Automatic screen presses work on the same principle. Flexible substrates such as T-shirts, however, must be individually positioned by hand before the automatic sequence begins.

copy for lithography. Consult a printer for details. The shop may want type on acetate instead of mounting boards or prefer overlapping colors instead of butting them. Screen printers vary in their preferences for halftone dot sizes, especially for billboards and other large signs.

Screen printing has several advantages over other methods in specific situations.

Short runs. If you need 20 lawn signs, 50 posters, or 200 bumper stickers, screen printing is the answer.

Heavy ink coverage. Screen printing lays down ink up to 30 times thicker than lithography and five times heavier than gravure. The result is color more dense and durable than from other processes. Silk screen is perfect for outdoor advertising.

Ink variety. Screen printing lends itself easily to ink with satin, gloss, or fluorescent finishes and to ink which accepts flocks or other decorative substances. There are special inks to print on glass, metal, cardboard, and other substrates. The electronics industry uses screen printing to etch circuits on copper-plated boards. Acid-resisting ink covers image areas, allowing acid to burn away the non-image copper surfaces.

Large images. Because the screen process is so simple, frames holding stencils can be made larger than the largest presses. Screen printers make huge posters and billboards.

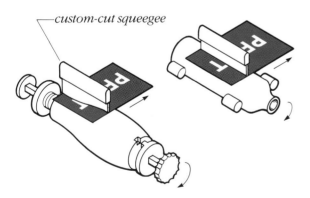
custom-cut squeegee

8-9 Screen printing irregular surfaces. Items such as bottles may be screen printed by a device that combines the motion of stencil and surface against a stationary squeegee. Many round items are made with notches so they can be held by such a mechanism.

Versatility. Advocates call screen printing "the print anything process." Clothing, wallpaper, panelling, metal signs, glass, and other materials that cannot be printed with lithography are easily screen printed. Inks go on so heavily they adhere to almost any surface. Applying ink requires only light pressure, so picking is rarely a problem.

Many products can be screen printed after being made. Ring binders, for example, will not go through an offset press, but can easily be screen printed. Plastic comb bindings can have screen printed titles on the spine. Some screen printers offer a related process called pad printing for transferring images to extremely uneven surfaces such as nutshells.

Screen printing does have limitations. It's slow both in printing and drying. Register can be difficult, especially with fabrics and other flexible materials.

Screen printers have their own classification in most classified directories. They are also listed under the products they make, such as outdoor advertising, book and catalog covers, and loose leaf binders. The industry is represented by its trade association, Screen Printing Association International.

Photocopy

Most printing systems use ink, a liquid. Photocopy uses toner, a powder. Copy machines place electrostatic charges on a belt or drum in the shapes of type and graphics. Toner sticks to the charged areas. When the toner comes into contact with paper, it is transferred and then fused by heat.

Photocopy machines vary greatly in the quality they produce. The best yield sharp, dense blacks similar to basic quality printing available from a small offset press. First generation copies are perfectly adequate as camera-ready copy for quick printing. Some machines even reduce and enlarge copy from 50% to 150%, giving users almost all the flexibility of stat cameras. Photocopies are extremely useful for making mockups of publications. Copies made by machines that will reproduce colors can be used for comprehensive layouts.

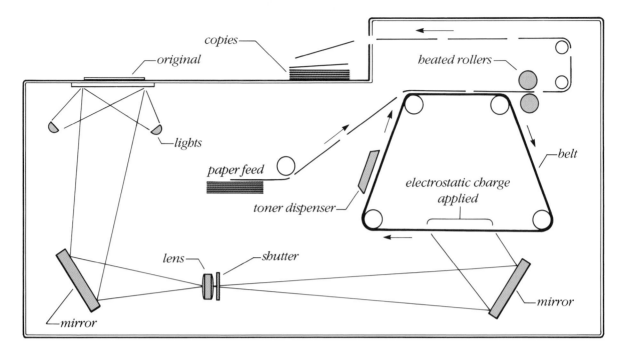

8-10 Photocopy. When lights flash onto an original, the reflected image passes through a lens and a shutter. Moving the lens reduces or enlarges the image. Adjusting the shutter controls the amount of light, making copies darker or lighter. Light striking the plastic belt is recorded as an electrostatic charge. An instant later the belt is dusted with toner, a black powder, that sticks only to the charged areas. When the belt comes in contact with paper, the toner transfers and it is then bonded as the sheet passes between heated rollers. With computer-driven photocopiers, digital commands drive laser beams that place charges on the belt. Because photocopy relies on a powder, images are never as sharp as typesetting or printing with ink.

Because of their speed and quality, photocopy machines compete with small offset presses for short runs at in-plant and quick printers. The machines give instant results, often can print on both sides of the paper during one pass, usually can be loaded with paper of the customer's choosing, and may reproduce passable halftones. Larger machines collate, side stitch, and even paste bind.

Getting the best quality possible from a photocopy machine requires the same attention to detail necessary for all forms of printing: clean original copy ready for lights and lens. The single light source characteristic of many photocopiers sometimes leads to shadow lines on copies. To avoid this problem, make originals as flat as possible. If cut lines continue to show up, try turning the original copy around on the glass or printing in "light copy" mode. If that doesn't work, clean up a first generation copy and use it as the original. And be sure the glass is clean. Specks may print.

Photocopy machines have an entirely different economy from printing presses. With presses, unit costs drop as print runs increase. With photocopiers, unit costs stay the same throughout the run. Copy number 1,000 costs the same as copy number one. Many customers use the rule of thumb that photocopy is the method of choice for less than 100 copies, although cost-efficient quantity levels go up each time manufacturers introduce new machines.

So-called intelligent copiers reproduce images from computer memories rather than copying from another sheet of paper. Coupled to word processors or driven directly from their own keyboard, these copiers use laser technology to produce basic quality printed pages at rates up to two per second. Type resolution isn't nearly as good as typesetting, but is adequate for reports, price lists, and business letters. Some intelligent copiers also have built-in halftone screens for black and white reproduction of photographs.

Computer-driven photocopiers are the basis of electronic publishing. Working at a screen, operators compose text and graphics into final page layouts. Small scanners may even digitize logos and other line art, allowing insertion of visuals on the screen. The final outcome is a fully-composed document ready for immediate printing. The technology works well with catalogs, newsletters, directories, manuals, and other kinds of publications that must be up-to-the-minute accurate and may be printed basic quality black and white.

Computer-driven photocopiers offer several advantages over offset presses yielding similar quality printing.

No pasteup or makeready. What you see on the screen is what you get from the machine.

Printing on demand. You get exactly the number of proposals or service manuals you need: inventory is on the disk.

Instant changes. Information can be changed before and during the run. Changing before the run means updating such material as price lists or contract terms to reflect today's conditions. Changing during the run means custom-making each copy by adding personal names or unique information such as the names of cities or companies.

Electronic transmission. Data can be sent via phone lines or satellites to machines elsewhere. Insurance policies written this morning in Chicago can print out this afternoon in Los Angeles and Houston. Electronic transmission is economical as well as fast: technical manuals go out by wire instead of in cartons.

Ink Jet

Another form of computer-controlled printing uses equipment with tiny nozzles that release ink droplets through an electrostatic charging unit onto paper. The charge shapes droplets into letters. Ink jet as a commercial process is common at mailing services, where the nozzles are mounted in line with collating, binding, and addressing equipment.

Ink jet printing is quiet and very fast. Nothing mechanical strikes paper. Speed comes from computer control. One nozzle might generate 66,000 drops a second and print a business letter in two seconds. Ink jet systems have few moving parts, so they are highly reliable and easily maintained.

The inks used for ink jet printing must dry instantly. Paper must be absorbent without allowing droplets to blur. Even with the right paper, ink jet printing yields very low quality. Imperfectly aimed droplets hitting an absorbent, moving substrate result in fuzzy characters.

Because ink jet technology is based on computers, the droplets can be patterned in the same variety as mechanical dot printers. Ink jet messages can be changed in a microsecond. A printer making catalogs might have six nozzles to print individual sales messages on bound-in order forms and another six nozzles for a different message plus address on the cover.

Catalogs and mailers processed through ink jet equipment need no labels because each address is printed directly onto the mailing piece. Addressing machines can be driven directly from magnetic tapes storing lists. This last feature is especially appealing when nine-digit zip codes appear in optical character recognition (OCR) patterns, qualifying for additional savings at the post office.

While ink jet is most useful for direct mail, its speed and economy make it practical for personalizing business forms, coding document entry systems, and numbering tickets. The process also works well with rough substrates.

Most printers and lettershops using ink jet offer one color only. Color work, however, is available. Using the four process colors, color ink jet systems can produce anywhere from 8 to 5,000 shades, depending on software. &

9

After printing, most jobs require more work to make them into the final product. Large sheets may need to be cut into individual pieces or folded to become parts of books. Printed sheets may need drilling, stitching, or some combination of a dozen possible ending steps.

Printers refer to everything that happens to paper after actual printing as bindery work. The category includes a process as simple as folding 100 fliers and as complicated as case binding 10,000 books.

Bindery operations take place in binderies that are either departments of a print shop or separate businesses. When they are separate businesses, they are known as trade binderies and are listed in classified directories under "bookbinders." In addition to having all the basic equipment, many trade binderies offer less common services such as tab sealing.

Binderies may be only a few machines in a back room or be multimillion dollar plants handling truckloads of printing per day. Trade binderies serve printers throughout their region.

Machines for bindery operations are the least accurate of graphic arts equipment. Even an average press can register to $1/100$ inch. In contrast, folding, trimming, and binding are seldom done to tolerances better than $1/32$ inch. Good design includes a clear understanding of what happens to a job in the bindery.

Mistakes in the bindery can be disastrous. A job that has been expertly managed and produced from design through preparation and

Bindery

press work can be ruined by a short trim or crooked fold. For that reason, it is imperative to take bindery requirements into account while the job is being planned. All bindery needs should be thoroughly discussed with the printer before work begins.

Many jobs are finished at a trade bindery instead of in the printer's bindery. When complicated work will go to a trade bindery, it pays to consult directly with its staff as well as with the printer who will send it.

In this chapter, we describe and illustrate common bindery operations. We also discuss management implications of packaging, final counts, shipping, and storage decisions.

Drilling and Punching

Drilling and punching holes in paper to put in ring or post binders is commonly done and easily specified. Hole diameters between $1/8$ inch and $1/2$ inch are readily available. State what size holes you want and how far they should be from each other and the edge of the paper. Better yet, give your printer an example of the binder the sheets must fit. Your printer may know sizes for a standard three-ring binder, but may not be familiar with drilling for five-ring binders or other less common formats.

Holes that are not round or are too small to be die cut must be punched. Punching for binding methods such as plastic combs and wire spirals costs quite a bit more than simple drilling.

Some binderies have equipment to reinforce holes in sheets that will undergo hard use. Round holes can have protective metal eyelets identical to those in shoes. As an alternative, areas of the sheet to be either punched or drilled can first be reinforced with mylar strips. Binderies can also lay strips of mylar or other plastic along the tabs of file folders.

It's easy to forget about drilling and punching during design and pasteup. Do not start copy so close to an edge that holes will pierce headlines or puncture borders. Avoid problems by drawing holes on roughs, mechanicals, and proofs in non-repro blue. Give the printer a drilled or punched dummy to show exact placement. Specify sizes in fractions of an inch. If the size or shape of the holes you need has a name unique to your industry, be sure your printer knows the correct pattern.

"I don't care what studio makes the mechanical, I want to see a dummy before the job goes into production. I want to see specifications, too. I wouldn't stay in the bindery business very long if my people didn't also re-measure trim and fold marks and check measurements against specifications. You'd be amazed at how many designs I see for work that won't fit our machines and has to be finished by hand. You can't be too careful! Whenever I inspect somebody's comp or mechanical, I try to imagine it reproduced 10,000 times. That helps motivate me to double-check for every possible flaw that I might be able to help avoid."

Cutting and Trimming

Most press runs use paper slightly larger than the finished piece or print several items on one large sheet. Waste must be cut away and items cut apart from each other.

All straight line cuts are called trims. Job specifications should include trim size as exact measurements of the final product and mechanicals should include trim marks. The trim size of this book is 8½ x 11.

Printers usually have a paper cutter at least large enough to handle sheets from the largest press in the shop. Cutters all work on the same principle: with the paper held tightly under pressure to assure an even cut, a guillotine blade slices down and across, cutting anywhere from one sheet to a stack three inches thick.

Some slight variations in trim size are inevitable, but not ragged edges or cuts that are out of square. The ragged look comes from dull blades or stacks not held under sufficient pressure. Jobs out of square are simply sloppy work.

The stack of paper on a cutter is known as a lift. Although the lift is held under pressure during cutting, some movement of the sheets is inevitable. The movement is called draw and leads to variations in trim size within the stack.

9-1 Trimming. Good design takes into account the lack of precision and inconsistency of bindery equipment. This example looks fine when properly trimmed, but is ruined by a trim that is slightly off.

Draw is held to a minimum by keeping blades sharp and lifts small. If specifications on mechanicals are clear, production trims should conform to the tolerances stated in Visual 7-8.

Printed sheets that are trimmed before their ink is completely dry may smear or offset while in the cutter. Your printer should insist on ample drying time, which depends on ink coverage and type of paper, and warn you if your schedule is too rushed.

Round cornering is available at most trade binderies. The process itself is fairly slow, so may require extra production time. Corners may be cut in a variety of standard sizes specified in radius from edge to edge. Round cornering prevents items such as membership cards from becoming dog-eared.

Scoring and Perforating

Scoring means to crease a printed piece so that it folds more easily. The procedure is necessary whenever paper thicker than .005 inch will be machine folded or when precise folding by hand is required. Scoring is typically done by equipment that presses paper against the metal edge of either a rule or a wheel. Coated stock, especially if printed with solids of a dark color, may require the softer touch of string scoring so that paper doesn't crack along the folds.

Perforating is simply punching a line of holes to make tearing easier. Most bindery machines can perforate in only one direction and

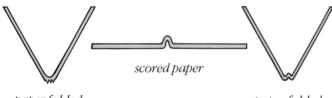

paper folded without scoring   *scored paper*   paper folded at score

9-2 Scoring. Thick paper, especially if it is coated or has heavy ink coverage across a fold, should be scored before folding.

perforations per inch

9-3 Perforating. Designers can control the tear strength of perforated lines by specifying the number of perforations per inch. Few perforations per inch mean longer individual cuts, less paper holding the two pieces together, and perforations relatively easy to tear. More cuts per inch result in a stronger bond.

only in straight lines. Perforating in more than one direction or in curved lines must normally be done on a press.

Specify scores and perforations on mechanicals by drawing a black line similar to a trim mark outside image areas. Label the line "score here" or "perforate here."

Scoring and perforating can each be done on offset and letter presses as well as specialized bindery equipment. When done as part of offset printing, they require attaching metal strips to the impression cylinder. The procedure saves time on long runs because it happens simultaneously with printing, but it ruins blankets and may adversely affect printing.

When done on a letter press, scoring and perforating can be done simultaneously with printing or die cutting.

Folding

The number of ways paper can be folded seem endless. Most printers have equipment to make common folds using sheets as large as their largest press. Trade binderies typically have machines with six or eight folding stations to accommodate complicated work.

Folding is not precise. Most folding machines can work within a tolerance of ¹/₃₂ inch per fold, but even that is not close enough for near-perfect crossovers. Plan your design to allow for tiny variations in folds just as you would for variations in trims.

On a large sheet that must fold several times, the accuracy of the first fold affects all subsequent folds. A ¹/₃₂ inch variation on the first fold may shift the second fold ¹/₁₆ inch and the third ¹/₈ inch. Even the thickness of the paper will cause a variation. Roll folds, for example, require that panel widths increase by at least ¹/₁₆ inch each as they move from inside panels to outside. To plan accurately for folds, make a dummy folded from the same paper that is called for in the specifications for your job.

Folding requires careful planning when a job is being designed and pasted up. Copy that is poorly positioned means products may not read correctly when folded or a fold might run through important visuals.

Paper less than 50# may be difficult to feed into the folder and may wrinkle going through; paper more than 80#, especially coated stock, often needs scoring before folding. Designing for printing on medium and heavy weight stock should anticipate folding by assuring that most folds run with the grain of the paper.

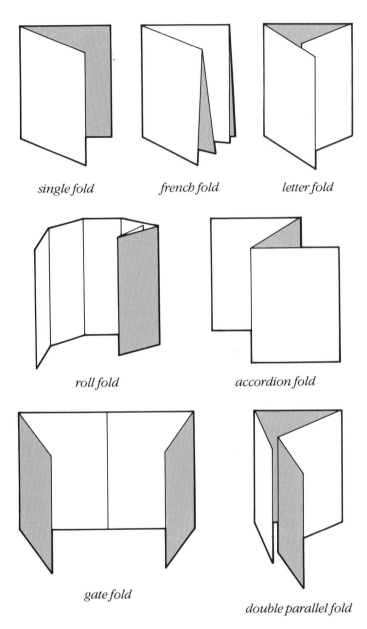

single fold *french fold* *letter fold*

roll fold *accordion fold*

gate fold

double parallel fold

9-4 Common folds. Referring to folds by their standard names ensures clear communication. While these seven folds are common, printers and trade binderies can often do many others, including some that are quite complicated. Binderies may have problems doing complicated folds with unusually light or heavy paper. When designing a printed piece that folds, always provide a folding dummy to the printer or bindery.

Although folding in a specific style may be easy for the bindery, it may lead to problems elsewhere. For example, machines that stuff envelopes for mass mailings may not handle items with accordion folds.

Collating and Gathering

Almost everyone has made endless trips around a table to assemble sheets for a book or report. Even for a printer or bindery, this hand method of collating may be the best for small jobs.

Collating can be done by equipment which holds stacks of sheets in pockets, then presents one sheet from each pocket for assembly. The machines have highly specific tolerances and capabilities. If you're designing for anything but the most standard 8½ x 11 job, consult with your printer or bindery first.

Products such as cookbooks with comb bindings look like assemblies of loose pages, but in fact were probably printed several pages to each large sheet. After folding, the sheets were trimmed on four sides to cut away folds and leave a pile of perfectly collated pages.

Such large sheets of pages, which are folded to become part of a catalog or book, are referred to as signatures. Gathering signatures means collating them so that, after they are trimmed, pages are in proper sequence. Gathering takes place on equipment that may also stitch and trim them in one operation.

Printers specializing in manufacturing books may print, fold, trim, and bind all in one machine sequence. Unit costs can be far lower than when working with printers who must set up new equipment for each stage of the job or who must send jobs to trade binderies.

"Our club publishes an updated cookbook every two years. Of course, every issue gets bigger. Last summer's book had so many recipes that we needed all six signatures and didn't have room for the order form. The printer's sales representative showed us how we could have order forms printed on card paper, perforated, and glued onto the end of the last signature. Our new forms are easier to use than the old ones that were printed along with the book itself."

Binding

There are several ways to attach loose sheets, folded sheets, or signatures to each other. Each method offers a different mixture of aesthetics, permanence, and convenience. Which one you choose depends on your design and budget as well as your requirements for durability.

Padding. Almost every printer can make pads from stacks of loose sheets, the most simple binding operation. For most printers it's a hand operation with brush and glue pot.

Gluing. Binderies and envelope makers must be able to apply adhesives in strips. Strips of adhesive that will be individually sealed by the user are available as either remoistenable glue or a sticky surface protected by a piece of peel-off paper.

Remoistenable glue strips are inexpensive to apply and can be moistened by automated machinery when necessary. Peel-off strips are handy for large envelopes and products that must be assembled by hand.

Tipping. When one sheet is glued to another sheet or signature, it's referred to as tipping. The sheet of order forms at the end of this book was tipped onto the last signature before binding. Tipping can be done by machines at most trade binderies.

Sealing. Often binderies have machines for sealing folded items. Binderies that do tab sealing apply an adhesive circle or strip of tape to the face of a booklet or self-mailer. Tab sealing is relatively inexpensive and helps products go through the mail in good condition.

Tinning. Tinning refers to clamping metal strips along the tops or bottoms of calendars. Although tinning machines are very simple, binderies that have them are hard to find. Begin by asking your printer.

Stitching. Stitch bindings are done with wire staples either through the crease of the spine or near one edge of the sheets.

Saddle stitching means staples go through the crease of the spine, allowing pages to lie nearly flat when opened. Most magazines are saddle stitched. The method is fast and inexpensive, but does not yield a flat outer spine that can show printing.

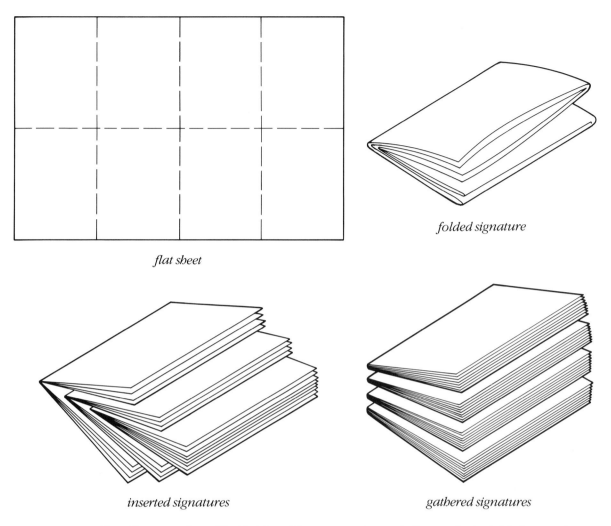

flat sheet

folded signature

inserted signatures

gathered signatures

9-5 Signatures. A booklet or catalog of 8, 12, 16, or 32 pages may be made from a single, folded press sheet, depending on the size of the press and trim size of the product. This sheet is referred to as a signature. Books and catalogs made from more than one signature can be bound by saddle stitching inserted signatures or by perfect or case binding gathered signatures. Note that page imposition is determined by how signatures will be assembled, so the method of binding must be known before stripping.

Booklets, small catalogs, and similar products up to about 20 sheets (80 pages) of 60# or 70# paper all lend themselves to saddle stitching. How well the stitching holds depends on the thickness of the sheets and length of the staples. Products having more than about 20 sheets may need some other kind of binding.

Saddle stitched products can easily accommodate special inserts such as envelopes, membership forms, or order blanks. Such inserts must be folded into four-page signatures or have a binding lip.

Because of the bulkiness of paper, designs for products to be printed on heavy stock and

end view of untrimmed signature

9-6 Creep. When a press sheet is folded into a signature, the inside pages creep away from the spine and push out on the opposite edge as shown here. The phenomenon may cause problems when using thick paper or too many inserted signatures. Creep can also happen with a design having narrow margins or bleeds on inner pages.

saddle stitched may need to allow for the effects of shingling, especially when the products have narrow outside margins. Mechanicals or flats must take shingling into account to assure equal margins throughout the printed piece. This may be more trouble than it's worth if slight variations in the margins will hardly be noticed. A dummy made before starting pasteup will show whether and how to adjust the mechanicals.

Loop stitching is a variant of saddle stitching where each staple has enough play outside the crease to go over the rings of a ring binder. The method is an alternative to drilling for catalogs that will insert into ring binders.

Side stitching puts staples through an entire stack of sheets near its edge. The method results in a strong bind, but means pages will not lie flat when open. Staples use some margin, so plan copy to start well in from the edge. Heavy-duty equipment can side stitch products up to 1½ inches thick, but the result would look and feel cumbersome. We suggest ½ inch maximum for side stitching. Stacks of paper that have been side stitched can have a wraparound cover applied with glue.

Paste binding. Booklets with just a few pages can be paste bound as an alternative to saddle stitching. With paste binding, a web press or folder lays thin strips of glue along fold lines. When the sheet is folded, glued creases meet glued folds to form the bond. After trimming, glue along the creased spine is the only binding. Some photocopiers paste bind by laying glue along the edge of single sheets, adhering them as they fall on top of each other.

Paste binding is much more economical than stitching for booklets of 8, 12, or 16 pages. The upper limit for the number of paste-bound pages depends on bulk of paper and capabilities of press or folder. High-bulk paper may be too thick to paste bind more than 16 pages.

"We used to spiral bind our technical manuals, but we were spending a fortune in reprinting because the field was changing so fast. We had a high initial investment when we switched to ring binders, but our print costs have gone way down. Now we just send out update sheets whenever there's new information."

Mechanical binding. Cookbooks or technical manuals intended to lie flat when open can be bound with plastic or wire shaped into either a spiral or comb. Two of these bindings are referred to by the brand names GBC (plastic comb) and Wire-O (wire comb) and cost more per unit than stitching. All mechanical bindings are well suited to short runs.

Spiral bindings tend to be the least costly per unit and Wire-O most costly, with GBC somewhere in the middle. The cost differences among all forms of mechanical bindings are not very great and cost relationships may change with large quantities.

The most important differences among mechanical bindings concern how they function. Spirals allow the product not merely to lie flat, but to be doubled over, a useful feature for technical manuals, notebooks, and calendars. Spiral bound products have lots of play between individual pages and cannot have pages added to them. Furthermore, the spirals may be damaged by crushing.

Comb bindings allow for less play in the pages, but are more subject to damage than spirals. They are relatively easy to install, thus can be done at many small printers and in-plant shops. Plastic combs come in a variety of colors and can be screen printed to put a message on the spine. They can be bent open to insert additional pages. GBC combs have the greatest capacity of any mechanical binding, some allowing for products up to three inches thick.

Plastic comb bindings have the disadvantage that products bound with them will not open past the point of lying flat. The combs are inserted by hand, which makes them very advantageous for just a few products and rather costly for large quantities. Unit costs do not drop very rapidly as quantities increase.

Wire-O bindings are double loops of wire that allow the product to be doubled over but, unlike spirals, keep the pages lined up across from each other. They are very durable, come in several colors of wire, and give a more finished look than spirals.

Double loop bindings have the disadvantages of not allowing for insertion of new pages and having a maximum capacity of about ⅞

saddle stitching

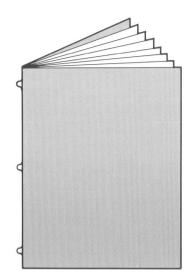

loop stitching

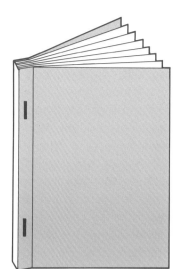

side stitching

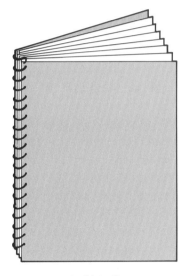

spiral binding

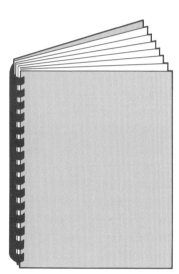

comb binding

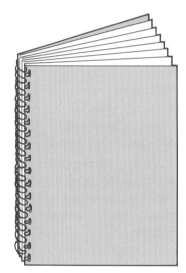

Wire-O binding

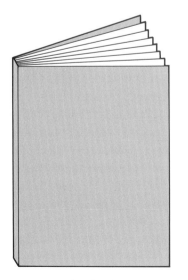

perfect binding

case binding

9-7 **Common bindings**. These eight bindings are commonly available at printing companies and trade binderies. Each has advantages and disadvantages, depending on page count, kind of paper, and how the product will be shipped and used. To assure correct imposition, the binding method must be known before stripping and platemaking.

inch. They cannot be printed on the spine, but can be case bound, yielding a handsome (and expensive) book. Most trade binderies can insert Wire-O, but not many printers can.

Printing designed for mechanical bindings, like side stitching, requires generous inside margins. Be sure your layout allows enough space.

Perfect binding. Perfect bound books, such as the common paperback, are made from signatures which have been gathered into a stack. The left side of the stack, the spine, is trimmed to get rid of the folds and expose the edge of each page. The stack is then roughened and notched along the spine to assure maximum surface for glue adhesion.

To bind the book, hot glue is applied along the spine. When the cover is pressed against the surface wet with glue, it adheres to the pad as well as forces some glue between the sheets. After the glue is dry, the assembled book is trimmed on the remaining three sides.

The glue for perfect binding should be even, free from lumps, and not forced too deeply between the sheets. Glues used for perfect binding must be somewhat flexible when dry, allowing books to open easily and without cracking. Some printers caution against perfect binding coated cover papers because coatings prevent glues from adhering strongly to fibers. If you're concerned about adhesion to coated cover stock, specify C1S cover grade so that the uncoated side may face inward.

Binderies that do burst perfect binding make slits along the the spines of signatures so glue is forced toward the inside pages. Burst perfect bound books look similar to sewn books because the signatures are not trimmed and roughened along the spine. They are almost as strong as sewn signatures and cost much less. If you are reading a soft cover copy of this book, it is burst perfect bound.

Case binding. Nothing beats case binding for durability, good looks, or high cost. The method, also known as edition binding, results in the common hard cover book.

Traditionally, case binding begins with sewing signatures along the spine. Thread makes a stronger and more elegant adhesive than glue. Because the machine most commonly used for sewing signatures is made by Smythe, most signatures are Smythe sewn. There are, however, other forms of sewing such as saddle, cleat, and McCain. If your book is for a market that has technical production specifications, such as those for school textbooks, be sure to check what kind of sewing is required.

After signatures are sewn, they are gathered and trimmed on three sides. The stack is put inside a case made of binder's board covered with paper, cloth, plastic, or leather. The case is held to the signatures by glue along the spine and between endsheets. Covers of case bound books can be printed in a variety of ways, although foil stamping is most popular.

To cut costs, some publishers skip the sewing by inserting perfect bound or burst perfect bound bodies into cases. Case binding can also mix with other techniques such as side stitching and mechanical bindings.

Printers and trade binderies who specialize in books customarily offer case binding. Most cities have a small bindery specializing in short runs, book restoration, and presentation volumes involving handcrafted case bindings. Leather coverings and handmade endsheets yield lavish books at equally lavish prices.

Because case binding combines so many components, writing specifications is quite complicated. You must decide about such elements as square or round backs, headbands, boards, cover material, and dust jackets. Sales representatives at trade binderies will help you make many of these decisions, although you might benefit from the point of view of an experienced book publisher as well.

"When we did our first book, we thought we did good market research, but we still guessed totally wrong about what percentage of the run should be perfect bound and what percentage case bound. In less than a year we ran out of the soft cover, but had 1,300 of the hard cover still sitting in our warehouse. With every book since then, we have only bound half the print run. We leave the other half as flat sheets stored on pallets at the bindery until we learn what kind of binding the market wants for that particular title."

Coatings and Laminates

Products such as book covers, menus, and folders may need coatings to protect them from scuffing, dirt, and fingerprints. Varnish or various plastic coatings can be applied for the necessary protection. Protective coatings can also add sheen and heighten contrast, making printing seem more dramatic.

Varnish is applied during printing rather than during binding. The liquid is carried on press like ink and may be applied in spots or as total coverage. Varnish is the most common, least expensive, and least durable coating.

Liquid laminates such as UV (ultraviolet) and IR (infrared) are applied in the bindery. Machines apply liquid plastic to paper, then pass sheets through drying units. As with varnish, you can ask for dull or gloss finishes. Liquid laminates give tough finishes similar to that on record jackets and the cover of this book.

Film laminates are applied by inserting paper between thin sheets of plastic, then pressing with hot rollers. Film laminating is a relatively simple operation available from many binderies. Although slow and costly, it yields an exceptionally strong surface that is also washable. Menus, membership cards, and luggage tags are often film laminated. Laminates are available in thicknesses from .001 inch to .010 inch and with either gloss or dull finishes.

Liquid and film laminates may affect foil stamping or embossing. Check with your printer before planning to combine processes.

Converting

A printed sheet that has been changed into a substantially new product, such as a box or envelope, has been converted.

Converting companies, like binderies, work primarily with printers. Unlike binderies, however, converters tend to specialize in products such as envelopes. Further specialization occurs in the category of boxes: some companies make boxes from corrugated paper while others make them from chipboard. The chipboard products are known in the trade simply as paper boxes.

As when working with any trade service, experience is the key to success. If you are a graphic arts novice, you will probably get the best quality and service by letting your printer be responsible for dealing with converters. As you gain experience, you will often benefit by dealing with converters personally.

Packaging

The method of packing the final product strongly affects shipping and storage and may also influence effectiveness and profit. No one is attracted to or wants to buy damaged goods. Materials should be tightly packed to prevent sliding and scratching. Rubber or paper bands or shrink wrap should go around small bundles before they are put into boxes. Specify how many items you want per bundle. Books that are not shrink-wrapped should have slip sheets between each book. Boxes should be banded when on skids.

Many industries have their own standards for shipping and storage which affect specifications to binderies. For example, buyers for retail outlets in some industries order by the half gross and gross, so binderies should be instructed to put products in boxes containing either 72 or 144 units.

At least part of almost every printing job will be stored in a warehouse, back room, or bottom drawer. Material must be packed to assure convenience and longevity. Convenience simply means in packages suitable for people who must deal with them. Bound materials should be stored horizontally, not standing on end. Light and moisture may affect quality during storage because paper absorbs moisture and ink fades. To avoid problems in six months or a year, discuss storage conditions thoroughly before specifying packaging.

"My printer puts an 'open last' label on one box of every job. Inside that box is a slip addressed to me with the job number, date, and quantity of the last printing. Our stock clerk sends me the slip and I just call the printer and re-order. We never run out and it's a winning situation for both the printer and my staff."

Printers and binderies offer several forms of packaging. Many jobs require a combination.

Bulk packing is the least expensive form of packaging and many jobs require nothing more. Bindery workers simply load pieces into boxes. Remember that boxes of printed matter can be heavy. A box containing 5,000 fliers on 8½ x 11 coated stock can easily weigh 50 pounds. And the weight adds up. If you plan to stack six or eight boxes on top of each other, be sure that the cartons are sturdy and the bottom ones are full.

We authors expect often to carry boxes filled with this book, so asked the publisher to specify that boxes weigh no more than thirty pounds. The U.S. Postal Service, UPS, and other carriers have their own limits on weight and size that you must keep in mind when planning how you want items packaged.

Shrink wrapping is the process by which a plastic film surrounds and seals products. You can see the items inside, but they are wrapped so tightly that they will not rub during transit. Wrapping with kraft paper is another option. Bindery workers wrap and label to your specifications, yielding individual packages that pack, store, and ship well.

Shrink and kraft wrapping are suitable for anything from fliers to books. Unless you specify some particular number, the bindery will wrap as it finds convenient—perhaps a handful to each package. Shrink wrapping also works for entire boxes and even pallets loaded with boxes. The plastic helps keep material fresh during long storage.

Pallets (also called skids) are standard wooden platforms used in every industry. They'll easily hold a ton of material packed in boxes. If you expect delivery on pallets and don't have a fork lift and loading dock, be sure you ask for delivery by truck with a lift gate.

Some trade binderies can handle retail packaging styles such as skin, bubble, and blister wrapping, although these techniques are more often done by specialized businesses. If your printing is part of a retail product, be sure you know packaging requirements. Organizations such as Goodwill Industries offer inexpensive retail packaging services.

Customers often don't think much about labels, so may simply get printing delivered with a sample of their product taped to the outside of boxes. To make labels clear, tell your printer what information you want on the outside of boxes and packages.

Final Counts

Whether orders are for 1,000 books, 5,000 posters, or 100,000 envelopes, they get counted —or estimated—for the last time while being packaged for delivery to the customer.

Quantity control is extremely difficult. Printers figure enough extra paper at the beginning of the job to allow for waste along the way. If everything goes smoothly, you'll have a few more pieces than you ordered and perhaps at no extra cost. If it's essential, however, that you have no less than the number you ordered, tell your printer as part of the specifications. Trade customs allow a 10% variation on orders unless you have negotiated a different percentage. To ensure that you get "no less than," your printer may insist on doubling the percentage tolerance for overruns.

Pay careful attention when you pick up materials or receive delivery. Trade customs and business ethics both dictate that you claim shortages promptly. The best time to check for problems is when the job is still on the printer's counter, loading dock, or truck. Take time to spot-check several boxes, then count the cartons to be sure everyone agrees on the totals.

Short counts can happen for several reasons. Perhaps the estimated ratio of waste to finished product just didn't work out. The ratio was, after all, only the printer's guess based on averages and experience. Perhaps some of your

---

"Our building only has a little freight elevator inside the front door. When the folders and other materials for our convention arrived by truck, the boxes were on a pallet with a steel band around it. We had to hunt all over for wire cutters, open the pallet inside the truck, and unload the boxes by hand. The driver was so frustrated that I finally called the printer to explain why he would be returning so much later than expected."

material is "lost"—still on a skid at the bindery or printer or in boxes on a truck headed for the other side of town. Perhaps there is a systematic error, such as boxes labeled as containing 500 really having 520.

On short counts you can either go back to press to complete the job or get a credit. From the printer's standpoint, going back to press costs far more than cutting the price. From the customer's standpoint, the printed pieces are probably more important than the money. Don't hesitate to insist on going back to press if the additional material is crucial. If you do insist, however, don't be surprised if that printer loses interest in you as a future customer.

Storage and Transit

Most printers and binderies are not in the warehouse business. When your job is done, they want you to have it. There are, however, two exceptions. Books and similar materials require a lot of storage space and may stay in inventory a long time. Printers who specialize in these products may offer inexpensive warehouse space. The other exception is material which must be later imprinted. It makes sense to keep that inventory at the printer's.

Storage at the printer's can be convenient and cheap, but also requires some common-sense precautions. Check actual warehouse conditions to be sure the space is reasonably secure and free from moisture, dust, and risk of fire. Double-check your insurance situation to learn who would pay for damaged or lost goods and how inventory would be verified. Finally, ask about accessibility. Don't wait until next summer's convention to learn the whole print shop goes on vacation in July.

Printers will happily send your goods wherever you like at standard shipping costs. If shipping is by common carrier, the printer's shipping department probably contracts with reliable services. If in doubt, check with a couple of freight companies yourself.

Customers need to keep track of jobs received and put into inventory. To assure the monitoring is done correctly, you should have a working relationship with storage and distribution people in your organization. You should tell them when to expect jobs that you have managed and how to handle them when delivered. They should tell you the best ways to have the job packaged and what their procedures are for handling packing slips, bills of lading, and other paperwork. ❧

10

To manage a variety of printing jobs, you need to know the capabilities of many printers. You may have two or three printers for routine work, but you should know how to identify and work with printers on a job-by-job basis when your regular shops are not appropriate.

Working with a variety of printers assures maximum control over quality, schedule, and price. To get the best price, you must be willing to shop among printers. Having a list of candidate printers does not, however, mean soliciting competitive bids for every job. Working with one of your regular printers is often the most convenient and dependable way to get a job done, even if it means that occasionally a job is subcontracted.

In this chapter we return to some of the themes about business relationships introduced in Chapter One. We emphasize working cooperatively with printers to achieve quality and service and offer guidelines for achieving good business relationships. For example, we present criteria for evaluating jobs and analyzing bills. Even with the guidelines, however, you'll often find yourself in a gray area where only experience can shape your judgment.

This chapter includes the Printer Equipment and Services form to help you keep a record of printing companies that might be suitable for your kinds of jobs. Like the forms in Chapter One, this form is presented slightly reduced and filled out with an example. The form ready to photocopy is in Appendix E.

Working with Printers

Near the end of this chapter we have reproduced a set of business guidelines known as printing trade customs. The customs are statements approved by the Printing Industries of America and other trade associations in the graphic arts. We wrote comments about the guidelines to make them more clear and useful.

Your Regular Printers

Many printing buyers find it practical to have printers they use regularly for routine work. When choosing regular printers from among shops that give satisfactory quality at prices that seem reasonable, what printers they select depends largely on service. Dependability and convenience become the key factors.

After establishing regular printers, you rely on their familiarity with what you expect and trust them to take care of your printing needs. Printing companies used regularly become part of a set of business relationships in the graphic arts that might also include a typesetter and trade camera service.

Having a quick printer as one of your regular printers can save time and money with basic quality, one-color jobs in relatively short runs. With those jobs, the average commercial printer would take longer and have to charge more than the job is worth to you.

As a consistent customer of a quick printer, you will usually have several advantages over the walk-in trade. You'll probably get monthly billings rather than individual invoices. The billings can include charges for photocopies that you recorded in a logbook. Priority service can include overnight printing, after hours pickup, and personal access to the light table and pasteup supplies.

As a consistent customer of a commercial printer, you may get priority press time and delivery scheduling. Staff may know your wishes with regard to halftones and packaging. You may get extended credit terms or be alerted to special values in paper.

Having regular printers helps plan jobs to take best advantage of press sizes and capabilities. Presses at quick printers are quite similar from one shop to the next, but it helps if you know your printer can run 12 x 18 paper so that 11 x 17 products can have bleeds.

The blend of presses and other equipment at commercial printers is more individual and complex than at quick printers. Being a regular customer helps you learn how to plan for a

"I don't want to write specifications and choose a new printer for every job. That's too much hassle. I just want to call the printer down the street and say, 'You know what I want' or 'Do another thousand like last time.' They take care of all of the typesetting and design and just show me photocopies so I can check that everything reads correctly. I like to meet my printer for coffee and don't want to worry whether I'm paying a little too much for dependable service."

press that may be a perfector, a multicolor unit, or both. Experience with the shop helps reveal its abilities regarding camera work and bindery operations as well as the printing itself.

People who buy a lot of printing may use five or six printers regularly. A book publisher must know about several book printers. The marketing director for a restaurant chain needs to know about menu printers and perhaps about some screen printers for aprons and T-shirts. Both types of buyers also need shops for forms, stationery, fliers, and other routine jobs.

Being a regular customer of any print shop does not mean getting bargain prices. While the staff may suggest ways to save money on a particular job, with most jobs you will pay as much as any other customer. Indeed, having regular printers may mean that you pay more for some jobs than you would have with competitive bidding. In our view, the service you should be getting is worth the few extra dollars.

Regular printers are especially convenient for reruns because they are already familiar with the job. The flats are probably on file and orders can be made over the phone and confirmed by mail. With routine jobs, therefore, your best choice is probably to let the original printer do the reruns.

The trade custom giving printers ownership of negatives and plates that they make exists to help printers get reruns. Printers who sense that reruns will come automatically may not, however, work at truly competitive prices the second time around. With major jobs it's to your advantage to have the negatives so you can solicit new quotes each time the job repeats.

If you want to own the negatives after the initial job is delivered, be sure your contract includes wording that gives you ownership. For more information about owning and storing negatives, see the end of Chapter Five.

"That week I had more printing than I could handle, so I deliberately quoted high to print the brochures for their warehouse sale. Someone in management must have liked me or thought I do good work, because I got the job anyway. I had to spend all weekend in my shop to get the work done on time."

Printers for Non-Routine Jobs

Most organizations and businesses need a wide variety of printed pieces. Many, such as forms, stationery, and newsletters, are almost always suited to one of their regular printers. Others, such as catalog sheets or presentation folders, might be done better, faster, and less expensively at another shop.

Knowing when to consider alternatives to your regular printers requires judgments about each individual job. You must decide whether a job is too large or small, must meet quality standards too high or low, or has some other aspect that makes it poorly suited to one of your regular printers. For example, if you want 5,000 booklets that are two-color, 16-pages, saddle stitched, and in the good quality category, your regular commercial printer is probably the best one for the job. If you want 50,000 booklets that include premium quality 4-color process work, it would make sense to get quotations from some other printers.

As you learn about commercial printers in your area, you will realize that they fall roughly into categories that reflect their capability for producing small, medium, and large jobs.

A shop suited to small jobs will have small presses capable of printing one or two colors at a time. The shop will also have simple preparation and bindery departments. At a print shop of this kind you would probably discuss jobs directly with the owner.

Printing companies suited to medium jobs have a blend of presses giving them great flexibility in scheduling and the kinds of items they can print. Shops of this size compete strongly for business and must operate efficiently to be profitable. Their customers deal mainly with sales reps, but they might also know some of the production supervisors.

At a print shop seeking big jobs, equipment and staff are geared to handle large amounts of paper and printed goods. There will probably be both web and sheetfed presses and press time must be scheduled days or weeks in advance. People in prep and bindery will be accustomed to dealing with very complicated jobs. Some larger printing companies are somewhat specialized because their web presses are configured to make specific products.

Only you can decide whether your routine printing needs or a non-routine specific job should be considered small, medium, or large. The key to intelligent buying is matching jobs with printers.

Selecting Printers

Experienced buyers can help you identify printers suited to your needs. Large companies, hospitals, banks, associations, and advertising agencies have one or two people who buy a lot of printing. Ask to speak with the printing buyer, marketing director, print production manager, or director of public relations. Using one of these titles when you inquire should get you to the right person who, perhaps over lunch, will be happy to give you leads.

You'll find knowledgeable printing buyers at local meetings of art directors and graphic designers and of organizations such as the International Association of Business Communicators, Public Relations Society of America, and American Advertising Federation. If you can't find these groups in your telephone directory, write to their national offices for names of local contacts. See Appendix C for addresses.

Classified directories do not distinguish between quick and commercial shops, but their ads and listings help tell who's who. The names of quick printers include words such as "jiffy," "rapid," and "instant." Commercial printers are more likely to include a family or regional name and to call themselves "full service" or "printers and lithographers."

In addition to listing companies under the classification "printers," classified directories have a variety of other categories for printing. Most are related to the names of products, such as "bags—paper," and "post cards." In Appendix A we refer to many of these classifications while discussing specific products.

Knowing the capabilities of printers helps put them into categories, but where you take a specific job depends more on the key factors of service, quality, and price. For most customers, service is the most important consideration. At a

small shop, you may get personal attention from the owner, who might also run a press. At larger printers you deal with a sales representative or someone in customer service. Of course, an efficient sales rep may give you better service than a harried shop owner.

The service that a shop gives includes how rapidly it can figure estimates and print your job, how conveniently it is located, and whether its staff will pick up and deliver. You should also take into account credit terms and additional services such as typesetting and pasteup.

The size of a printing company is a poor guide to the quality of work it can do. Shops with small presses as well as those with large presses may do showcase work. Both kinds of shops may also turn out work that is very disappointing. Routine work from one may be identical to another's maximum effort. Intelligent buying means knowing what you can reasonably expect from a specific printer. Don't settle for less, but don't ask for more unless higher than normal standards were part of the contract.

Press size is often a fairly good guide to price. Press sizes and styles are the primary factors that determine which printer can handle a specific job most efficiently. For example, large presses produce high quantity jobs faster than small ones. Of course, quantities must be sufficient to make setting up the machines cost effective for both printer and customer.

When thinking about press sizes and features, keep in mind that the most important considerations are how well you want your job done, when you want it delivered, and how much it will cost. Knowing about presses helps you select possible printers, but doesn't guarantee quality, speed, or economy.

"I thought I was doing my printing sales rep a favor by giving his shop our company Christmas card job every year, even though I knew I could probably get it cheaper somewhere else. I figured the rep always gave us good service and deserved every job I could arrange. Last year I learned from a mutual friend that the job always got farmed out to a smaller printer better suited to the short run and that even though we paid a markup, the job was more trouble than it was worth to them."

To learn about printers who might suit your needs, simply call likely candidates and ask for information. Use the Printer Equipment and Services form to record relevant information. Ask for samples of the kind of work the shop does best. Explain that you are calling simply to become better acquainted with shops whose services you might use.

As a prospective customer, you may get invitations to tour printing companies. We suggest that you accept the first two or three to get a feel for how various printers set up their shops and how jobs flow from one department to another. We believe, however, that plant tours lose their value after the first few except for an occasional visit to a specialty shop or trade service. Tours are educational and build good business relations, but they don't help much in making specific buying decisions.

If you are considering a shop from the standpoint of becoming a regular customer, ask previous customers if quality is consistent and quoted prices are dependable. Ask the printer about any plans for buying new equipment or adding new services. Discuss how to design jobs that take advantage of particular machines. Inquire about credit arrangements.

Printer Equipment and Services

Knowing the capabilities of a wide range of printers helps build control over quality, schedule, and costs. Learning these capabilities requires systematic effort. Using the Printer Equipment and Services form will make the effort more effective.

The form in this chapter is filled out with information representing a typical commercial printer. In this example, we invented a printer appropriate for the summer catalog job that is

organized, scheduled, and specified in Chapter One. The blank form ready for you to photocopy for your own use is in Appendix E.

Knowledgeable printing buyers know that the brand name of a press speaks volumes about the quality of work that its owner expects to turn out. We did not feel it appropriate in this book to distinguish among press manufacturers, so used fictional press names. The information about maximum and minimum sizes, number of colors, and perfecting ability is relevant to presses of any brand.

The second side of the form takes into account the wide variety of equipment and services falling under such categories as bindery and prepress. The information you enter on these lines will reflect your kind of jobs and your needs for quality, speed, and economy. With any printer, however, it is important to know financial terms and to talk with one or two previous customers. We urge you to be careful in filling out those portions of the form.

When you talk with customers of a printing company, use the Printer Equipment and Services form to guide the discussion. Ask whether the quality of work met their expectations. Previous customers are especially helpful for evaluating how much service a printer offers and how well a printer stays on schedule.

Specialty Printers

Many printing jobs are routine enough for almost any printer to handle easily. Some shops, however, specialize in certain kinds of work. Their prices for that type of work will usually be lower than elsewhere.

The most common way for a printer to specialize is to have machinery and supplies geared to a specific product. For example, most urban areas have at least one envelope printer. Any shop with a small press can print envelopes, but one that specializes in printing them can print long runs faster and less expensively. Other products for which there are specialty printers include business forms, labels, magazines, direct mail, and books.

Specialty printers are sometimes listed in classified directories under the products in

---

"More customers should tell me when they are unhappy with our work. When we print a job that they find unsatisfactory for whatever reason, whether it's overdue or a poor ink match or just not decent quality, it's mostly because one of us wasn't clear with the other. A good percentage of any job turning out right is both the customer and the printer knowing what to expect."

Date compiled ___1-15-86___

Printing company ___ZIEDOFF LITHO___

address ___491 INDUSTRIAL WAY___

city, state, zip ___ANYTOWN, USA 84638___

Contact ___SARAH ALCOTT___ or ___ALLEN STEPHENS___

title ___SALES REP___ title ___CUSTOMER SERVICE___

phone ___348-5672___ phone ___348-5674___

Type of printer

☐ quick

☐ in-plant

☐ small commercial

☑ medium commercial

☐ large commercial

☐ specialty in _____

Routine quality ☐ basic ☐ good ☑ premium ☐ showcase

Possible quality ☐ basic ☐ good ☐ premium ☑ showcase

Union shop

☐ yes ☑ no

Comments about samples ___SEVERAL CONSUMER CATALOGS AT PREMIUM;___
___ANNUAL REPORTS AT PREMIUM AND SHOWCASE; MINOR___
___BINDERY PROBLEMS___

Sheetfed offset presses

brand ___FRANKLIN 320___ max sheet size __23__ x __29__ min size __11__ x __17__ # colors __2__ ☐ perfector

brand ___FRANKLIN 580___ max sheet size __26__ x __40__ min size __14__ x __20__ # colors __4__ ☑ perfector

brand _____ max sheet size ___ x ___ min size ___ x ___ # colors ___ ☐ perfector

brand _____ max sheet size ___ x ___ min size ___ x ___ # colors ___ ☐ perfector

brand _____ max sheet size ___ x ___ min size ___ x ___ # colors ___ ☐ perfector

Web offset presses

brand ___MONK 516___ maximum roll width __36__ cutoff __23½__ # colors __6__

brand _____ maximum roll width ___ cutoff ___ # colors ___

Letterpresses

brand ___GUTENBERG___ max size __12__ x __18__ min size __3__ x __5__ primary function ___FOIL STAMP___

brand _____ max size ___ x ___ min size ___ x ___ primary function _____

Other printing processes (engraving, thermography, photocopy, etc.) _____

10-1 Printer equipment and services. Getting appropriate quality, schedule, and costs for each job requires knowing the capabilities of many printers. Using this form to record information will prove helpful when selecting printers for

Bindery

cutter maximum sheet dimension __42__   folder maximum sheet size __26__ x __40__   min size __8__ x __10__

folding capabilities __STANDARD__

binding abilities (wire, paste, saddle stitch, perfect, case, etc.) __SADDLE STITCH; PERFECT BIND__

other bindery abilities __UV COATER__

Prepress services (halftones, separations, stripping, platemaking, etc.) _____

__ALL PREPRESS INCLUDING COLOR SCANNER FOR SEPARATIONS__

Miscellaneous in-house services (design, typesetting, pasteup, pick up and delivery, storage, fulfillment, direct mailing, list management, etc.) __2 DESIGNERS (ONE ALSO PHOTOGRAPHS PRODUCTS); PICKUP AND DELIVERY__

Negatives (ownership, storage conditions, insurance, etc.) __GOOD STORAGE FACILITIES; CUSTOMERS OWN FLATS__

Credit terms __50% DOWN ON FIRST JOB; INVOICE WITH JOBS; 2% FOR PAYMENT IN TEN DAYS__

Previous customer references

name __RALPH HARRIS__   name __ALLISON GREEN__

organization __NORTHWEST ADVERTISING__   organization __MONEY BY MAIL__

phone __267-3968__   phone __284-9000__

Comments __SHOP HAS DELIVERY TRUCK WITH LIFT GATE AND PALLET MOVER. GOOD CUSTOMER PARKING, BUT TRICKY ROUTE TO GET THERE: TAKE VERA STREET OFF RAMP, TURN LEFT AT SECOND. BOTH PREVIOUS CUSTOMERS SAY QUALITY AND PRICES GREAT, BUT WATCH THEM ON SCHEDULE, ESPECIALLY IF SALES REP IS S.A.__

specific jobs. The data entered on this example include fictional brand names for presses. A full-size, blank version of this form ready for you to photocopy is in Appendix E.

which they specialize and sometimes along with general printers. They also advertise in periodicals oriented to potential buyers of their products. For example, several printers who specialize in large quantities of 4-color fliers advertise in magazines aimed at people in gift and jewelry businesses.

Developing a customer base with a special interest is another way for a printer to focus sales and service. One small shop in our area prints waterproof identification numbers worn by runners. (Runners racing in Oregon spend a lot of time in the rain.) The owner of this shop doesn't limit himself to this product, but does know how to print consecutive large numbers on a special paper better and faster than anyone else. This is the kind of shop to look for whenever you need an uncommon product.

Many of the product descriptions in Appendix A of this book include tips for learning names of specialty printers.

Often a specialty printer is too far away to visit. For products such as catalogs, books, direct mail, and showcase quality annual reports, printers compete in a national market. Customers using printers who specialize in methods such as gravure and flexography also sometimes deal at a distance.

Experienced printing buyers routinely send specifications, mechanicals, and art over long distances and deal with proofs and shipments over the same distances. They may travel personally to the printers only for a press check.

Specialty printers in the national market can frequently produce a job at 30% or 40% less than the lowest local bidder. With large jobs, the savings may be much greater than the extra costs of doing business at a distance. Moreover, distant printers are often represented locally by brokers or sales representatives in daily contact with the shop.

Many customers feel nervous about sending jobs to out-of-town shops, recognizing they will have less contact with the printer. Dealing with a distant printer does indeed limit close supervision. Whether it is worth the risk depends on your quality requirements, schedule, and the cost savings. If in doubt, ask for references to local customers. Specialty printers

base their reputations on economical and timely production of selected products. Most previous customers are happy they learned to work with distant printers under the right circumstances and may urge you to do the same.

The typical production schedules for specialty printers are different from schedules for commercial printers. Some specialty printers deliver much faster than would a commercial shop for the same job, but others deliver more slowly. When dealing with a specialty printer, it always pays to ask about delivery times.

Sometimes experienced printing buyers who need long runs of multicolor or 4-color process work shop internationally. Low labor costs and favorable exchange rates may mean lower prices than from a printer in the U.S.

Printers abroad may use paper with unfamiliar sizes and weights, factors discussed in Appendix E. Dealing with them also requires some expertise in international financing and customs arrangements. Furthermore, there are restrictions about what can be printed outside the U.S. and copyrighted by a U.S. citizen.

Some large printers in Asia and Europe have sales offices in major U.S. cities. You may find them listed in a directory under "printers" or you may have to contact the consulates of countries such as Hong Kong, Italy, Japan, Singapore, and Spain. Some nations maintain trade development councils in New York City that are sources of information about printers.

In-Plant Printers

Many businesses, governments, and school systems have their own print shops, called in-plant printers. Employees that use them should know what facilities the shop has and how it operates from a business standpoint.

"As our business grew, our catalog grew, too. I used my original printer until last year when a catalog broker asked to quote the job. Was I surprised! The broker's price was 30% less than what I thought I would pay my regular printer and the broker delivered a good quality job in plenty of time for our mailing. That broker saved me the cost of our new computer."

In-plant print shops are an administrative arrangement unrelated to the size, skill, equipment, or specialization of the shop. Both the U.S. Government Printing Office and a mimeograph machine in a church fit the definition.

The in-plant printer for a state government or large private company might perform the same full range of services as many large commercial printers. The typical in-plant, however, more closely resembles a quick or small commercial printer. Using small offset presses, the shop handles routine jobs.

The number of in-plant shops is large because of the availability of equipment that is relatively easy to operate for routine jobs. In-plant print shops exist for reasons of convenience, cost, and security.

Taking the job down the hall or to a nearby building, especially for people in large, non-commercial areas such as college campuses, is more convenient than going outside. Staff at in-plant printers also build their inventories, equipment, and services to fit the needs of the host organization.

Because in-plant printers do not operate for profit and have no costs for sales or marketing, printing jobs should cost less than from independent printers. Further savings occur when staff at the in-plant know postage regulations and paper needs as they relate to products made by the host organization.

For many businesses, security is the main reason for having an in-plant print shop. In-plants do not serve the public, so information such as new prices can more easily be kept confidential during printing.

Some users of in-plants argue that the advantages sound fine in theory, but don't work out so well in practice. They claim their in-plant may prove less convenient than working with a nearby printer, especially when the in-plant seems part of a complex bureaucracy. They say the security question is irrelevant for most jobs. Most important, they assert that in-plants don't have to compete for work, and are not as aware of cost and quality control as outside printers.

Sometimes the complaints are justified, but they must be viewed in their proper context. Although they may be using the same equipment and materials as the world of independent printers, in-plants have a different set of management problems.

Customers often bring in-plants incomplete and poor mechanicals that independent printers would either reject or correct at additional costs. People at in-plants may patch things together, even though they know the result is poor quality work.

In-plants tend to get the routine jobs such as forms, pads, and staff directories. Interesting work goes outside, contributing to the stereotype that in-plants can't do quality printing. Some in-plants do excellent work on material that demands it, even winning awards for products such as annual reports.

Because in-plant printers don't have to compete in the commercial market, they often have old equipment that wasn't very high quality to begin with. They may be getting the best possible work from the machines, but that still may not be very good.

To get the best possible work from your in-plant, give its staff good mechanicals, adequate time, and appropriate respect. Equally important, know what you can reasonably expect. Ask to see the shop and learn about what various presses can do. Think about your in-plant as you would any other printer: right for some jobs and wrong for others.

The typical manager of an in-plant print shop has a background in printing and is familiar with local printers. The manager can help you write specifications, prepare copy, and make decisions regarding your jobs that are not suitable for in-plant printing. Taking advantage of this knowledge leads to managing all printing jobs better.

"People in our stockroom thought they were doing me a favor when they'd call to report they had just sent over the last box of forms. I could never get them reprinted in time, especially with changes in copy. I finally took the time to explain my situation to them and toured the stockroom to see the operation from their side of things. We put a sign with my phone number over the storage area for my department. Now they call me when they get down to three boxes."

BROCHURES AND FLIERS

Prices are based on customer-furnished, actual size, camera-ready, line copy. No bleeds, no large solids, no 4-color process printing. Please see next page for additional sizes and papers, color tinting information, and extra charges for halftones and other available options. For prices over 50,000 or for color combinations not shown below please request special quotes.

Sheet Size	Maximum Image Size
8½ x 11	8¼ x 10½
8½ x 14	8¼ x 13½

8½ x 11 Printed on 50# White Book, Minimum Quantity 5M, No Bleeds

First Side	Black Ink	Black Ink	Black and 1 Color	1 Color	Black and 1 Color	Black and 2 Colors	Black and 1 Color	Black and 2 Colors	2 Colors
Second Side	No Printing	Black Ink	No Printing	1 Color	Black Ink	No Printing	Black and 1 Color	Black Ink	2 Colors
5M	$140	$220	$240	$265	$300	$310	$365	$365	$385
6 to 9M	+16/M	+17/M	+18/M	+19/M	+18/M	+18/M	+19/M	+19/M	+22/M
10M	220	305	330	360	390	400	460	460	495
11 to 49M	+14/M	+14/M	+16/M	+17/M	+16/M	+16/M	+17/M	+17/M	+19/M
50M	780	865	970	1040	1030	1040	1140	1140	1255

For 8½ x 14 add 2/M to 8½ x 11 prices above, 50# book only

10-2 Formula pricing facsimile. This price chart simulates a page from the 1986 catalog of a printer specializing in catalogs, books, and self-mailers. Prices are based on standard formats, quantities, colors, and papers that the company can print most efficiently. If your job deviates from the standards, you would pay about the same as using a custom printer. Like many such companies, this specialty printer also offers mailing services.

Getting Prices

Printers offer either formula or custom pricing. Formula pricing is based on specifications that fit the printer's price chart. Quick printers, for example, typically have price charts showing costs per hundred copies using black ink and standard papers. Formula pricing means you know exactly what the job will cost before you hand mechanicals across the counter.

Many specialty printers use formula pricing. You can order envelopes, self-cover direct mailers, 4-color fliers, and even books whose unit costs you compute from price lists. These printers keep costs low by using a limited choice of paper weights, sizes, formats, and trims, and often by ganging jobs of different customers onto the same press sheets.

When you can use one of the formats that a shop offers, formula pricing can save you hundreds or thousands of dollars on jobs where the message is more important than customized production. Deviating from the standard format, however, may mean that your job will cost the same as it would at any commercial printer.

Most commercial printers figure a custom price for each job. Using specifications prepared by customers, their estimators compute the costs of paper, preparation and press time, and other factors they consider relevant to the job. They calculate what each job will cost the printer and, therefore, what the printer should charge to make a profit. Estimators may also take into account how fast you want work finished, the quality level you want, and your reputation as an easy or demanding customer.

Printers give custom prices as estimates and as firm quotes. Estimates are guesses about what the job will cost based on your guesses about specifications. They are appropriate for jobs where you're using an unfamiliar process or need options for budget review. Estimates also reveal when you are dealing with a printer or project that you can't afford and help expose potential production problems.

Estimates are not contract offers. Firm quotes, however, may be. Printers base firm quotes on complete and final specifications. If you sign the quote form without changing any specifications, usually you have a contract.

Some printers give firm quotes only on seeing mechanicals, not specifications. They know that customers often overlook factors while writing specifications. Printers who follow this practice should make it clear by writing on the quotation forms that the price is subject to review of mechanicals.

Every printing job is unique and every print shop has a special blend of machines and skills. Moreover, some shops want business more than others. These factors mean that prices on the same job may vary widely from shop to shop. Quotes from printers looking at identical specifications can vary as much as 50% even when every shop is well-suited to the job.

Some customers go through the work of writing specifications and getting quotes too often. They would be better off simply handing most jobs to their regular printers and paying the bills. Other customers don't get quotes often enough. They are losing money by not shopping and by not keeping their regular printers competitive.

"We have millions wrapped up in presses, so we have to keep them running. We hustle to find new customers and are always willing to negotiate. Once in a while I spot a new account that's worth quoting the first job at less than our cost. We make up our lost profit by spreading the costs among our regular customers."

Here are some guidelines telling when it is appropriate to solicit quotations.

Costs. Get quotes when you think the job will cost an amount of money that you consider significant. For some customers, that figure is $500; for others, it is $10,000.

Familiarity. Get quotes when you're dealing with a printer, product, or process that's new to you. With your first job using color separations or perfect binding, you probably lack sufficient experience to judge whether costs from your regular printer are reasonable.

Quantities. Get quotes when there might be significant savings at different quantities. The printer that bids low on 10,000 brochures might be high bidder on 25,000. Quantity price breaks can vary greatly from one printer to the next.

Competition. Get quotes on a routine job every couple of years just to remind your regular printer not to take your business for granted.

Business conditions affecting individual printers influence what they will quote on a job from one week to the next. A small shop owner might be hungry for business and give you a terrific price. A month later that same shop might be so busy that the quote on the same job is double because doing your work would involve paying overtime. A large shop might have an opportunity to gang your job with others or run it on paper it bought by the carload.

A printer may actually produce only one job for every five quoted. If you're a customer asking for quotes but never contracting a job, you'll soon be ignored. Don't abuse printers' willingness to figure costs. For example, don't ask a small printer to bid on 4,000 copies of a 200-page, perfect bound book. Only ask for quotes from printers suited to the job, let each shop know who else is quoting, and tell everyone who got the job and at what price.

The printer whose quote was too high today may still be right for tomorrow's job. Thank the unsuccessful bidders and tell them you look forward to dealing with them again.

How many quotes you should get depends on how familiar you are with general printing costs, particular printers, and the specific job. For most jobs, three quotes should be enough —assuming each comes from a printer well suited to the job. With complicated jobs that might run either sheetfed or web, and jobs where you might use an out-of-town printer, four or five quotes are appropriate. If you've picked your possible printers wisely, you should rarely need more.

Each printer quoting your job must have identical information. If your specifications vary, you can't compare prices. Specifications should be on a form such as the one in Chapter One and must be precise and complete. Even when they are, printers may interpret requests differently. To ensure clear understanding, ask that samples of paper and examples of previous work accompany quotations.

While insisting that printers give quotes based on identical specifications, don't hesitate to ask about additional costs on a small number of alternatives. It's often a good idea to ask the cost of equivalent paper that may be a house sheet or for prices on one or two alternate quantities. Keep an open mind about alternatives that would cut costs, but insist on seeing prices on your specifications as well.

Printers figure their costs using complicated formulas that take into account the capabilities of equipment, costs of paper and other supplies, wages and salaries, overhead needs, and profit goals. You can't know all these figures, but you can learn prices for specific items such as tints and halftones. With that information, you can refigure some costs yourself as you consider certain kinds of changes.

Evaluating Quotations

When evaluating quotes from printers, check first that the price is actually based on your specifications. The quote should refer to your job number or product name from your request for quotation.

The professionalism of the quote tells a lot about a print shop. Quotes should be neatly organized and typed and answer every relevant question about cost, condition of copy, type of proofs, packaging, and delivery time. They should arrive when promised. A printer that is efficient, thorough, and on time with quotations is likely to be that way with jobs, too.

When confirming a quotation or contracting with a printer, be sure you agree on the cost for additional copies. That figure is the amount you should pay per unit for an overrun or be credited for an underrun. For example, if your quotation for 5,000 books is $10,000 and for 6,000 books is $11,000, the cost of additional copies is one dollar each.

Printing jobs often include services such as foil stamping or case binding that a printer must subcontract to another business. Printers should know what these buyouts will cost before quoting the price of the total job. Quotes shouldn't leave any open lines saying something like "plus cost of dies."

The cost of paper and other supplies may be an exception to the above rule about open price lines. Printers may not be able to anticipate price increases, so be forced to tell you "paper prices subject to current rates."

Most printers hold quoted prices firm for 30 or 60 days. It may be unclear, however, whether the time limit means you must sign the contract within that number of days or actually bring in the job. Ask if you are unsure, and don't hesitate to ask if you need a little more time to think things over.

Remember that dollar amounts on quotation forms are not the only costs of printing. If working with the low bidder means considerable travel time and expense or if it means dealing with each other only through the mail, the price might not look so attractive after all. The peace of mind that comes with close control over a job may be worth a lot, especially when you are new to a process or product.

As the last step in evaluating quotes, remember our advice in Chapter One about setting your budget. Ask yourself what the job is worth to you and whether dollar amounts seem

"There's one studio in town whose buyer is never satisfied with price. No matter what we quote, he always tries to squeeze. He thinks he has a lot of clout because he insists on good work. It's true the studio does premium design, but that doesn't mean printers feel honored to work with it. At least, I don't. I told our estimator just to ignore requests for quotations from him."

reasonable. Concentrate on value to yourself. For example, if selling a new product depends on a premium quality brochure, don't risk using a printer whose quality is doubtful. If your membership drive is keyed to a mailing on the first of the month, don't risk using a printer who may not deliver on time.

When you solicit quotations, one of your regular printers may not be low bidder. If the difference is slight, ignore it. Business relationships that stay reliable over time are worth far more than a few dollars saved on a particular job. If, however, your regular printer is much too high, offer a chance to quote again. Maybe the printer will reduce the price to keep your steady business.

A quote should be accepted in writing to assure the contract is clear and enforceable. Sign the form and return it along with a purchase order or letter of agreement.

Sales and Service

In most medium and in all large shops, your contact with the printer is a sales or customer service representative.

Good sales reps ensure jobs are done properly and on time. They suggest ways to raise quality and cut costs, pick up and deliver copy and samples, and answer technical questions. A good rep will even occasionally point out that a particular job might be done better, cheaper, or faster elsewhere.

Sales reps work on behalf of their customers within the printing company. They monitor estimates to keep costs down, work with strippers and press operators to keep quality up, and check with production supervisors to keep jobs on schedule. As your advocate, your rep may compete with other reps working for the same company for press time or delivery priority.

Good representatives make everything go smoothly from planning to delivery. Take your rep to lunch once in a while just to say thanks.

Sales reps spend much of their time working with customers away from the printing company, so larger shops also have customer service reps. Customer service reps remain in the shop to support the sales force. Call them with technical questions or to learn about the status of a particular job.

Sales and customer service reps earn salaries and commissions from the printers who employ them. Printing brokers are independent agents who make their living by adding a markup to jobs they sell. Brokers are familiar with a number of printers and shop among them for service, quality, and price.

The difference between using a sales rep and a broker may be crucial. On the plus side, a good broker knows the industry intimately and puts the knowledge to work for you. A broker, for example, may know about printers hungry for business who can meet a very tight deadline. On the negative side, if the broker makes a mistake, the printer is not obligated to reprint the job or give you credit.

People selling specialty printing are often brokers rather than sales reps. When dealing with specific people, ask about their status. Insist on recommendations from previous customers before signing anything but the most routine order.

Authorizing Payment

Regardless of how carefully you plan and monitor printing jobs, final bills are often higher than you expect and quality may not match your expectations. Before you authorize payment, it's a good idea to check every aspect of the job very carefully. When you find a problem, discuss it with your printer and, if necessary, your accounting or purchasing department.

If you doubt the fairness or accuracy of an invoice, you should discuss the matter candidly

"After we wrote specifications, we decided to make a complete test of book printers in our region. We sent requests for quotations to 14 companies. The prices we got ranged from $3415 to $5865, with the average at $4170. Three printers quoted on some variation of our specifications that they thought we needed, but hadn't asked us about first. We ignored those, figuring they didn't have much respect for our ability to plan our own books. The job went to the one with the third lowest price, but who guaranteed delivery in twenty days."

with the printer. You must be able to explain your position clearly and show that you are correct. The evidence is obvious if the specifications and invoice both called for printing on Wonder Gloss, but the product showed up printed on Wonder Dull. There's clearly a problem if the blueline showed a tint on page seven, but the tint never got onto the plate.

Final costs are often different from quotations because customers made changes as the job was in progress. Charges for alterations are usually straightforward. If you were late with mechanicals or changed the schedule, your printer may have paid overtime and should pass that cost on to you. If your printer bought paper you specified but decided not to use, it may not be returnable or may be sent back only with a hefty restocking charge.

Quality is more subjective. When you chose the printer, it was your responsibility to match your expectations to the shop's ability to produce and to explain your needs clearly. To verify that you got what you wanted, use the quality features listed in Visual 7-8 to analyze the piece. If you are unhappy with its quality, tell your printer exactly what you think is wrong with it.

In addition to evidence of mistakes and knowledge of reasonable quality expectations, negotiating requires that you assess how strongly you feel. Arguing with your printer may save some money and enhance your reputation as a sophisticated customer. It will also take time and energy and may detract from an otherwise smooth business relationship. Make sure the rewards are worth the effort.

The U.S. Government Printing Office rates problems with printing as critical errors, major defects, or minor flaws. The system and the logic behind it are applicable throughout the graphic arts industry.

Critical errors. Errors are critical when they render the product useless. If key elements are totally missing or the text is illegible, the printing has no value.

Major defects. The printed piece will be less effective or attractive when there is a major defect, but nothing will be missing and readers will still understand its message.

How to Analyze a Job for Payment

Completeness. Examine one piece closely to be sure it has the reverses, tints, photos, and other features that the invoice says you should pay for.

Quality. Study several pieces to verify that the job was printed to the correct standard of quality.

Paper. Verify that the job is on the paper specified.

Quantity. Confirm that you have the right amount. Compare delivery records with your invoice and count the contents of a box or two.

Alterations. Make sure that charges for alterations or corrections cover only those changes that you asked for or that the printer suggested and you agreed to.

Extra charges. Evaluate extra charges to make sure you understand what they are for and agree that you should pay them.

Schedule. Note whether delivery was on time and, if not, whether the contract with the printer included a penalty clause for late delivery.

Shipping. If charges seem out of line, ask for copies of postal receipts or bills of lading.

Taxes. If your bill includes a sales tax, verify that you are liable according to local laws.

Arithmetic. Check that all percentages and totals have been correctly figured.

10-3 How to analyze a job for payment. Before authorizing payment of an invoice, the invoice, random samples from the job, and its specifications should be carefully examined with the above points in mind.

Minor flaws. When only sophisticated readers will notice, and even they may not comment, the flaw is minor. These little mistakes are unfortunate, but won't cause any trouble.

This system of categorizing errors helps you decide how seriously to consider a specific problem. Using it, you can decide whether you can live with a problem or whether it seriously impairs your image, profit, or message. Keep your audience in mind. Most readers will not notice or care about minor flaws. There's no need for you to be quarrelsome if a mild dose of assertiveness will notify your printer that you expect better work in the future.

If you feel you must negotiate the amount on an invoice, do it without delay. When talking with your printer, explain how the problem affects your message and aim for accord on specific points. Write a list of things that you and the printer agree went wrong.

You have a right to reject a job that doesn't match the specifications on which your contract was based. Only exercise that right in the face of critical errors. Rejecting a job is very hard on your printer and probably hard on you, too. Printers work on very small profit margins that are totally destroyed by jobs that are refused. From your standpoint, refusing a job means missing your deadline and, if you are a graphic designer, perhaps losing a client who was depending on you.

Situations involving major defects usually can be settled by negotiating reduced payment. Most printers will be fair, especially when you have samples and proofs. Agree on some dollar amount to deduct from the bill, then consider the matter closed. Another approach is for the printer to offer a discount on a future order, an arrangement that lets both printer and customer come out winners.

Some disputes involve the question of who is responsible for settling the matter with the printer. If a graphic designer, account executive, or broker coordinated the job and brokered the printing, that person is the printer's customer and should settle any problems. If the poor work took place at a bindery or other subcontracted trade service, the customer deals with the printer, not the trade shop.

Responsibility and money go hand in hand. The person who presents you with the bill is the person to confront about problems.

"I specify quantities rather generously to be sure our community relations department always has enough handouts. If the final counts are a little too low, I don't worry about it. I'll probably make up for it some other time with a box of overs. Sometimes, though, the count is simply too low to ignore. That's when I summon my best mix of friendship and assertiveness and say to the printer, 'We both agree the count is short this time. What shall we do about it?'"

Trade Customs

Every industry has practices concerning issues such as credit, delivery, and insurance. Often the practices are published by a trade association. Some companies use the published practices as policy, others simply as guidelines.

The PIA (Printing Industries of America) is a trade association for printers that publishes a list of 18 trade customs. Those customs, presented as Visual 10-4, concern technical issues unique to the graphic arts as well as business issues common to all commercial relationships.

Printers are not obligated to follow the PIA standards and practices vary greatly from one shop to another. Indeed, many printers rewrite the PIA list to reflect their business preferences, then print their own version of the customs as terms on the backs of quotation forms and contracts. When you sign a quotation form or contract with terms on the back, you accept those terms as part of the contract.

When printing is bought using a purchase order form, the business terms on the purchase order may be different from those on a printer's quotation form. In that case, it may be unclear whether the buyer's terms or the printer's terms govern the contract. The printer's terms prevail when they were part of the offer to supply the service and the buyer accepted them by signing the quotation form.

Sometimes a printer will refer to a trade custom to settle an argument. If that happens, be sure the custom is truly customary. A trade custom has legal standing only if the guideline is uniform. If Superior Litho says you would own flats, Great Graphics insists they would own them, and Ultimate Image doesn't care, then no one can claim there's a trade custom governing ownership of flats.

The PIA trade customs reveal a set of reasonable concerns for both printers and customers. Having a good business relationship with any printer requires that you know how management in the shop views the issues that the customs try to settle. Printers should give customers copies of the trade customs. Customers should know the customs as part of their dealing with the graphic arts industry.

1. *Quotation.* A quotation not accepted within sixty (60) days is subject to review. All prices are based on material costs at the time of quotation.

2. *Orders.* Orders regularly placed, verbal or written, cannot be cancelled except upon terms that will compensate the printer against loss incurred in reliance of that order.

3. *Experimental work.* Experimental or preliminary work performed at the customer's request will be charged for at current rates and may not be used until the printer has been reimbursed in full for the amount of the charges billed.

4. *Creative work.* Creative work, such as sketches, copy, dummies, and all preparatory work developed and furnished by the printer, and not expressly identified and included in the selling price, shall remain his exclusive property and no use of same shall be made, nor any ideas obtained therefrom be used, except upon compensation to be determined by the printer.

10-4 **Printing trade customs.** The 18 customs on this and the following pages were adopted by the Printing Industries of America and other graphic arts organizations in 1985. The statement of customs that they replace may still be found on handouts and forms used by many printers. The old customs deal with the same business and technical issues as the new ones. There are, however, some specific differences between the old customs and the new ones, so concerned printing buyers should carefully examine statements on any form that, when they sign or agree to it, would become part of a contract.

For the rest of this section, we discuss the 18 PIA trade customs. We refer to the custom by number and assume you will read the appropriate paragraph in Visual 10-4.

Please note that our comments are based on our years of experience in the graphic arts. We believe our interpretations are valid, but emphasize that we are not lawyers and these are not legal opinions.

Custom #1 means a printer's quotation constitutes a legal offer good for 60 days. After that, prices may change. To protect themselves against the impact of inflation while a customer is evaluating a quote, printers may state that prices are subject to change due to the changing cost of paper and other supplies.

It may be uncertain whether the 60 days of the offer means you must sign the contract within that time or actually bring in the job. Ask if you are not sure.

Custom #2 is clear. If you cancel an order, you must compensate the printer for work and expenses incurred to date. Note the words "verbal or written." It's good policy to give orders in writing, not verbally. Some printers insist on it, refusing to work from oral instructions.

One of the reasons why orders and contracts should be in writing involves the Uniform Commercial Code. The code states that contracts for sales of goods worth more than $500 must be in writing and signed by both parties to be enforceable. Printing involves the sale of goods and is therefore governed by the code.

The experimental work covered by custom #3 seldom causes confusion. Both printers and customers expect to pay for time and materials used while developing a job. Note that the final phrase of custom #3 leads into the ownership issues covered by #4 and #6.

Both customs #4 and #6 contain only one basic idea: printers own everything they create while getting the job ready for press.

Trade customs deal with ownership in two ways. First, printers own physical property they make such as dummies, sketches, and negatives. In Chapter Five we discussed the implications of owning negatives. We suggested that you specify in your contract that they become your property, even when they are stored at your printer's shop.

The second implication of ownership involves rights. When printers make sketches,

---

5. *Condition of copy.* Upon receipt of original copy or manuscript, should it be evident that the condition of the copy differs from that which had been originally described and consequently quoted, the original quotation shall be rendered void and a new quotation issued.

6. *Preparatory materials.* Working mechanical art, type, negatives, positives, flats, plates, and other items when supplied by the printer, shall remain his exclusive property unless otherwise agreed in writing.

7. *Alterations.* Alterations represent work performed in addition to the original specifications. Such additional work shall be charged at current rates and be supported with documentation upon request.

8. *Prepress proofs.* Prepress proofs shall be submitted with original copy. Corrections are to be made on "master set," returned marked "O.K." or "O.K. with corrections," and signed by the customer. If revised proofs are desired, request must be made when proofs are returned. The printer cannot be held responsible for errors under any or all of the following conditions: if the work is printed per the customer's O.K.; if changes are communicated verbally; if the customer has not ordered proofs; if the customer has failed to return proofs with indication of changes; or if the customer has instructed printer to proceed without submission of proofs.

---

dummies, or mechanicals, they claim they own copyrights to their creations. Their reasoning is the same as designers and photographers who own copyrights to their work even when specifically commissioned. We described the concepts and rules of copyright in Chapter One.

If you want to own copyrights as well as property made for you by printers, say so before signing the contract.

Custom #5 deals with typesetting and means that no bid on typesetting is binding until the printer sees the copy. Typesetters operate this way too, and with good reason. Some customers have very low standards for what constitutes clean copy.

Many printers receive copy on disks or via modem or satellite. While custom #5 does not specifically refer to electronic copy, a printer has a right to change typesetting prices if keyboarding or formatting is not done correctly.

Printer's quotes are usually based on specifications written before completion of mechanicals and loose art. Custom #7 protects a printer from customers whose copy doesn't match their specifications or who make changes after preparation has begun. Experienced customers know that changes almost always mean increased costs and leave a few dollars in their budgets to cover them.

Note that custom #7 refers to a printer's obligation to be able to document charges for alterations. If your invoice includes a charge for two hours of additional stripping, the printer should have evidence that an alteration you requested required two hours to accomplish.

Customs #8, #9, and #10 reinforce what we've said throughout this book about the value and cost of proofs. If you have questions, read about evaluating color in Chapter Four, proofs in Chapter Five, and press checks in Chapter Seven. Note also that custom #8 reinforces the advice that customers and printers confirm every specification and alteration in writing.

Read custom #11 carefully and note that the 10% over and under rule is subject to negotiation before the job begins. It always pays to ask about the guidelines used by a specific printer. As a general rule, the percentage tolerances should decrease as runs get longer. For a run of 6,000 or 8,000 10% would be reasonable, but 5% might be appropriate for a run of 50,000.

Custom #11 also says that printers may charge for overruns just as they should credit the customer for underruns. Some charge and credit, but others simply bill for the job at whatever they quoted.

Printers use rather generous spoilage percentages to make sure they can provide the full

---

9. *Press proofs.* Unless specifically provided in the printer's quotation, press proofs will be charged for at current rates. An inspection sheet of any form can be submitted for customer approval, at no charge, provided the customer is available at the press during the time of makeready. Lost press time due to customer delay, or customer changes and corrections, will be charged at current rates.

10. *Color proofing.* Because of differences in equipment, processing, proofing substrates, paper, inks, pigments, and other conditions between color proofing and production pressroom operations, a reasonable variation in color between color proofs and the completed job shall constitute acceptable delivery.

11. *Over runs and under runs.* Over runs or under runs not to exceed 10% on quantities ordered, or the percentage agreed upon, shall constitute acceptable delivery. The printer will bill for actual quantity delivered within this tolerance. If the customer requires guaranteed exact quantities, the percentage tolerance must be doubled.

12. *Customer's property.* The printer will maintain fire, extended coverage, vandalism, malicious mischief, and sprinkler leakage insurance on all property belonging to the customer, while such property is in the printer's possession; the printer's liability for such property shall not exceed the amount recoverable from such insurance. Customer's property of extraordinary value shall be insured through mutual agreement.

amount ordered, so you are likely to be delivered more than you ordered rather than less. Be sure, however, to tell your printer if your order requires "no less than" a certain number. To guarantee that figure, printers can reasonably increase percentages allowed for spoilage.

Custom #12 deals with insuring customers' property, a topic we discussed in Chapter Five with respect to negatives. In our experience, few printers follow this custom. Many shops disclaim liability for customer property.

Printers should carry liability insurance similar to any other business. In addition, they should carry insurance to cover risks unique to the graphic arts. Those risks stem from actions by the printer that damage customer property or business.

Customers leave valuable property such as manuscripts, mechanicals, and photographs in the care of printers. Trade custom #12 mentions only a few of the ways that property might be lost or damaged. Property in the care of printers may also be in transit or at a typesetter, trade shop, or bindery instead of on the premises of the print shop.

Your printer should be able to tell you exactly how your property is insured while being worked on or stored and regardless of where the property is located. The insurance should also cover the printed pieces themselves until you actually take possession.

Even the best insurance may not cover the true cost of replacing a manuscript, mechanical, or transparency. As physical objects, these are worth only a tiny fraction of their replacement value as creative works. Making a duplicate when possible is the only true insurance.

Custom #13 can cause problems because of how it defines "delivery." If you're in town, a job is delivered when you pick it up or receive it. If you're an out-of-town customer, the job may be considered delivered when it gets to the printer's loading dock or the printer mails you the invoice. For purposes of billing, many printers consider a job delivered when work is complete and the customer has seen samples.

For purposes of insurance coverage, printed pieces belong to the printer until the job is given to you or to a shipping company that will bring them to you. Then they belong to you. The custom does not deal with insurance on a job 99% complete.

Unless you have contracted for delivery FOB your address, a job is your property while

---

13. *Delivery.* Unless otherwise specified, the price quoted is for single shipment, without storage, F.O.B. local customer's place of business or F.O.B. printer's platform for out-of-town customers. Proposals are based on continuous and uninterrupted delivery of complete order, unless specifications distinctly state otherwise. Charges related to delivery from the customer to the printer, or from the customer's supplier to the printer, are not included in any quotations unless specified. Special priority pickup or delivery service will be provided at current rates upon the customer's request. Materials delivered from the customer or his suppliers are verified with delivery ticket as to cartons, packages, or items shown only. The accuracy of quantities indicated on such tickets cannot be verified and the printer cannot accept liability for shortage based on the supplier's tickets. Title for finished work shall pass to the customer upon delivery to the carrier at shipping point or upon mailing of invoices for finished work, whichever occurs first.

14. *Production schedules.* Production schedules will be established and adhered to by the customer and the printer, provided that neither shall incur any liability or penalty for delays due to state of war, riot, civil disorder, fire, labor trouble, strikes, accidents, energy failure, equipment breakdown, delays of suppliers or carriers, action of Government or civil authority, and acts of God or other causes beyond the control of the customer or the printer. Where production schedules are not adhered to by the customer, final delivery date(s) will be subject to renegotiation.

15. *Customer-furnished materials.* Paper stock, inks, camera copy, film, color separations, and other customer-furnished material shall be manufactured, packed, and delivered to the printer's specifications. Additional cost due to delays or impaired production caused by specification deficiencies shall be charged to the customer.

---

on a common carrier from the printer to you. If the job is being delivered in a vehicle belonging to the printer, you don't take possession until it's unloaded at your place of business.

Note that custom #13 deals with deliveries made to the printer as well as those made from the printer. When receiving shipments of paper or other materials ordered by the customer, the printer will verify arrival but will not be responsible for checking the accuracy of quantities.

Custom #14 says customers and printers will abide by production schedules, but nothing about what happens if things go wrong. Printers are entitled to change delivery dates when customers are late with mechanicals, but very few printers will accept a penalty if the delay is their fault.

Printers know the kinds of films, papers, and other supplies that work best in their own shops. Custom #15 simply says that customers who provide their own materials must pay the costs if the materials delay or impair production because they are not what the printer specified.

Custom #16 recognizes that printers have

a wide variety of payment plans and credit arrangements. Many commercial printers give regular customers 30 days to pay for routine jobs. Some offer discounts for early payment and most impose penalties for being late.

Many printers ask for down payments from new customers to cover costs of paper and pre-press work: 50% when the order is entered and 50% on delivery is common. As with any business, terms are flexible for steady customers, big spenders, and good credit risks.

Custom #16 also deals with defective goods. We hope you'll never have to claim "defects, damages, or shortages." If you do, make your claim at once. Don't even wait 5 days, much less 15. And if you believe you have defective goods, do not pay the invoice, distribute any of the pieces, or do anything else that implies that you find them acceptable.

The first sentence of trade custom #17 acknowledges that damaging or losing customer property or failing to perform a contract can have disastrous business implications for the customer. Most printers follow this custom.

16. *Terms.* Payment shall be whatever was set forth in the quotation or invoice unless otherwise provided in writing. Claims for defects, damages, or shortages must be made by the customer in writing within a period of fifteen (15) days after delivery of all or any part of the order. Failure to make such claim within the stated period shall constitute irrevocable acceptance and an admission that they fully comply with terms, conditions, and specifications.

17. *Liability.* Printer's liability shall be limited to stated selling price of any defective goods, and shall in no event include special or consequential damages, including profits (or profits lost). As security for payment of any sum due or to become due under terms of any agreement, the printer shall have the right, if necessary, to retain possession of and shall have a lien on all customer property in the printer's possession including work in process and finished work. The extension of credit or the acceptance of notes, trade acceptance, or guarantee of payment shall not affect such security interest and lien.

18. *Indemnification.* The customer shall indemnify and hold harmless the printer from any and all loss, cost, expense, and damages (including court costs and reasonable attorney fees) on account of any and all manner of claims, demands, actions, and proceedings that may be instituted against the printer on grounds alleging that the said printing violates any copyrights or any proprietary right of any person, or that it contains any matter that is libelous or obscene or scandalous, or invades any person's right to privacy or other personal rights, except to the extent that the printer contributed to the matter. The customer agrees, at the customer's own expense, to promptly defend and continue the defense of any such claim, demand, action, or proceeding that may be brought against the printer, provided that the printer shall promptly notify the customer with respect thereto, and provided further that the printer shall give to the customer such reasonable time as the exigencies of the situation may permit in which to undertake and continue the defense thereof.

They can, however, buy liability insurance covering the risk of your business being adversely affected by their errors and omissions.

Errors and omissions liability insurance is also important when considering the content of the printed piece. The simplest typo or other mistake could cost you thousands of dollars and result in seeing your printer in court. Errors and omissions coverage protects printers from settlements based on their own negligence or failure to perform because it reimburses customers for their loss.

Custom #18 states the very reasonable precaution that printers are not responsible for violations of copyrights, libel, invasion of privacy, or similar problems associated with materials provided by customers. This custom also requires customers to defend in court a printer being sued over the reproduction of copy that the customer provided.

Although they are not legislation, trade customs clarify issues important to both printing buyers and printers. Knowing about the customs and how printers may interpret them helps assure good business relationships.

Working effectively with printers begins with selecting appropriate printing companies to ask for quotations and contract for jobs. It continues with consultation while planning, preparing copy properly, and delivering mechanicals and proofs on schedule. When the job is done, you should be prompt about assessing its quality and quantity and paying the invoice.

If you follow the guidelines in this book about working with printers, you will be rewarded with the service you deserve and the quality you want at a reasonable price. Working cooperatively with printers also rewards both you and your printer with the satisfaction of creative work well done.

APPENDICES

APPENDIX A

Glossary of Printed Products

In this appendix we give information about printing, or buying ready made, over 100 printed products. The entries focus on what is unique about the printed pieces, thus supplement the information found in the body of this book.

The descriptions of products often mention magazines, other books, and trade associations. You will find full references for books and addresses for magazines and trade associations in Appendix C.

While writing these descriptions, we assumed that readers would be familiar with graphic arts terms and concepts. Those terms that you find unfamiliar are defined in Appendix B.

When buying many of these products in large quantities, you will often find the best prices at specialty printers known to people in the businesses that the printers wish to serve. Speaking with experienced printing buyers in your profession is a good way to locate specialty printers.

In this appendix we refer often to listings in classified directories. No classified directories, not even those for the largest cities, include all the headings. They are, however, standard headings used by the National Yellow Pages Service Association, so are good places to start looking for names of printers and other graphic arts services.

A

Album covers. See *Record jackets.*

Announcements. You can order announcements and invitations of a stock design or you can have them custom made. Stock announcements are available from catalogs found at printers and stores that sell stationery and paper products, especially those that cater to the wedding trade.

Printing on stock announcements may include engraving, thermography, or foil stamping. Prices are reasonable when compared with the cost of custom announcements, especially for small quantities.

Announcements are usually printed on text paper that may have a deckle edge. Some formal announcement cards come with an embossed panel ready for imprinting. If your announcement will be French folded, be sure paper isn't too heavy or can be scored first.

Unfolded or single-folded announcements work best on cover paper. Some cover papers are available as two sheets of different colors pasted together and called by names such as duo and duplex.

If you want matching envelopes for custom announcements, be sure you can get them before authorizing printing of the announcements. Envelopes made from the grade or color of paper you want and in the correct size may be hard to find.

Most classified directories include the listing "invitations and announcements."

Annual reports. The U.S. Securities and Exchange Commission (SEC) requires that publicly-held companies make annual reports to their investors. The SEC publishes guidelines about format, type size, and deadlines. (The SEC publications also give guidelines for quarterly reports, proxy statements, prospectuses, and similar legal documents.)

Many companies treat the requirement for an annual report as an opportunity to create a sales and public relations tool. To produce an impressive report, these companies hire top writers, photographers, and designers, and pay for showcase printing.

Because so many annual reports are showpieces, paper mills and distributors are well supplied with examples. Annual reports are available free from the companies producing them.

Quality printers that do a variety of jobs handle annual reports. Picking the right shop depends on needs for quality and quantity. Because most annual reports are produced during the first three months of the year, the better grades of paper and the press time at popular printers are in high demand and may need to be scheduled months in advance.

For specialized information about annual reports, consult the book by Elmer Winter listed in Appendix C.

Art reproductions. Reproducing fine art by offset printing is a commercial process not to be confused with original etchings, serigraphs, or lithographs made by artists. Any commercial printer can make a reasonable facsimile of original art, but some printers specialize in making the finest possible reproductions. Those printers consider themselves artists striving for perfection before profit.

When looking at proofs or press sheets, remember that the pigments in artists' colors are different from those in printing inks. Exact color matches are often impossible.

Art reproductions on coated papers show the fine details and bright colors of the original, but lack its depth or texture. Using uncoated book or text papers enhances the texture, but at some loss of detail and brightness. Reproductions needing to last for years must be on archival or acid-free paper. The paper is not commonly stocked by distributors, but printers who do such work know where to get it.

Art may require printing by the collotype method. Emulsion on collotype plates is a gelatin that reproduces continuous-tones without converting them to halftones. Sharpness is equivalent to 1200 line halftones.

To locate printers capable of reproducing fine art, inquire at the publications office of a museum or gallery or ask people who produce showcase quality posters. Another source of leads is a paper representative who sells archival papers.

B

Badges. Self-adhesive badge stock is available in cut sizes and large sheets and can be printed on any offset press. Preparation of camera-ready copy and quality considerations are the same as for any other printing on paper. Most nametags are printed on small offset presses. Stock nametags and badges are available at stationery stores.

Classified directories include the listings "badges" and "buttons."

Bags. Producing a small number of paper bags or getting bags made quickly calls for working with a local letterpress printer.

When you have plenty of time and want large quantities, paper can be printed before being made into bags. Paper distributors represent bag manufacturers and can quote you prices. You must know the kind of material you want, number of ink colors, and size of bag and its gusset.

Plastic bags are printed using flexography and are available either from companies that specialize in packaging or from paper distributors.

Most classified directories include the listing "bags." Some have subcategories such as "paper" and "specialty." Small quantities of specialty bags are also available from advertising specialty companies.

Balloons. See *Specialty advertising.* Some classified directories include the listing "balloons."

Banners. Most banners and flags are big and made in relatively short runs, so are screen printed. Screen printing also allows banners to be made on strong, weather-resistant materials of the kind seen outside gas stations and car dealerships.

Banners for indoor use can be printed offset, but are limited in size to the size of the press. Offset banners are often on kraft and cover papers.

Copy and art for banners is often prepared by companies that do the printing. To find them, look in classified directories under "flags and banners."

Billboards. Because of their size, billboards are a specialty of screen printers. Printers who make them are listed under "advertising—outdoor."

Binders. See *Loose-leaf binders.*

Board games. See *Games.*

Bonds. See *Certificates; Currency.*

Booklets. Booklets are saddle stitched or paste bound and have covers printed on paper different from that inside. Any printer can make them, so the choice of printer depends on format, quality, quantity, and schedule.

Books. There may be more variety in the specifications for books and large catalogs than with any other printed product. Any commercial printer can make them and even some quick printers do short runs. (In the book business, a short run is anything below 5,000 copies.) The best price, however, comes from printers who specialize in books.

Book printers have equipment and production techniques tailor-made to the needs of publishers and catalog companies, including presses and production schedules suited to short runs. Many book printers offer typesetting designed to interface with word processing done by writers and editors.

The papers on which books are printed are as varied as the titles. Publishers like using high bulk sheets that make books thick, off-white papers for novels and biographies with long copy, and coated stock for books with lots of photos and art. Choice of paper is also affected by type of binding.

How books are bound depends on how they will be used, the paper on which they are printed, and the production budget. Writing binding specifications can be quite complicated, especially for case binding. Books that are not produced by specialty book printers usually are bound at a trade bindery whose sales rep should be consulted early in the planning stages.

Books are made from sheets folded into signatures containing a number of pages divisible by four. The most common signature sizes are 8, 16, and 32 pages. Economical book production requires editorial, design, and production decisions that make efficient use of signatures.

In addition to requirements of printing, book design is influenced by the need for standard elements such as contents and copyright pages. Anyone producing a book should read one of the books in the field such as those by Marshall Lee, Stanley Rice, Hugh Williamson, or Adrian Wilson, cited in Appendix C. Prospective self-publishers should consult the book by Dan Poynter.

Printers specializing in books tend to be located outside of major urban areas and concentrated in the midwestern and eastern United States. The larger ones have sales representatives located in various parts of the country. Book publishers and catalog companies deal routinely with these sales reps and, through them, with printers who might be hundreds of miles away.

To find names of book printers, look in *Literary Market Place*, available in most libraries, or the *Directory of Short Run Book Printers.*, by John Kremer. You could also inquire from the American Book Producers Association or the Book Manufacturers Institute. When you identify a few with whom you might work, ask for production samples and references to previous customers.

Boxes. The box business is divided between companies making paper boxes and those making corrugated boxes. Both types are available ready made in a huge selection of styles and sizes. Having boxes custom made includes the cost of a die as well as other special setup costs.

Paper boxes such as shoe boxes are made from chipboard (grey throughout), coated box board (white outside and grey inside), or sulphite box board (white throughout). Stock can be printed via offset, screen, flexography, or gravure before being made into boxes. For a higher quality or special effect, paper boxes can have fancy, colored paper laminated to them.

Corrugated boxes and cartons normally come in kraft (brown) or oyster (white). Like paper boxes, they can be laminated with label papers.

The board from which corrugated boxes is made can vary in strength and durability. Corrugated boxes also vary in the construction of their flutes and walls. Strength increases with the number of flutes per inch and number of walls. Before ordering boxes, ask for a sample or prototype.

To find sources of boxes, look in classified directories under "boxes" and the various subheadings such as "paper," "corrugated," and "wooden."

Brochures. See *Booklets; Rack brochures.*

Bumper stickers. Any offset printer can make bumper stickers on self-adhesive label paper. Water and sun, however, cause offset inks to fade quickly and are hard on the paper as well. Stickers printed offset may last only a few weeks. More durable and more expensive stickers can be made by screen printing vinyl label stock.

Papers for bumper stickers are available with adhesives that allow stickers to peel away from metal easily when necessary.

Business cards. Some printers and stationery stores offer business cards with standard designs, type styles, paper stocks, and ink colors. Usually cards from these sources are printed by a company that specializes in business cards, especially when the printing involves thermography. Standard cards are very inexpensive and turnaround time is quick. Your logo can be included for a small extra cost.

Business cards are usually printed in small quantities, thus custom cards are best obtained from a quick or small commercial printer that specializes in stationery.

Most business cards are printed on either cover or bristol paper. Cover papers come in a wide variety of colors and weights, but some fray rather easily. Some bristols are made especially for the card business and have names such as Thin Card or Thin Plate. Bristols are smooth, white, and stiff so cards stay in good condition.

Unusual custom cards can be made from anything from wood veneer to rice paper, can include photographs and special colors, and may be engraved, embossed, or foil stamped as well as lithographed. Regardless of the method of printing, cards will probably be printed three or four at a time, then cut apart.

When ordering custom business cards, remember that the standard size is 2 x 3½. Larger cards will not fit card holders. Also keep in mind how your card will look with your letterheads and envelopes. Many papers are available that allow matching these three products as part of your identity program.

Business reply cards. See *Post cards.*

Buttons. Some classified directories include the listing "buttons—advertising." Machines that make buttons are inexpensive and easy to operate.

C

Calendars. Office supply catalogs, stationery stores, and some printers offer a wide variety of stock calendars on which you can imprint your name and message. Stock calendars are also available through specialty advertising companies. Some classified directories include the listing "calendars."

Any printer can make a custom calendar. If you go the custom route, proofread extra carefully. Every printer has a story about the customer whose calendar had 31 days in June.

The common calendar stapled in the middle and hanging from a hole in the top requires only 28 pages (including cover). If your print run is small, the sheets will probably be done individually or two-up and the unusual page count will not affect cost. If your run is on a large press, however, you might find that you can get 32 pages for the same price as 28.

Calendars can be bound by padding, stitching, tinning, spiral, or comb. Desk calendars need an easel back that your printer can get from a trade bindery or paper box company.

Caps. See *Clothing; Specialty advertising.*

Cartons. See *Boxes.*

Catalog sheets. See *Fliers.*

Catalogs. From the standpoint of their printing and binding, catalogs are similar to two other products described in this appendix: perfect or case bound catalogs are like books; medium-size saddle stitched catalogs are like magazines.

Most catalogs are printed offset, but very long runs of consumer catalogs are often printed gravure. To find printers that specialize in long runs of catalogs, read *Catalog Age* magazine, look in classified directories under "rotogravure" and "catalog compilers," or inquire from the National Catalog Manufacturers Association.

Certificates. Standard forms for certificates, awards, and diplomas are available at stationery and legal stores and from many printers. They can be imprinted in short runs via offset or letterpress. Art supply stores sell clip art border patterns as the basis for custom-made certificates.

Corporate bonds and other legal certificates are printed on 100% rag bond paper. Many awards and diplomas are printed on parchment papers. To locate specialty printers, look in classified directories under "stock certificates," "engravers—bank note," or "law and financial printers."

Charts. See *Maps.*

Checks. Most checks are ordered through banks that deal with specialty check printers. Any printer, however, can make custom checks by using the correct paper and magnetic inks. Printers can buy safety check paper in different colors and with or without carbonless coatings. Checks may also be printed on a variety of bond and text papers.

If you plan to have checks printed by a shop that doesn't specialize in them, be sure to consult with someone at your bank as you prepare specifications.

Many check printers are members of the Financial Printers Association. Some classified directories include the listing "checks—printing."

Circulars. See *Fliers.*

Clothing. Caps, shirts, and other fabric items are either screen printed or printed using heat transfer. To find printers, look in classified directories under "screen printing" or "garments—printing and lettering," or inquire at retail stores selling athletic wear or decorated T-shirts.

Comic books. Comic books are printed and bound like magazines, but on groundwood paper via letterpress. Almost all comic books produced in the U.S. are produced by one printer in Illinois. For references, consult a comic book publisher or Printing Industries of America.

Cookbooks. The difference between many cookbooks and other kinds of books lies only in the fact that they are bound with combs or spirals to lie flat. Cookbook covers should have a plastic coating or film lamination that can be wiped clean.

Some printers specialize in cookbooks for churches and clubs. Those printers provide layout pages and other guidelines and usually print short runs very inexpensively. To locate one of these printers, inquire at an office of a local Junior League or church headquarters.

For detailed information about producing cookbooks, consult the book by Doris Townsend cited in Appendix C.

Coupons. Simple, one-color coupons print well on 16# or 20# bond paper. Quick printers can do short runs. Short runs that need numbering can be done letterpress. For longer runs with or without numbering, consider a business forms printer.

Multicolor or 4-color process coupons may require coated stock and more sophisticated printers. Shops with large presses may run as many as 100 coupons per impression.

If your coupon printing includes perforating, be sure you allow enough room between copy and perf lines. Discuss design ideas with your printer.

Currency. The U.S. government has strict regulations about printing photographs and illustrations of currency, stamps, and bonds. If these rules are violated, printers as well as customers can be held liable. The printing trade custom that holds customers alone liable for copy that violates laws does not apply. For that reason, both the U.S. Treasury Department and Printing Industries of America have publications telling printers what is legal. Read one of these publications before printing anything, especially an advertisement that reproduces or simulates money, stamps, or bonds.

D

Decals. Most decals are made from self-adhesive label stock with a metallic or plastic surface and printed via offset, screen, or flexography. Printers that make or sell labels are the place to start looking. Some directories list "decals."

Diplomas. See *Certificates.* Some classified directories include the listing "diplomas."

Direct mailers. Any piece of mail that solicits a response is considered direct mail. The piece must attract the reader's attention and make it appealing and easy to respond.

The traditional direct mail package consists of an outer envelope, brochure, order coupon, and reply envelope. Printing of these four elements can be done at any printer. As the direct mail industry has grown, specialty printers have developed products that combine in one piece the features of all four separate elements. Those products are known as self-mailers or response vehicles and are dealt with separately in this glossary. See *Self-mailers.*

The design of direct mail pieces must take into account how they will be addressed. Mailing lists are available on self-adhesive labels, Cheshire labels, and magnetic tapes. Self-adhesive labels are the most expensive and must be applied by hand. Cheshire labels are on ungummed paper and are designed to be applied automatically by machines made by the Cheshire company. Magnetic tape is the least costly way to get mailing lists having upwards of 50,000 names. Addresses digitally stored on tape are applied by ink jet printing.

Direct mailers and reply envelopes or cards must conform to postal regulations governing size, color and thickness of paper, direction of folds, and content and placement of indicia. Check very thoroughly before proceeding.

Directories. Economically produced directories begin with well-organized data because they repeat most of the information in their previous versions. New information may include only a few new names or address changes. For these reasons, all but the smallest directories benefit from having information handled by a computer that allows type to be updated without keyboarding all data over again.

Computers suited for directory information might be part of a word processor, address maintenance system, or typesetter. Some organizations have such large memberships that maintaining mailing lists on personal computers would not be practical. List maintenance companies with large computers can handle the job. Many of those companies also offer directory design and printing services that are very economical because of their relationship to the list data base.

Readers think of directories as reference tools not needing sophisticated design or printing. Basic quality is sufficient. Laser printers coupled to computers make adequate camera-ready copy. Small directories can be done at a quick print shop, larger ones at a book printer.

To locate a specialty directory printer, ask the publications director at a college alumni office or large trade association or look in classified directories under "publishers—directory and guide."

E

Envelopes. Any printer with a small offset or letter press can print ready-made envelopes, so runs of a few hundred or thousand are handled like any other printing. Ready-made envelopes can also be thermographed, embossed, engraved, or foil stamped.

Any commercial printer with a small press can print envelopes economically in quantities up to about 50,000. On larger quantities, it may prove cost effective to deal with paper distributors or envelope makers. If you are getting envelopes with a custom design or made from dark paper, be sure to check that they are acceptable to postal officials.

Envelopes that require special paper, size, or shape, or whose printing calls for close register, bleeds, or embossing that doesn't show on the back may require custom production. Normally custom work involves printing flat sheets, then die-cutting them to fold into envelopes.

Most classified directories include the listing "envelopes—wholesale and manufacture." You can also locate envelope makers by asking the Envelope Manufacturers Association.

F

Fliers. Rather simple in design, fliers, handbills, and leaflets are single sheets of 8½ x 11 paper often printed basic quality one color on one side. Circulars and catalog sheets are the same size, but usually printed in colors on coated paper.

For press runs up to about 5,000, a quick printer will probably give the best service and price. For more than 5,000, shopping pays. Inquire at medium-sized commercial shops. For more than 50,000 impressions, inquire at large commercial shops and also at printers with a business forms web press. A forms web can run two or three colors on 16# or 20# bond very inexpensively.

If you need upwards of 50,000 4-color pieces, the best price will probably come from the gang-run printers that do catalog sheets and statement stuffers.

Folders, file. Standard file folders can be imprinted on a letter press. A custom folder requires having a die made to cut and score the sturdy paper, usually a heavy index, tag, or bristol. Many letterpress shops have standing dies.

If you need a message on the tabs of only a few hundred folders, consider printing on labels, then putting the labels on the tabs.

Folders, folded. See *Fliers; Rack brochures.*

Folders, presentation. Sometimes called pocket folders, presentation folders hold several 8½ x 11 sheets or booklets in pockets. The typical folder is 9 x 12 with three-inch pockets and begins as a sheet of cover or bristol at least 15 x 18. The sheet is printed first, then sent for die-cutting and scoring. Folding and gluing are usually done by hand.

How the folder will be used influences design. Folders are available with gusseted spines and pockets to allow for expansion. They may be UV coated or film laminated for extra durability. Many large cities have printers that specialize in presentation folders.

Forms. Of the 15 largest printers in the U.S., seven specialize in business forms. In addition, most cities have one or two printers with the same specialty. Most directories include the listings "business forms and systems" and "sales and order books."

Catalogs showing standard business forms are available from large forms printers and from stores selling office and computer supplies. Standard forms can be inexpensively imprinted and numbered to meet your needs.

Custom forms can involve hundreds of design decisions. Some of the most obvious include whether you need individual or continuous forms, whether they should use carbon paper or be carbonless, and how many copies they must yield. Other choices include colors of papers, punches and perforations, numbers, short sheets, and, of course, quantity.

Forms that will include sensitive information can be made so that the data go onto some copies, but not others. Carbon paper can come with uncoated windows that will not copy. Nocopy windows can be made on the back of certain sheets of carbonless forms by printing them with chemicals that desensitize the coating.

There are three kinds of business forms suppliers, each quite different from the other. Large forms printers have facilities at several locations around the nation. They seek large volume customers, offer highly competitive prices, and need about six weeks to deliver. Smaller local or regional forms printers specialize in rapid service and shorter runs. The third source is a forms broker who works with a variety of printers to give the best combination of price and service.

All three sources of business forms may offer inventory control by having a staff person visit your place of business to monitor supplies.

The market for forms is so vast that the industry has three major trade associations. The Business Forms Management Association specializes in analysis and design; International Business Forms Industries consists of printers and their suppliers; The National Business Forms Association services distributors and sales people. All three associations publish guides for designing and specifying forms.

G

Games. The boards for board games are often printed on C1S label paper and converted by paper box companies that laminate the label paper to chipboard. Cards and other paper parts of games are printed on large sheets of cover or bristol. Often plastic coating is applied to protect cards and other game components.

To find specialty game printers, ask for references from the art or production manager of a company already well established in the game business.

Gift wrap. Flat sheets of gift wrap can be made by any printer whose presses can run paper 20 x 26 or bigger. The most common papers used are 60# gloss coated book and 60# C1S label, although other sheets work as well.

Rolls of gift wrap are produced by specialty web printers using flexography or gravure. Papers tend to be 30# or lighter. Only a few web printers can handle stock this light. To find one, look in trade publications for the gift and premium market.

Some classified directories include the listing "gift wrapping materials."

Greeting cards. Any commercial printer using sheetfed presses can mass produce greeting cards. Questions of quality control and schedule are similar to any other printing job.

Greeting cards are gang printed on sheets that may yield as many as 32 cards in one impression. Imposition is the key to economy because, ideally, flats would remain stripped for exact reruns. It may pay to strip negatives for each card into individual flats, then make multiple burns for platemaking when quantity needs are clear.

When choosing paper for cards that will sell retail, keep in mind how customers handle cards in the store before buying them. Coated cover, uncoated bristol, and heavy textured papers dominate the field because they are stiff and strong.

Names of specialty printers may be learned by looking in directories under "greeting cards—wholesale and manufacture" or by inquiring from the Greeting Card Association.

H

Handbills. See *Fliers*.

I

Inserts. The cardinal rule when designing newspaper or magazine inserts is to know the inserting requirements of the periodical.

Newspaper inserts must have correct dimensions, be thick enough to conform to automatic inserting equipment, and arrive precisely on schedule. Most papers need at least a week lead time and want a line of copy on the insert stating that it is not published by the newspaper itself.

Magazines have the same requirements as newspapers plus additional concerns about folded size and trim margins. Smaller, saddle stitched magazines may be able to handle a single sheet insert only by tipping in rather than stitching in. Single sheets work easily with perfect-bound magazines. Small sheets such as reply cards can be inserted loose by blowing in.

Inserting machines do not work at 100% accuracy. Some have so much trouble with skips and doubles that only 80% of the newspapers or magazines receive just one single insert as planned. Take accuracy into account as part of your inserting contract.

Many inserts are printed very inexpensively at the same shop that prints the host publication. When getting prices, don't overlook this possibility.

Invitations. See *Announcements*.

J

Journals. Scholarly organizations refer to their trade periodicals as journals. Most are made like perfect bound books, are printed in small quantities, and can be most economically manufactured by a short run book printer.

L

Labels. The most common kind of labels or stickers are called self-adhesive or pressure-sensitive and have peel-off backing sheets. These labels come in sheets ready to offset print like any other paper and in rolls that must be printed by a specialty label printer. Blank labels on sheets can be purchased already kiss die cut and are available in a wide range of sizes. Labels in rolls are usually printed via flexography that allows kiss die cutting at the same time.

Self-adhesive labels can have a variety of adhesives depending on the surface to which they must adhere and how permanently they must stick.

Dry-gum labels are commonly known as lick and stick because they have glue on the back like postage stamps. They are less expensive than self-adhesive labels. Bookplates are a dry-gum item.

Non-adhesive labels for boxes, cans, bottles, or to be applied by addressing machines receive their glue when they go onto the product. Printed on uncoated or C1S label paper, they may be treated to withstand a variety of conditions. For example, paper for labels on bottles that will be refrigerated has extra sizing to resist puckering from moisture.

Non-adhesive (laminated) labels for application to boxes must meet strict guidelines governing trim sizes, margins, grain direction, and protective coatings. Consultation with the box maker is imperative. Labels for use on retail packages need to be varnished or UV coated and may need to include a Uniform Product Code.

Label printers using flexography are limited to basic and good quality results. They can, however, get very bright inks onto foil stocks, yielding vivid colors impossible to produce using offset printing.

Heat-seal labels of the kind used in grocery stores on meat packages require heat-sensitive paper and can be preprinted by commercial and label printers. Using them requires a heat applicator.

Any printer can print self-adhesives, dry-gums, and non-adhesives in sheets. For labels in rolls, specialty labels, and large quantities, find printers under the listings "decals" and "labels" in classified directories. Large directories list label printers and brokers in subgroups such as "fabric," "paper," and "plastic." Printers that specialize in laminated labels may be found by asking at box making companies.

Specialty printers may also be found by inquiring from the Tag and Label Manufacturers Institute.

Lawn signs. Because lawn signs must be on strong material that resists weathering and are usually made in very small quantities, they are screen printed on wood or specialty board stock. Every city has screen printers who specialize in lawn signs. To find them, ask people familiar with political campaigns or real estate. Printers who make lawn signs usually provide stakes and hardware.

Leaflets. See *Fliers*.

Letterheads. One of the most common printing jobs, letterheads are part of stationery packages that include envelopes and business cards. They can be done by any offset printer and often include foil stamping, thermography, embossing, or engraving. Most stationery is made by commercial printers using small presses.

Letterheads are usually printed on bond paper, but could also be on uncoated book or lightly-patterned text. Only a few book and text papers, however, offer matching envelopes in business sizes.

Most classified directories include the listing "stationery—wholesale and manufacture." For further information about prestige letterheads, consult the Engraved Stationery Manufacturers Association.

Loose-leaf binders. Suppliers of ring binders and report covers offer custom printing by screen printing or foil stamping. To find them, look in office supply catalogs or ask at stationery stores. Classified directories may also include the listing "loose-leaf equipment, systems, and supplies." Listings in most directories are for brokers, not manufacturers.

Binders may come with padded covers and spines, interior pockets, heavy-duty rings, lifters, and other quality features. They are also available with clear plastic sleeves for insertion of printed cards as an option to printing on the binders themselves.

M

Magazine inserts. See *Inserts*.

Magazines. Magazines with large, national circulations are printed on web presses using light weight paper. Short run magazines, however, are usually printed sheetfed, and thus can be handled by many medium and large commercial printing companies.

Most magazines are trim size 8⅜ x 10⅞, saddle stitched, and printed in multiples of eight pages. Printers that specialize in magazines often handle addressing and distribution as well. They are familiar with the tight deadlines of publication printing and work with customers to keep on schedule.

Many magazine printers are more interested in economy and speed of printing than quality. If your magazine must be higher than average quality, make sure your printer knows your needs.

If you need a magazine printed, consider hiring a publications consultant familiar with the business. The production manager for another magazine would be a candidate. To locate a specialty printer, read the ads in *Folio* magazine or inquire from the Magazine Printers Section of the Printing Industries of America, or the Magazine Publishers Association. For design ideas, consult books by Allen Hurlburt, Roy Paul Nelson, and Jan White.

Maps. Proper preparation of copy is the key to printing good maps. Ideal copy for maps are plate-ready acetate overlays instead of camera-ready mechanicals. Images on the overlays should be prepared in negative form and at finished size. Contact printing the overlays to make plates eliminates all risk of distortion by the lens of a process camera.

Cartographers know how to prepare overlays correctly. They usually consult with the printer to ensure that pin register systems are compatible between light table and platemaker.

Printers familiar with map work may be able to prepare the art and will know about special papers and folding needs. Maps must withstand hard use and often bad weather, so may need to be printed on very durable stock. Only large printers or trade binderies have folders capable of making the series of accordion folds required for most maps.

Some classified directories include the listing "maps—custom made."

Matchbooks. See *Specialty advertising*.

Membership cards. Cards are ganged and printed offset on cover or bristol paper. For extra durability, they can be film laminated, although lamination prevents them from being signed or numbered later. Round cornering helps prevent cards from becoming bent or ragged.

Large supplies of membership cards can be printed offset, then imprinted or numbered via letterpress in the same fashion as business cards.

Organizations large enough to have their member files on computer data bases can print cards that snap out of perforated sheets. Cards from that paper are not as sturdy as those made from cover or bristol.

Menus. Because they are usually made in very short runs and may be frequently changed, menus are best done at quick or small commercial printers. Unless made to be disposable, they should be on cover or bristol paper and possibly have the additional protection of UV coating or film lamination.

When designing a custom menu, pay particular attention to how colors of papers and inks and type size affect readability.

Printers who specialize in menus advertise in restaurant trade publications and may be listed in classified directories under "menu service." Menu services also offer stock menus ready for imprinting.

Money. See *Currency.*

Monographs. Highly specialized books by scholars are known as monographs. They may be perfect or case bound, are printed in short runs, and are most economically made by a short run book printer.

Music. Any commercial printer can produce sheets and books of music. Standard trim size is 9 x 12, meaning that sheet music folds from 12 x 18 sheets.

Some classified directories list "music printers and engravers." Those companies concentrate on preparing camera-ready copy and do not usually do the printing. They have special typewriters, pens, and layout sheets made for the music trade.

N

Name plates. Name plates, plaques, and signs can be made from metal or plastic and are printed via silk screen or a routing process called engraving. To find printers, look under "name plates" in directories.

Nametags. See *Badges.*

Napkins. Special occasion napkins can be ordered from the catalogs and paper supply stores that also sell wedding invitations and party goods. Large quantities of printed napkins can be ordered from paper distributors.

Newsletters. Any quick or commercial printer can print newsletters, depending on the need for quality and quantity. One economical format is 8½ x 11 with four-page issues made from an 11 x 17 sheet or eight-page issues made from two 11 x 17 sheets.

Many newsletters have a colored nameplate preprinted in large quantities, then stored at the printer's. Copy for individual issues is then imprinted in black ink. Preprinting can be done offset, then imprinting done via offset or photocopy.

Some classified directories include the listing "newsletters." The category is for people who supervise newsletter production, not specialty printers. For more about newsletters, read the books by Mark Beach and Polly Pattison listed in Appendix C.

Newspaper inserts. See *Inserts.*

Newspapers. Most newspaper publishing companies own their printing facilities and use their papers and presses to do outside commercial printing, sometimes called job printing. If your job fits one of their standard formats, such as tabloid, one of these shops may print it at an exceptionally low price even for a short run.

Owners of many smaller newspapers operate multicolor presses capable of basic and good quality printing. Prices for job printing, however, vary greatly depending on work loads, so shopping pays.

The trade organizations of the newspaper industry are the American Newspaper Publishers Association and the National Newspaper Association.

Notebooks. If you want enough notebooks to justify making them yourself or want your message on the covers of notebooks, any printer that can print 10 or 12 point cover stock can do the job. More sturdy covers can be made from chipboard. Mechanical bindings are installed at a trade bindery and are usually spiral or Wire-O.

Novelties. See *Specialty advertising.*

P

Pads. Any printer can make pads that have sheets printed with your form or message. You state how many sheets per pad, the end on which to apply the glue, and whether you want a chipboard backing. For large quantities of pads, check prices at a business forms printer.

Pamphlets. Pamphlets are saddled stitched or paste bound and self-covered. Any printer can make them economically in short runs. Large quantities might be bought most inexpensively from a printer specializing in self-mailers.

Pennants. See *Banners; Specialty advertising.*

Placemats. Both printers and paper distributors supply placemats and tray liners. Printers use uncoated book paper or placemat stock. The stock is sometimes called monks cloth and can have either straight or scalloped edges.

For large quantities, check the price of having a paper distributor supply mats already printed.

Playing cards. See *Games; Specialty advertising.*

Point of purchase displays. A point of purchase (POP) display is any printed display that either holds or advertises merchandise. It could be a box holding books or an easel with a pocket for coupons.

Point of purchase displays are converted or constructed by box companies. The converter receives printed sheets from your printer and mounts them to chipboard or corrugated cardboard. As with box labels, production guidelines are strict to assure good results. Converting companies have standing dies for common designs.

To find POP makers, look in classified directories under "boxes—paper" and the various categories of "display." For design ideas, see the book *Point of Purchase Design*, by Robert Konikow.

Post cards. To accentuate bright colors or a good photograph, post cards are often printed on C1S cover paper. They can, however, be done on any cover or bristol paper thick enough to meet postal regulations. The regulations also govern minimum and maximum size. Business reply cards (BRCs) are subject to even more strict regulations.

Some classified directories include the listing "post cards" that includes distributors, printers, and full service brokers.

Posters. Few products are produced in a greater range of quality and quantity than posters. A neighborhood event might be advertised with 50 one color 8½ x 11 sheets, while a commercial poster might run 100,000 copies in six colors on 23 x 35 paper.

Many posters are printed offset with the same quality considerations as any printing job. For many others, however, quality must be good, but only a few hundred are needed. They are screen printed.

Ink on outdoor posters must resist fading and be in colors bright enough to attract attention. Paper can be any stock that will yield a good image. Using thick papers (more than .024 inch) may mean that screen printing will work better than offset. Screen printing can also handle sheet sizes too big for the presses of most offset printers.

Most classified directories include the listing "posters." Companies included in that listing can design and do photography for posters as well as print them. Some also handle distribution.

Premiums. See *Specialty advertising.*

Press-on letters. See *Transfer lettering.*

Programs. Depending on their size and binding, programs are similar to fliers, brochures, or booklets. Many church and organizational headquarters offer preprinted programs that can be imprinted by quick printing or mimeograph. When folded, they look like a custom printing job that has color photos.

Puzzles. Puzzles are usually printed on coated book paper that is later laminated to chipboard. The product is cut into pieces at a trade bindery or paper box company using a die. Companies that make puzzles have standing dies that offer a range of frustrations in putting the puzzle together. Custom making a die for a puzzle would be very expensive.

R

Rack brochures. The standard size for brochures designed to fit racks in hotel lobbies and information centers is 4 x 9. A brochure 8½ inches high may cost less, but it also may look odd next to the others. The most common paper used is 70# coated book.

Rack brochures are folded into panels, with the most common sizes being three panel (9 x 12 sheet), four panel (9 x 16 sheet), and five panel (9 x 20 sheet). More than five panels requires special folding equipment and should be discussed first with your printer.

When designing a rack brochure, keep in mind that its placement on the rack behind other brochures can mean that only the top three inches of the front panel are visible.

Record jackets. Record jackets and album covers are printed on C1S board ranging from 18 to 30 points, then liquid coated or film laminated. Small runs can be hand assembled after printing, but runs of all lengths are more economically made at specialty printers located in cities with active recording industries. Get references from local recording companies or by reading music trade magazines.

Response vehicles. See *Self-mailers; Direct mailers.*

Resumes. Classified directories list "resume services" that will write and print your resume by quick printing or photocopy. Dress up your resume by using a premium paper such as a 100% cotton bond or 70# text. Buy a ream at a stationery story or paper outlet that caters to quick and in-plant printers. Remember these sheets work fine in most photocopy machines as well as on offset presses.

Ring binders. See *Loose-leaf binders.*

Rubber stamps. Almost every quick print shop and office supply store takes orders for rubber stamps. You can select from their standard type or, for slightly more money, provide your own camera-ready copy. The stamps are actually made by only a few local companies. To find one of them, look in a classified directory under "rubber and plastic stamps."

Rub-off lettering. See *Transfer lettering.*

S

Self-mailers. Response vehicles and self-mailers are made from one sheet of paper printed, folded, and gummed to include the message, order information, and reply envelope. Usually they are printed in two or three colors on small web presses.

Any commercial printer can make self-mailers, but many customers use either a mailing service or a specialty printer. The argument for having printing done by the mailing service is that they understand postal regulations and do the whole sequence of printing, addressing, and mailing under one roof. Specialty printers, on the other hand, can produce millions of pieces quickly at rock bottom prices.

Many large cities have printers that specialize in response vehicles. To find them, ask a paper distributor, sales rep at a mailing service that does not offer printing, or printing buyer at a company that relies on direct mail. You could also inquire from the Direct Marketing Association or at an agency listed under "advertising—direct mail." For design and additional production tips, consult *Direct Marketing Design*, a book compiled by the Direct Marketing Creative Guild.

Specialty advertising. This is a very general category including such items as pencils, balloons, mugs, ashtrays, and matchbooks. Local businesses that supply the items contract for the printing with companies that make them. The printing itself may be offset, foil stamp, or screen, depending on the item.

Directories include the listing "specialty advertising" and also listings for "premium goods" and "novelties." Sources are also available by writing to the Specialty Advertising Association International.

Stamps. See *Labels; Currency.*

Statement stuffers. Like small newsletters, statement stuffers commonly mail along with bills and bank statements. They are usually printed on light weight paper and in large quantities, so run on web or large sheetfed presses. Statement stuffers must meet the technical requirements of automatic stuffing machines, so should be designed in consultation with your mailing service.

Stationery. See *Letterheads; Envelopes; Business cards.* For design ideas, see books by David Carter or Motoo Nakanishi cited in Appendix C. See also the many printed promotion samples offered by the leading makers of bond papers.

Stickers. See *Labels.*

Stocks. See *Certificates.*

T

Table tents. C1S cover or cover weight text paper is commonly used for table tents. Being on a table or bar, table tents are handled often and may benefit from having a protective coating. Assembling table tents requires inserting tabs into slots (both die cut) or using tape.

Tabloids. See *Newspapers.*

Tags. Paper distributors, office supply catalogs, and office supply stores sell wire and string tags that can be printed letterpress. Offset printers can make tags from cover, bristol, or tag paper. A few printers and trade binderies have machines that will insert and loop wire or string in each tag.

Specialty printers may be found under the classification "tags" and by inquiring from the Tag and Label Manufacturers Institute.

Technical manuals. Technical manuals give operating instructions for products and systems such as electronic and mechanical equipment, computer software, appliances, and tools. Their format varies from small booklets to 500-page tomes.

Technical manuals explaining computer hardware and software are called user guides. Many user guides are bound in loose-leaf binders to facilitate adding or replacing pages.

Because technical manuals and user guides are often written shortly before a product enters the market, many are produced on word processors and may be electronically published to speed production. Technical information must be presented clearly, but rapid production leaves little time for design. For layouts applicable to typewritten and word processed manuals and guides, consult the book by Daniel Felker in Appendix C.

Companies that publish technical manuals and user guides usually hire technical writers, editors, and illustrators to produce them. For further information about their work, consult the Society for Technical Communication.

Tickets. Pads of identical tickets can be made like any other pads. Tickets that must be numbered or perforated require production on a letter press or forms web press. When you need large quantities or tickets in rolls, look under the classification "tickets and coupons" to locate specialty printers.

Transfer lettering. Logos and special typography can be custom made into transfer sheets (also known as rub-off or press-on sheets) by the companies that produce standard commercial transfer lettering.

Camera-ready art requirements are the same as for any offset printing job. Sheets can be printed in a variety of colors as single or multicolor jobs. For ordering information, read transfer lettering catalogs and inquire at stores that sell stationery or art and graphics supplies.

Tray liners. See *Placemats.*

T-shirts. See *Clothing.* Many classified directories include the listing "T-shirts."

U

Uniform Product Code. The dark bars in a light square on many consumer products are codes that give computers information about prices and inventories. Codes are assigned and the system is managed by the Uniform Product Code Council, Inc., 7051 Corporate Way, Suite 201, Dayton OH 45459.

User guides. See *Technical manuals.*

Y

Yearbooks. The typical print run for a yearbook of only a few hundred copies is very short for book printing. Any printer that makes books could do it, but there are several large printers that specialize in yearbooks and print them very inexpensively. Those printers will provide layout guidelines and arrange a production schedule that they guarantee to meet.

To learn names of yearbook printers, ask a teacher who is the yearbook advisor, or inquire from the Yearbook Printers Association.

Z

Zebras. Inquiries at our local zoo confirmed our suspicion that zebras are really horses with screen printed stripes. Zoo officials would not reveal whether they started with white or black horses.

APPENDIX B

Glossary of Graphic Arts Terms

This glossary includes all the technical and business terms used in this book with the exception of terms about typesetting, which may be found on pages 32 and 33. In addition, this glossary has a few terms which are not used in the book but which are part of the graphic arts lexicon.

Because the meaning of many terms is more fully understood in context or when the term is illustrated, you may wish to examine a portion of text in which a term is used. The index identifies pages in the text where a term occurs.

A

Acetate. Thin, flexible sheet of transparent plastic used to make overlays.

Against the grain. At right angles to the grain direction of paper.

Agent. Alternate term for *Artist's representative*.

Airbrush. Pen-shaped ink sprayer used to retouch photographic prints and create illustrations.

Alley. Space between columns of type on a page.

Alteration. Change in copy or specifications made after production has begun.

Amberlith. Ulano trade name for orange masking material.

Artboard. Alternate term for *Mechanical*.

Art director. Employee, often of advertising agency, who supervises creation and preparation of copy to give printers.

Artist's representative. Person who handles marketing and other business matters for designers, illustrators, and photographers.

Artwork. Images, including type and photos, prepared for printing.

ASCII. Acronym for American Standard Code for Information Interchange, a standard code used to help interface digital equipment.

B

Backbone. Alternate term for *Spine*.

Back up. To print on the second side of a sheet already printed on one side. Such printing is called a backup.

Banding. Method of packaging printed pieces using paper, rubber, or fiberglass bands.

Base negative. Negative made from copy pasted to mounting board, not overlays.

Basic size. The one standard size of each grade of paper used to calculate basis weight.

Basis weight. Weight in pounds of a ream of paper cut to the basic size for its grade.

Baud rate. Number of bits of information transmitted per second from one digital device to another.

Benday. Alternate term for *Screen tint*.

Bind. To fasten sheets or signatures and adhere covers with glue, wire, thread, or by other means.

Binder's board. Very stiff paper board used to make covers of case bound books.

Bindery. Print shop department or separate business that does trimming, folding, binding, and other finishing tasks.

Blanket. Thick rubber sheet that transfers ink from plate to paper on an offset press.

Blanket cylinder. Cylinder of a press on which the blanket is mounted.

Bleed. Printing that extends to the edge of a sheet or page after trimming.

Blind emboss. To emboss without added ink or foil on the embossed image.

Blow up. To enlarge photographically. Such an enlargement is called a blowup.

Blueline. Prepress, photographic proof where all colors show as blue image on white paper.

Board. Alternate term for *Mechanical*.

Board paper. Grade of paper commonly used for file folders, display, and post cards.

Bond paper. Grade of paper commonly used for writing, printing, and photocopying.

Bookbinder. Alternate term for *Trade bindery*.

Book paper. Grade of paper suitable for books, magazines, and general printing needs.

Brightness. Characteristic of paper referring to how much light it reflects.

Bristol. Type of board paper used for post cards, business cards, and other heavy-use products.

Broken carton. Less than one full carton of paper.

Broker. Agent who supplies printing from many printing companies.

Bulk. Thickness of paper, expressed in thousandths of an inch or pages per inch (ppi).

Bulk pack. To pack printed pieces in boxes without prior wrapping in bundles.

Burn. In photography, to give extra exposure to a specific area of a print. In lithography, to expose a blueline proof or printing plate with light.

Burnish. To smooth and seal by rubbing elements adhered to a mechanical.

Burst perfect bind. To bind by forcing glue into notches in spines of signatures, and then adhering a paper cover.

Butt. To join without overlapping or space between.

Butt fit. Ink colors overlapped only a hairline so they appear perfectly butted.

Buyout. Subcontracted service.

C

C1S. Paper coated on one side.

C2S. Paper coated on both sides.

Calender. To make paper smooth and glossy by passing it between rollers during manufacturing.

Caliper. Thickness of paper, expressed in thousandths of an inch.

Camera-ready copy. Mechanicals, photographs, and art fully prepared to be photographed for platemaking according to the technical requirements of either quick or commercial printing.

Camera service. Business using a process camera to make PMTs, halftone negatives, printing plates, etc.

Cardboard. General term for stiff, bulky paper such as index, tag, or bristol.

Carload. Usually 40,000 pounds of paper.

Case bind. To bind by gluing signatures to a case made of binder's board covered with fabric, plastic, or leather, yielding hard cover books.

Cast coated. Coated paper with a surface similar to that of a glossy photograph.

Center marks. Lines on a mechanical, negative, plate, or press sheet indicating the center of a layout.

Chipboard. Inexpensive, single-ply cardboard, usually brown or gray.

Chrome. Alternate term for *Transparency*.

Cleat bind. Alternate term for *Side stitch*.

Clip art. High-contrast drawings printed on white, glossy paper and made to be cut out and pasted to a mechanical.

Coarse screen. Screen with ruling of less than 133 lines per inch.

Coated paper. Paper with a coating of clay that improves ink holdout.

Collate. To assemble sheets into proper sequence.

Collateral. Ad agency term for printed pieces, such as brochures and annual reports, that are not directly involved in advertising.

Collotype. Method of printing continuous tones using a plate coated with gelatin.

Color bar. Strip of colors printed near the edge of a press sheet to help evaluate ink density.

Color break. In multicolor printing, the point or line at which one ink color stops and another begins.

Color correct. To retouch or enhance color separation negatives.

Color Key. 3M trade name for overlay color proof.

Color matching system. System of numbered ink swatches that facilitates communication about color.

Color process. Alternate term for *4-color process printing.*

Color separation. Set of four halftone negatives for making plates for 4-color process printing.

Color separation service. Business making separation negatives for 4-color process printing.

Color swatch. Sample of an ink color.

Comb bind. To bind by inserting teeth of a flexible plastic comb through holes in a stack of paper.

Commercial artist. Artist whose work is planned for reproduction by printing.

Comp. Short for *Comprehensive dummy.*

Composite film. Graphic arts negative made by combining two or more images.

Composite proof. Proof of color separations in position with graphics and type.

Comprehensive dummy. Complete simulation of a printed piece.

Consignment memo. Alternate term for photographer's *Delivery memo.*

Contact print. Photographic print made by exposing a negative in direct uniform contact with paper.

Contact sheet. Alternate term for *Proof sheet.*

Continuous-tone copy. All photographs and those illustrations having a range of shades.

Contrast. Range of gradations in tones between lightest white and darkest black in continuous-tone copy or the abrupt change between light and dark in line copy.

Converter. Business that combines printed sheets with other materials to make boxes, displays, etc.

Copy. For an editor or typesetter, all written material. For a graphic designer or printer, everything that will be printed: art, photographs, and graphics as well as words.

Copyboard. Part of a process camera that holds copy in position to be photographed.

Copy preparation. In typesetting, marking up manuscript and specifying type. In pasteup and printing, making mechanicals and writing instructions to ensure proper placement and handling of copy.

Copyright. Ownership of creative work by the writer, photographer, or artist who made it.

Copywriter. Person who writes copy for advertising.

Corner marks. Lines on a mechanical, negative, plate, or press sheet showing the corners of a page or finished piece.

Corrugated. Characteristic of board for boxes made by sandwiching fluted kraft paper between sheets of paper or cardboard.

Cotton content paper. Paper made from cotton fibers rather than wood pulp.

Cover paper. Grade of paper made for covers and post cards.

C print. Color photographic print made from a negative on Kodak C Print paper.

Crash printing. Letterpress printing on carbon or carbonless forms so image prints simultaneously on all sheets in the set.

Creep. Phenomenon of middle pages of a folded signature extending slightly beyond outside pages.

Cromalin. DuPont trade name for integral color proof.

Crop. To eliminate portions of an illustration or photograph so the remainder is more clear, interesting, or able to fit the layout.

Crop marks. Lines near the edges of an image showing portions to be eliminated.

Crossover. Image that continues from one page of a publication across the gutter to the opposite page.

Cutoff. The circumference of the impression cylinder of a web press, therefore also the length of the sheet the press will cut from the roll of paper.

Cut stock. Paper distributor term for paper 11 x 17 or smaller.

CWT. Paper distributor abbreviation for 100 pounds.

Cyan. One of the four process colors; also known as process blue.

D

Dampener fountain. Alternate term for *Water fountain* on a press.

Dampening solution. Alternate term for *Fountain solution*.

Data conversion. To change digital information from its original code so that it can be recorded by an electronic memory using a different code.

Deboss. To press an image into paper so it lies below the surface.

Deckle edge. Feathered edge on specially-made sheets of text and cover paper.

Delivery memo. Form sent by photographers and stock photo services to clients for signature to verify receipt of photos and agreement to contract terms.

Densitometer. Instrument used to measure light reflecting from or transmitted through copy.

Density. Relative darkness of copy, ink on paper, or emulsion on film, as measured by a densitometer.

Density range. Expression of contrast between darkest and lightest areas of copy.

Depth of field. Photographer term for relative sharpness of features in an image regardless of their distance from the camera when photographed.

Design brief. Written description of how a printed piece is intended to look and the requirements for reproducing it.

Diazo. Light-sensitive coating on paper or film for making contact prints of technical drawings.

Die. Sharp metal rule used for die cutting or block of metal used for embossing or foil stamping.

Die cutting. Cutting irregular shapes in paper using metal rules mounted on a letter press.

Dimensional stability. Ability of paper and other substrates to retain their exact size despite the influence of temperature, moisture, or stretching.

Direct mail. Mail designed to motivate readers to respond directly to senders with a purchase, donation, or other action.

Doctor blade. Flexible metal strip that cleans excess ink from a gravure plate prior to each impression.

Dodge. To block light from selected areas while making a photographic print.

Dot etching. Chemical or photographic method of color correcting separation negatives.

Dot gain or spread. Phenomenon of dots printing larger on paper than they are on negatives or plates.

Double bump. To print a single image twice so it has two layers of ink.

Double burn. To expose a plate or proof to two negatives to create a composite image.

Draw down. Sample of specified ink and paper, used to evaluate color.

Drill. To bore holes in paper so sheets fit over posts of loose-leaf binders.

Drop out. To eliminate halftone dots or fine lines due to overexposure during camera work or plate-making. The lost copy is said to have dropped out.

Dropout halftone. Halftone in which the highlight areas contain no dots.

Dry gum paper. Label paper with glue that can be activated by water.

Dull finish. Characteristic of paper that reflects relatively little light.

Dull ink or varnish. Alternate term for *Matte ink or varnish.*

Dummy. Preliminary drawing or layout showing visual elements. Also a simulation of a printed piece using paper specified for a job.

Duotone. Photograph reproduced from two halftone negatives and usually printed in two ink colors.

Duplex paper. Paper with a different color or finish on each side.

Duplicator. Small offset press using paper 12 x 18 or smaller (not to be confused with spirit duplicator).

Dylux. DuPont trade name for photographic paper used to make blueline proofs.

E

Edition bind. Alternate term for *Case bind.*

Electronic image assembly. Assembly of new image from portions of existing images or elements using a computer.

Electronic memory. Disk, magnetic tape, or other memory device that holds digital information.

Electronic page assembly. Assembly and manipulation of type, graphics, and other visual elements on a computer screen.

Electronic publishing. Publishing by printing with a computer-controlled photocopy machine.

Electronic retouching. Using a computer to enhance or correct a scanned photograph.

Emboss. To press an image into paper so it lies above the surface.

Emulsion. Coating of chemicals on papers, films, and printing plates that, prior to development, is sensitive to light.

Enamel paper. Alternate term for *Coated paper* with gloss finish.

End sheets. Sheets that attach the inside pages of a case bound book to its cover.

Engraver. Person who makes a plate for engraving. Also may refer to trade camera service.

Engraving. Method of printing using a plate, also called a die, with an image carved into it.

Estimate. Price that states what a job will probably cost based on initial specifications from customer.

Etch. Using chemicals or tools, to carve away metal leaving an image or carve an image into metal. Also, alternate term for *Fountain solution.*

Exposure time. Time required for light to record an image while striking light-sensitive emulsion.

F

Fake duotone. Halftone in one ink color printed over screen tint of a second ink color.

Fast film. Film that requires relatively little light to record an image.

Film coat. Paper with a very thin coating.

Film laminate. Thin sheet of plastic adhered to printed paper for protection.

Filter. Colored glass or gelatin used to reduce or eliminate specific colors from light before it strikes film or paper.

Final count. Number of printed pieces delivered and charged for.

Fine screen. Screen with ruling of more than 150 lines per inch.

Finish. Surface characteristic of paper.

Finishing. Inclusive term sometimes used for all bindery operations.

Finish size. Size of printed product after production is complete.

Fixer. Chemical that prevents deterioration of images on photosensitive paper.

Flat. In photography, characteristic of an image that lacks contrast. In printing, an assembly of negatives taped to masking material and ready for platemaking.

Flexography. Method of printing on a web press using rubber plates with raised images.

Flood. To cover a sheet with ink or varnish.

Flop. To reproduce a photograph or illustration so that its image faces opposite from the original.

Flush cover. Cover that is trimmed to the same size as inside pages, as with paperback books.

Flute. Paper pleat between the walls in corrugated cardboard.

Foil emboss. To foil stamp and emboss an image.

Foil stamping. Method of printing on a letter press using thin metallic or pigmented film and a die.

Form. One side of a press sheet.

Format. Size, shape, and overall style of a layout or printed piece.

Formula pricing. Printing prices based on standard papers, formats, ink colors, and quantities.

Fountain. Reservoir for ink or water on a press.

Fountain solution. Mixture of water and chemicals that dampens a printing plate to prevent ink from adhering to its non-image area.

4-color process. Technique of printing that uses the four process colors of ink to simulate color photographs or illustrations.

Free sheet. Paper made from cooked wood fibers mixed with chemicals and washed free of impurities.

French fold. Two folds at right angles to each other.

Fully saturated. Photographer term for rich color.

G

Gang. To reproduce two or more printed pieces or multiple copies of the same piece simultaneously on one sheet of paper. Also, to halftone or separate more than one image in only one exposure.

Gather. To assemble signatures into the proper sequence for binding.

GBC binding. General Binding Corporation trade name for plastic comb binding.

Generation. A first generation image is the original; second generation is made from the original; third generation is made from the second generation. Print on this page is fourth generation: type (first), negative (second), plate (third), print (fourth).

Ghost halftone. Halftone that has been screened to produce a very faint image.

Ghosting. Phenomenon of a faint image on a printed sheet where it was not intended to appear.

Gloss. Characteristic of paper, ink, or varnish that reflects relatively large amounts of light.

Glossy. Photographic print made on glossy paper.

Goldenrod. Alternate term for *Flat*.

Grade. One of seven major categories of paper: bond, uncoated book, coated book, text, cover, board, and specialty.

Grain. In paper, the direction in which fibers are aligned. In photography, crystals that make up emulsion on film.

Grain long or grain short. Paper whose fibers parallel the long or short dimension of the sheet.

Graphic arts. The crafts, industries, and professions related to designing and printing messages.

Graphic arts film. Film whose emulsion responds to light on an all-or-nothing principle to yield high contrast images.

Graphic arts magnifier. Lens, mounted in a small stand, used to inspect copy, negatives, and printing.

Graphic designer. Professional who conceives of the design for, plans how to produce, and may coordinate production of a printed piece.

Graphics. Art and other visual elements used to make messages more clear.

Gravure. Method of printing using etched metal cylinders, usually on web presses.

Gray scale. Strip of swatches of tone values ranging from white to black used by process camera operators to calibrate exposure times.

Gripper edge. Edge of a sheet held by the grippers, thus going first through a sheetfed press.

Groundwood paper. Newsprint and other inexpensive papers made from pulp created by grinding wood mechanically.

Gusset. Expandable portion of a bag, file folder, or envelope.

Gutter. Space between columns of type where pages meet at the binding.

H

Hairline. Very thin line or gap about the width of a hair: $1/100$ inch.

Halftone. To photograph continuous-tones through a screen to convert the image into dots. The result is also called a halftone and may be either positive or negative and on film or paper.

Halftone dots. Dots that by their varying sizes create the illusion of shading or a continuous-tone image.

Halftone screen. Piece of film containing a grid of lines that breaks light into dots as it passes through.

Half web. Web press whose width and cutoff allow printing eight $8^{1}/_{2}$ x 11 pages on one press sheet.

Hard bind. Alternate term for *Case bind*.

Hard cover. Bound with a case of binder's board.

Head stops. Adjustable posts on register unit of a press that properly position leading edge of a sheet.

Heat-set web. Web press equipped with oven to make ink dry faster, thus able to print coated paper.

Hickey. Donut-shaped spot or imperfection in printing, most visible in areas of heavy ink coverage.

High-bulk paper. Paper made relatively thick in proportion to its basis weight.

High contrast. Few or no tonal gradations between dark and light areas.

Highlights. The lightest areas in a photograph or halftone.

Holding fee. Charge made to clients who keep photograph longer than agreed to.

Holdout. Alternate term for *Ink holdout*.

House sheet. General-use paper ordered in large quantities and kept in stock by a printer.

Hypo. Alternate term for *Fixer*.

I

Image area. Portion of a negative or plate corresponding to inking on paper; portion of paper on which ink appears.

Image assembly. Alternate term for *Stripping*.

Imposition. Arrangement of pages on mechanicals or flats so they will appear in proper sequence after press sheets are folded and bound.

Impression. One pressing of paper against type, plate, blanket, or die to transfer an image.

Impression cylinder. Cylinder on a press that presses paper against the blanket (offset) or plate (gravure).

Imprint. To print additional copy on a previously printed sheet.

Index paper. Light weight board paper for writing and easy erasure.

Indicia. Postal permit information printed on objects to be mailed and accepted by USPS in lieu of stamps.

Ink fountain. Reservoir on a printing press that holds ink.

Ink holdout. Characteristic of paper allowing ink to dry on its surface rather than by absorption.

Ink jet. Method of printing by spraying droplets of ink through computer-controlled nozzles.

In-plant printer. Department of an agency, business, or association that does printing for the parent organization.

Integral proof. Color proof of separation negatives exposed in register on one piece of proofing paper.

Interface. To link two or more electronic devices so they can function as one unit.

Internegative. Negative made from a transparency for the purpose of making photographic prints.

IR coating. Liquid laminate coating bonded and cured with infrared light.

ISBN. International Standard Book Number assigned by the book's publisher using a system administered by the R. R. Bowker Company in New York City.

ISSN. International Standard Serial Number assigned by the Library of Congress in Washington DC to magazines, newsletters, and other serials requesting it.

J

Job shop. Commercial printing company.

Job ticket. Alternate term for *Work order*.

Jog. To straighten or align sheets of paper in a stack.

K

Key. To code separate pieces of copy to a layout or mechanical using a system of numbers or letters.

Keyline. Alternate term for *Mechanical*.

Keylines. Lines on a mechanical or negative showing the exact size, shape, and location of photographs or other graphic elements.

Keys. Screws on an ink fountain that control ink flow.

Kill fee. Charge made by writers and photographers for work done on assignment, then not used.

Kiss die cut. To die cut the top layer, but not the backing layer, of self-adhesive paper.

Knock out. Alternate term for *Mask out*.

Knockout film. Alternate term for *Masking material* such as *Rubylith*.

Kraft paper. Strong paper, usually brown, used for wrapping and to make bags.

Kromekote. Champion Paper Company trade name for a high-gloss, cast-coated paper.

L

Laid finish. Grid of parallel lines on paper simulating surface of handmade paper.

Laminate. To bond plastic film to paper, or to glue paper to chipboard or corrugated cardboard.

Large-format camera. Camera that makes negatives 4 x 5 or larger.

Laser printing. Method of photocopying using a laser beam to charge the drum.

Layout. Sketch or drawing of a design for a proposed printed piece showing position, size, and color of copy.

Leading edge. Edge of a sheet of paper that enters the press first, also known as the *Gripper edge*.

Ledger paper. Strong, smooth bond paper used for keeping business records.

Legible. Characteristic of copy having sufficient contrast with the paper on which it appears and determined by such features as typeface, size, leading, and quality of printing.

Letterpress. Method of printing from raised surfaces. A letter press is the kind of press used.

Lettershop. Alternate term for *Mailing service*.

Light table. Translucent glass surface lit from below, used by production artists and strippers.

Light weight paper. Book grade paper of basis weight 40# or less with high opacity for its weight.

Line conversion screen. Piece of film containing line patterns that break light into those patterns as it passes through.

Line copy. Type, rules, clip art, and other images that are high contrast.

Line negative. High contrast negative usually made from line copy.

Linen tester. Alternate term for *Graphic arts magnifier*.

Lines per inch. The number of lines or rows of dots there are per inch in a screen and therefore in a screen tint, halftone, or separation.

Linotype. Mergenthaler trade name for machine that sets lines of metal type.

Liquid laminate. Plastic applied to paper as a liquid, then bonded and cured into a hard, glossy finish.

Lithography. Method of printing using a chemically-coated plate whose image areas attract ink and whose non-image areas repel ink.

Live area. Alternate term for *Image area*.

Logo. Assembly of type and art into a distinctive symbol unique to an organization, business, or product.

Long grain. Alternate term for *Grain long* (paper).

Loop stitch. To saddle stitch with staples that are also loops which slip over rings of binders.

Loose proof. Proof of one color separation.

Loupe. Alternate term for *Graphic arts magnifier*.

M

M. Roman numeral for 1,000.

Magenta. One of the four process colors; also known as process red.

Mailing service. Business specializing in addressing and mailing large quantities of printed pieces.

Makeready. All activities required to set up a press before production begins. Also refers to paper used in the process.

Making order. Order for custom-made paper.

Manila paper. Strong, buff-colored paper used to make envelopes and file folders.

Margin. Space forming border of a page or sheet.

Masking material. Opaque material, often film, used in pasteup to outline photographs or in plate-making to withhold light from non-image areas.

Mask out. To cover selected copy or art so it will not appear on a negative or plate.

Master. Paper or plastic offset printing plate. Also, paper plate for spirit duplicating.

Matchprint. 3M trade name for integral color proof.

Matte finish. Slightly dull finish on coated, lightly-calendered paper.

Matte ink or varnish. Ink or varnish that appears dull when dry.

Mechanical. Camera-ready assembly of type, graphics, and other line copy complete with instructions to the printer.

Mechanical artist. Alternate term for *Production artist.*

Mechanical separation. Mechanical prepared using a separate overlay for each color to be printed.

Media conversion. Alternate term for *Data conversion* from one digital coding to another.

Medium format camera. Camera that makes 2¼ x 2¼ negatives.

Medium screen. Screen with ruling of 133 or 150 lines per inch.

Metallic ink. Ink containing powdered metal that sparkles in light.

Micrometer. Instrument used to measure thickness of paper.

Middle tones. Tones in a photograph or illustration about half as dark as its shadow areas and represented by dots between 30% and 70% of full size.

Mike. To measure the thickness of a sheet of paper using a micrometer.

Mill swatch. Paper sample book provided by a mill.

Mimeograph. Method of printing using a plastic stencil mounted on a rotating drum containing ink.

Mimeograph bond. Highly absorbent paper made for the mimeograph method of printing.

Mockup. Alternate term for *Dummy.*

Model release. Contract authorizing commercial use of a photograph that includes image of a recognizable person or private property.

Modem. Short for modulator/demodulator, a device that converts digital signals to analog tones and vice versa so that systems based on electronic memories can interface over telephone lines.

Moire. Undesirable pattern in halftones and screen tints made with improperly aligned screens.

Mottle. Spotty, uneven ink coverage especially noticeable in large solids.

Mounting board. Any thick, smooth piece of board paper used to paste up copy or mount photographs.

Multicolor printing. Printing done in more than one ink color.

Mylar. DuPont trade name for polyester film.

N

Negative. Characteristic of an image on film or paper in which blacks in the original subject are white or clear and whites in the original are black or opaque. Also, piece of film on which negative image appears.

Negative space. Alternate term for *White space.*

Non-image area. Portion of mechanical, negative, or plate that will not print.

Non-reproducing blue. Light blue color that does not record on graphic arts film, therefore may be used to write instructions on mechanicals.

Novelty printing. Printing on products such as pencils, balloons, and ashtrays.

O

Offset. Alternate term often used for *Setoff*.

Offset paper. Alternate term often used for *Uncoated book paper*.

Offset powder. Fine powder sprayed on freshly printed sheets to prevent transfer of wet ink as they accumulate in the delivery stack.

Offset printing. Method of lithographic printing that transfers ink from a plate to a blanket, then from the blanket to paper.

OK sheet. Printed sheet representing final inking adjustments approved before production run begins.

Opacity. Characteristic of paper that helps prevent printing on one side from showing on the other.

Opaque. Not transparent. Also, a verb meaning to cover flaws in negatives with paint or tape. Also, the paint used for this purpose.

Opaque ink. Heavily pigmented ink that blocks out color of underlying ink or paper.

Open web. Web press without a drying oven, thus unable to print on coated paper.

Outline halftone. Halftone in which background has been removed to isolate or silhouette an image.

Overlay. Sheet of tissue or acetate taped to a mechanical so that it covers the mounting board.

Overlay proof. Color proof consisting of acetate sheets covering each other in register, one for each color to be printed.

Overprint. To print over a previously printed image.

Overrun. The number of pieces that were printed in excess of the quantity specified.

Overs. Printed pieces in an overrun.

P

Pad. To bind by applying glue along one edge of a stack of sheets.

Page count. Total number of pages, including blanks and printed pages without numbers.

Pages per inch. Number of pages per inch of thickness of a bound publication. Each sheet has two pages.

Pagination. Assembly of type with other line copy into page format. When done by hand, this is make-up or pasteup; when done electronically, it is computer aided pagination (CAP).

Pallet. Wooden platform used as a base for loading and moving paper and printed products.

Paper distributor. Merchant selling paper wholesale to printers and other buyers of large quantities.

Paper dummy. Unprinted sample of a proposed printed piece trimmed, folded, and, if necessary, bound using paper specified for the job.

Parchment. Paper that simulates writing surfaces made from animal skins.

Parent sheet. Paper distributor term for sheet 17 x 22 or larger.

Paste bind. To bind by adhering sheets with glue along the fold of the spine.

Paste up. To adhere copy to mounting boards and, if necessary, overlays so it is assembled into a camera-ready mechanical.

Pasteup. The process of pasting up. Also, alternate term for *Mechanical*.

Percentage wheel. Alternate term often used for *Proportional scale*.

Perfect bind. To bind sheets by trimming at the spine and gluing them to a paper cover.

Perfecting press. Press capable of printing both sides of the paper during a single pass.

Photocopy. Method of printing that transfers images electrostatically and creates them on paper with powder bonded by heat.

Photosensitive. Characteristic of paper, film, and printing plates coated with light-sensitive chemicals.

Photostat. Process used to make positive paper prints of line copy and halftones. Often used as alternate term for *PMT*.

Picking. Undesirable phenomenon of bits of fiber or coating coming loose from paper during printing.

Pigment. Finely-ground particles giving color and opacity to ink.

Pinholes. Tiny holes in the emulsion of negatives or printing plates.

Pixel. Short for picture element, referring to a part of a dot made by a scanner or other digital device.

Plate. See *Printing plate*.

Plate cylinder. Cylinder of a press on which the printing plate is mounted.

Platemaker. In quick printing, process camera that makes plates automatically after photographing mechanicals. In commercial printing, machine used to expose plates from flats.

Platen press. A letter press that opens and closes like a clamshell.

Plate-ready film. Alternate term for *Flat*.

Pleasing color. Color that is satisfactory even though it doesn't match original samples, scenes, or objects.

Plugged up. Undesirable characteristic of printing when ink fills in around halftone dots, causing loss of shadow detail.

PMS. Abbreviation for PANTONE MATCHING SYSTEM, a check standard trademark for color reproduction and color reproduction materials owned by Pantone, Inc.

PMT. Abbreviation for photomechanical transfer, a Kodak trade name for a process used to make positive paper prints of line copy and halftones.

Point. In paper, unit of thickness equalling $1/1000$ inch. In typesetting, unit of height equalling $1/72$ inch.

Portfolio. Collection of best work by an artist, photographer, or designer for showing during meetings with prospective clients.

Position stat. Photocopy or PMT made to size and pasted to a mechanical showing how to crop, scale, and position loose art or photos.

Positive. Characteristic of an image on film or paper in which blacks in the original subject are black or opaque and whites in the original are white or clear. Also, the image itself.

PPI. Short for pages per inch.

Preparation. Camera work, stripping, platemaking, and other activities by a trade camera service or printer before press work begins. Also called prep.

Prepress. Alternate term for *Preparation*.

Preprint. To print work in advance to be ready for inserting or imprinting.

Press check. Event at which test sheets are examined before production run is authorized to begin.

Press proof. Proof made on press using the plates, paper, and ink specified for the job.

Press run. The number of pieces printed.

Press sheet. One sheet as it comes off the press.

Price break. Quantity level at which unit cost of paper or printing drops.

Printer. In printing trade, person who owns or manages print shop or runs printing press. In 4-color process printing, one of the separation negatives.

Printing. Any process that repeatedly transfers an image from a plate, die, negative, stencil, or electronic memory.

Printing plate. Surface carrying image to be printed.

Printing trade customs. See *Trade customs*.

Process blue. Alternate term for *Cyan*.

Process camera. Graphic arts camera used to photograph mechanicals and other camera-ready copy.

Process colors. The colors needed for 4-color process printing: yellow, magenta, cyan, and black.

Process inks. Inks in the four process colors.

Process printing. Alternate term for *4-color process printing*.

Process red. Alternate term for *Magenta*.

Production artist. Person who does pasteup.

Prog. Short for *Progressive proof*.

Progressive proof. Press proof showing each color of a job separately or several colors in combination.

Proof. Test sheet made to reveal errors or flaws, predict results, and record how a printing job is intended to appear.

Proof OK. Customer signature approving a proof and authorizing the job to advance to the next stage.

Proofread. To examine copy or a proof for errors in writing or composition.

Proof sheet. Photographer term for sheet of images made by contact printing negatives.

Proportional scale. Device used to calculate percent that an original image must be reduced or enlarged to yield a specific reproduction size.

Publish. To produce and sell or otherwise make available printed communication to the public.

Pulp. Mixture of wood and/or cotton fibers, chemicals, and water from which mills make paper.

Q

Quick printer. Printer whose business attitude emphasizes basic quality, small presses, and fast service.

Quotation. Printer's offer to print a job for a specific price calculated from specifications and dummies provided by customer.

R

Railroad board. Heavy board paper used for posters and signs.

Raised printing. Alternate term for *Thermography*.

RC paper. Resin-coated paper for typesetting and PMTs that, when properly processed, will not yellow.

Readable. Characteristic of messages that are written and edited and set in type selected and composed to make them easy to understand.

Ream. 500 sheets of paper.

Recto. Right-hand page of an open publication.

Reflective copy. Copy that is not transparent.

Register. To position printing in proper relation to edges of paper and other printing on the same sheet. Such printing is said to be in register.

Register marks. Cross-hair lines on mechanicals and negatives that guide strippers and printers.

Reprographics. General term for xerography, diazo, and other methods of copying used by designers, engineers, and architects.

Retouch. To enhance a photo or correct its flaws.

Reverse. Type or other image reproduced by printing the background rather than the image itself, allowing the underlying color of paper or previously printed ink to show in the shape of the image.

Right reading. Copy reading correctly (normally) from left to right.

Rights. Conditions and terms of licensing agreement between copyright owner and client.

Rotogravure. Gravure printing using a web press.

Rough layout. Simple sketch giving general idea of size and placement of type and art.

R print. Color photographic print made from transparency without using internegative.

Rubylith. Ulano trade name for red masking film.

Rule. Line used for graphic effect.

Ruling. See *Screen ruling*.

Run. Total number of copies ordered or printed.

Running head or foot. Title or other information at the top or bottom of every page of a publication.

S

Saddle stitch. To bind by stapling sheets together where they fold at the spine.

Scale. To identify the percent by which images should be enlarged or reduced.

Scaling wheel. Alternate term for *Proportional scale*.

Scanner. Electronic device used to make color separations and sometimes halftones and duotones.

Score. To compress paper along a line so it will fold more easily.

Screen. Piece of film with dots of uniform density, used to make plates that will print screen tints. See also *Halftone screen*.

Screen density. Amount of ink, expressed as percent of coverage, that a specific screen allows to print.

Screen printing. Method of printing by forcing ink through a mesh stencil.

Screen ruling. The number of rows or lines of dots per inch in a screen for tint or halftone.

Screen tint. Area of image printed with dots so ink coverage is less than 100% and simulates shading or a lighter color.

Scribe. To scratch lines into emulsion of a negative.

Scum. Undesirable thin film of ink covering non-image area of printed sheet.

Self-cover. Publication made entirely from the same paper so that cover is printed simultaneously with inside pages.

Self-mailer. Printed piece designed to be mailed without an envelope.

Separation. Alternate term for *Color separation*.

Setoff. Undesirable transfer of wet ink from the top of one sheet to the underside of another as they lie in the delivery stack of a press.

Sew. To use thread to fasten signatures together at the spine of a book.

Shadows. Darkest areas in a photograph or halftone.

Sharp. Characteristic of an image in clear focus.

Sheeter. Device to cut roll of paper into sheets.

Sheetfed press. Press that prints sheets of paper.

Shingling. Allowance made during pasteup or stripping to compensate for creep.

Short grain. Alternate term for *Grain short* (paper).

Show through. Printing on one side of paper that can be seen on the other side.

Shrink wrap. Method of tightly wrapping packages or products in plastic film.

Side guides. Adjustable mechanism on register unit of a press that properly positions a sheet side to side.

Side stitch. To bind by stapling through sheets along one edge.

Signature. Sheet of printed pages which, when folded, become part of a publication.

Silhouette halftone. Alternate term often used for *Outline halftone*.

Sizing. Chemicals mixed with pulp that make paper less able to absorb moisture.

Skid. Alternate term for *Pallet*.

Slip sheet. Blank sheet placed between newly-made printed products to prevent setoff or scuffing during handling and shipping.

Slit. To cut paper using a disk or wheel.

Slow film. Film that requires a relatively large amount of light to record an image.

Slur. Undesirable phenomenon of halftone dots becoming slightly elongated during printing.

Small-format camera. Camera making negatives 35mm or smaller.

Smyth sewn. One pattern of sewn binding.

Soft bind. Alternate term for *Perfect bind*.

Soft cover. Bound without a case; usually perfect bound, but also sewn and bound with a paper cover.

Solid. Any area of the sheet that has received 100% ink coverage.

Special effects. General term for reproduction of photographs using techniques such as line conversion and posterization.

Specialty advertising. Printed advertising on products such as mugs, matchbooks, jewelry, and pencils.

Specialty papers. Paper distributor term for carbonless, pressure-sensitive, synthetic, and other papers made for special applications.

Specialty printer. Printer specializing in making a particular product.

Specifications. Complete and precise descriptions of paper, ink, binding, quantity, and other features of a printing job. See also *Type Terms*, page 33.

Spec sheet. Short for sheet on which specifications are written.

Spine. Binding edge of a signature or publication.

Spiral bind. To bind using a spiral of wire or plastic looped through holes.

Spirit duplicating. Method of printing that uses a chemical fluid to dissolve a trace of carbon from the plate to make each impression.

Split fountain. Technique of printing more than one ink color at a time from a single printing unit.

Spoilage. Paper wasted during makeready, printing, or bindery operations.

Spot varnish. Varnish applied to portions of a sheet.

Stabilization paper. Paper for typesetting and PMTs that begins deteriorating a few weeks after use.

Stamping. Alternate term for *Foil stamping.*

Stat. General term for inexpensive photographic print of line copy or halftone.

Stat camera. Small process camera.

Stationery. Letterhead, envelopes, cards, and other printed materials for business correspondence.

Stencil. Piece of fabric or film carrying image for screen printing or mimeograph.

Stitch bind. To bind with wire staples.

Stock. Paper or other substrate.

Stock photo. Photograph in a collection maintained for commercial purposes.

Stripper. Person who strips negatives.

Stripping. Assembling negatives in flats in preparation for making printing plates.

Substance weight. Alternate term for *Basis weight* used when referring to bond papers.

Substrate. Any surface on which printing is done.

Sub weight. Short for substance weight.

Supercalender. To calender paper extensively until very glossy.

Surprint. Alternate term for *Overprint.*

Swatch book. Book with small samples of paper or ink colors.

Synthetic paper. Plastic or other petroleum-based paper.

T

Tack. Characteristic of ink making it sticky.

Tag. Board grade paper used for products such as tags and file folders.

Text paper. Grade of paper characterized by textured surfaces.

Thermography. Method of printing using colorless resin powder and heat applied to wet ink yielding raised images.

Thumbnail sketch. Rough sketch of a design.

Tick marks. Alternate term for *Crop marks.*

Tinning. Method of binding by crimping a metal strip along edges of sheets.

Tint. Alternate term for *Screen tint.*

Tip in or on. To glue one edge of a sheet to another sheet or signature.

Tissue. Thin, translucent paper used for overlays.

Tonal range. Photographer term for density range.

Toner. Powder forming the image in photocopy.

Toning. Alternate term for *Scumming.*

Trade bindery. Business specializing in trimming, folding, binding, and other finishing operations.

Trade camera service. Alternate term for *Camera service.*

Trade customs. Business terms and policies followed by businesses in the same field and often codified by a trade association.

Trade shop. Printer or other service working primarily for other graphic arts professionals.

Transfer key. 3M trade name for integral color proof.

Translite. Piece of glass or plastic lit from behind and on which a photographic image has been reproduced for display.

Transparency. Positive photographic image, usually in color, on film allowing light to pass through.

Trap. To print one ink over another.

Trim marks. Lines on a mechanical, negative, plate, or press sheet showing where to cut edges off of paper or cut paper apart after printing.

Trim size. Size of the printed product after last trim is made.

Turnaround time. Amount of time needed to complete a job or one stage of it.

U

Uncoated paper. Paper that is not clay coated.

Undercolor removal. Technique of making and printing color separations that minimizes amount of cyan, magenta, and yellow ink in shadow areas.

Underrun. Production run of fewer copies than the amount specified.

Up. Printing two up or three up means printing the identical piece twice or three times on one sheet of paper in one impression.

UV coating. Liquid laminate bonded and cured with ultraviolet light.

V

Varnish. Clear liquid applied like ink on press for beauty and protection.

Vellum finish. Relatively rough finish on uncoated paper.

Velox. Kodak trade name for high-contrast photographic paper. Also refers to a positive made by contact printing a negative to such paper.

Verso. Left-hand page of an open publication.

Vignette halftone. Halftone whose background gradually fades into white.

W

Wash up. To clean ink from rollers, fountains, and other components of a press.

Waste. Alternate term for *Spoilage.*

Water fountain. Reservoir on a press to hold fountain solution.

Watermark. Distinctive design created in paper during manufacture.

Web. Roll of printing paper.

Web break. Break in paper running through a web press, causing production to stop.

Web press. Press that prints paper from a roll.

Weight. See *Basis weight* (of paper).

White space. Designer term referring to non-image area that frames or sets off copy.

Window. Block of masking material on a mechanical that shows position of a photograph or other visual element. Also, an area cut out of masking material.

Wire-O. Trade name for method of mechanical binding using double loops of wire.

With the grain. Parallel to the grain direction of paper.

Working film. Graphic arts negatives still loose or not composited.

Work order. Form used by printing companies to specify and schedule production of jobs and record the time, materials, and supplies that each job requires to complete.

Wove finish. Relatively smooth finish on paper achieved by moderate calendering.

Wrong reading. Image that is backwards compared to the original.

X

Xerography. Alternate term for *Photocopy.*

APPENDIX C

Publications and Associations

Books, periodicals, and trade associations are sources of additional information about the graphic arts. This appendix deals with all three.

The list of books is divided into the categories business and legal, design, photography, production, reference, and typography. Titles within each category are listed alphabetically by author and are briefly annotated. When a book has been published by a company whose address is not given in *Literary Market Place*, which is available in most libraries, we include the address as part of the citation.

Books: Business and Legal

American Society of Magazine Photographers. *Professional Business Practices in Photography*. American Society of Magazine Photographers, 1981. The photographers' trade association tells how members should work with clients.

Beil, Norman. *The Writers Legal and Business Guide*. Arco Publishing, 1985. How to deal with contracts, agents, and taxes.

Brackman, Henrietta. *The Perfect Portfolio: Professional Techniques for Presenting Yourself and Your Photographs*. Amphoto, 1985. How to set goals, analyze markets, edit photos, and deal with the 20 questions clients most often ask.

Corbett, Ruth. *Art as a Living*. Art Direction Book Co., 1985. Business-smart information from the school of hard knocks.

Craig, James. *Graphic Design Career Guide: How to Get a Job and Establish a Career in Design*. Watson-Guptill, 1983. Tells how to handle portfolios, resumes, and interviews.

Crawford, Tad. *Legal Guide for the Visual Artist*. Robert Silver Associates, 1985. (307 East 37th Street, New York NY 10016.) Explains copyright, contracts, taxation, grants, estate planning, and collecting.

Crawford, Tad, and Arie Kopelman. *Selling Your Graphic Design and Illustration*. St. Martin's, 1981. A guide to marketing, business, and law.

Duboff, Leonard. *The Law in Plain English for Craftspeople*. Madronna Publishers, 1984. Covers forms of organizations, taxes, copyrights, insurance, contracts, and other topics essential to doing business.

Gold, Ed. *The Business of Graphic Design*. Watson-Guptill, 1985. Tells how to start and manage a studio, complete with interviews of leading designers discussing promotion and management.

Graphic Artists Guild. *Handbook of Pricing and Ethical Guidelines for Graphic Artists*. Graphic Artists Guild, 1984. (Distributed by Robert Silver Associates, 307 East 37th Street, New York NY 10016.) Deals with trade customs, copyrights, contracts, and other business matters.

Grill, Tom, and Mark Scanlon. *Photography: Turning Pro*. Watson-Guptill/Amphoto, 1985. Tells how to create a portfolio, work with clients, establish fees, and manage a studio.

Grode, Susan. *The Visual Artists Manual*. Doubleday, 1984. How to choose agents and other professional services and deal with leases, insurance, and taxes.

Marquand, Ed. *How to Prepare Your Portfolio*. Art Direction Book Co., 1985. Shows how to organize and present your best work.

Poynter, Dan. *The Self-Publishing Manual*. Para Publications, 1984. The standard guide to writing, publishing, and selling books on your own. PO Box 4232-67, Santa Barbara CA 93103.

Rosen, Frederic. *The Professional Photographers Business Guide*. Amphoto, 1985. How to handle financing, studio space, marketing, and publicity.

Stasiowski, Frank. *Negotiating Higher Design Fees*. Watson-Guptill, 1985. Deals with strategies, settings, presentations, and ethics. Written for architects, but ideas and tactics apply to graphic designers, too.

Strong, William. *The Copyright Book*. Massachusetts Institute of Technology Press, 1984. Practical guide for publishers, programers, designers, composers, and all creative people.

Weil, Ben H. *Modern Copyright Fundamentals*. Van Nostrand Reinhold, 1985. Special emphasis on relationship of copyright law to electronic publishing.

Books: Design

Beach, Mark. *Editing Your Newsletter: A Guide to Writing, Design, and Production*. Coast to Coast Books, 1982. (2934 NE 16th Avenue, Portland OR 97212.) The standard book in the field.

Biegeleison, Jack I. *Design and Print Your Own Posters*. Watson-Guptill, 1976. How to make as well as plan effective posters.

Carter, David E. *Corporate Identity Manuals*. Art Direction Book Co., 1984. How to design and carry out a program, complete with 13 CI manuals.

Carter, David E. *Designing Corporate Identity Programs for Small Corporations*. Art Direction Book Co., 1985. Gives 37 illustrated case histories.

Direct Marketing Creative Guild. *Direct Marketing Design*. PBC International, Inc., 1985. Large photos show award winning envelopes, boxes, stuffers, and other components of direct mail.

Evarts, Susan. *The Art and Craft of Greeting Cards*. North Light/Writers Digest, 1985. How to design, paste up, produce, and market cards, announcements, and invitations.

Felker, Daniel. *Guidelines for Document Designers*. American Institutes for Research, 1981. (1055 Thomas Jefferson Street NW, Washington DC 20007.) Shows how to organize text and use typography, layout, and visuals with reports and similar documents.

Holmes, Nigel. *Designer's Guide to Creating Charts and Diagrams*. Watson-Guptill, 1985. Shows how to extract information from a mass of detail and portray it clearly in visual form.

Industrial Design Magazine. *Packaging Design II*. PBC International, Inc., 1985. Visual dictionary in areas such as cosmetics, housewares, and food.

Konikow, Robert B. *Exhibit Design*. PBC International, Inc., 1984. Trade show and traveling exhibits.

Konikow, Robert B. *Point of Purchase Design*. PBC International Inc., 1985. Shows 400 display units for beverages, health and beauty aids, paper goods, and other products.

Laing, John. *Do-it-Yourself Graphic Design*. MacMillan Publishing, 1984. Design theory and practice clearly presented and beautifully illustrated in color.

Lee, Marshall. *Bookmaking: The Illustrated Guide to Design, Production, and Editing*. R. R. Bowker Co., 1979. The standard in the field.

Lefferts, Robert. *Elements of Graphics: How to Prepare Charts and Graphs for Effective Reports*. Harper and Row, 1981. When, why, and how to use visuals to communicate numerical data.

Maas, Jane. *Better Brochures, Catalogs, and Mailing Pieces*. St. Martin's, 1981. Guide for organizations and small businesses.

Marcus, Aaron. *Managing Facts and Concepts: Computer Graphics and Information Graphics from a Graphic Designer's Perspective*. National Endowment for the Arts, 1983. (1100 Pennsylvania Avenue NW, Washington DC 20506.)

Nakanishi, Motoo. *Corporate Design Systems*. PBC International, Inc., 1985. Nine case studies and 325 color photos show how graphic artists for corporations created logos, signs, and other design entities.

Nelson, Roy Paul. *Publication Design*. William C. Brown, 1983. College textbook about designing magazines, newspapers, and books.

Newcomb, John. *The Book of Graphic Problem Solving: How to Get Visual Ideas When You Need Them*. R. R. Bowker, 1984. Presents a systematic method for generating effective designs.

Pattison, Polly. *How to Design a Nameplate*. Pattison Productions, 1983. (5092 Kingscross Road, Westminster CA 92683.) Ideas and examples.

Porter, Tom, and Bob Greenstreet. *Manual(s) of Graphic Techniques for Architects, Graphic Designers, and Artists*. (4 volumes) Scribner's, 1980, 1982, 1983, & 1985. Each volume deals with five topics, such as perspective drawing and simulation.

Radice, Judi. *Menu Design*. PBC International, Inc., 1985. How to market a restaurant through graphics.

Rice, Stanley. *Book Design*. R. R. Bowker, 1978. Standard in the field.

Schmid, Calvin. *Statistical Graphics: Design Principles and Practice*. John Wiley and Sons, 1983. A textbook for people in accounting and statistics using case studies to explain design choices.

Sutter, Jan. *Slinging Ink: Guide to Producing Booklets, Newspapers, and Ephemeral Publications*. William Kaufmann, 1982. Concentrates on writing and distribution.

Townsend, Doris. *The Way to Write and Publish a Cookbook*. St. Martin's Press, 1985. Includes a chapter about cookbooks for churches, community organizations, and clubs.

White, Jan. *Designing for Magazines*. R. R. Bowker, 1982. Deals with specific problems such as front covers and tables of contents.

White, Jan. *Editing by Design: A Guide to Effective Word and Picture Communication for Editors and Designers*. R. R. Bowker, 1982. Shows how to combine type, graphics, and color into effective layouts, mainly for magazines.

White, Jan. *Graphic Idea Notebook*. Watson-Guptill, 1980. Hundreds of examples and comments about mugshots, rules, and other design elements.

White, Jan. *Mastering Graphics: Design and Production Made Easy*. R. R. Bowker, 1983. Simple format, 480 drawings, and 80 photos cover the essentials.

White, Jan. *Using Charts and Graphs: 1000 Ideas for Visual Persuasion*. R. R. Bowker, 1984. Examples of pie, bar, and dot charts, organizational tables, and other formats for presenting numerical data.

Williamson, Hugh. *Methods of Book Design: The Practice of an Industrial Craft*. Yale University Press, 1983. Covers design plus much more about type, preparation, printing, and binding.

Wilson, Adrian. *The Design of Books*. Peregrine Smith, 1974. Large-format, profusely-illustrated model of book design.

Winter, Elmer. *Complete Guide to Preparing a Corporate Annual Report*. Van Nostrand Reinhold, 1985. Deals with everything from writing copy to design and production.

Books: Photography

American Society of Magazine Photographers. *Stock Photography Handbook*. American Society of Magazine Photographers, 1984. Describes sources and business practices for individuals and agencies.

Brodatz, Phil. *Photo Graphics: A Workshop in High Contrast Techniques*. Amphoto, 1981. High contrast films, photograms, special effects screens, and other methods to turn photos into line copy.

Douglis, Philip N. *Pictures for Organizations: How and Why They Work as Communication*. Ragan Communications, 1982. (407 South Dearborn, Chicago IL 60605.) Presents 100 large photographs together with comments about why they work and other ways the shots might have been made.

Sanders, Norman. *Photographing for Publication*. R. R. Bowker, 1983. Tells professional photographers how to make pictures and work with printers. Book is example of premium quality printing.

Vandermeulen, Carl. *Photography for Student Publications*. Middleburg Press, 1979. (PO Box 166, Orange City IA 51041.) How to visualize, capture, develop, print, and reproduce black and white photos for all kinds of publications, not just student.

S.D. Warren Paper Co. *Black Halftone Prints*. S.D. Warren Paper Co., 1980. (225 Franklin Street, Boston MA 02101.) Identical photographs printed on a variety of papers using a range of screen rulings.

Books: Production

Adams, J. Michael, and David Faux. *Printing Technology*. Wadsworth Publishers, 1982. College text about how to be a printer. Excellent illustrations.

Bureau, William. *What the Printer Should Know About Paper*. Graphic Arts Technical Foundation, 1982. (4615 Forbes Avenue, Pittsburgh PA 15213.) Emphasis on characteristics, printability, handling, and ordering.

Campbell, Alastair. *The Graphic Designer's Handbook*. Running Press, 1983. Handy guide with lots of color, including color tint charts.

Cardomone, Tom. *Advertising Agency and Studio Skills: How to Prepare Art and Mechanicals for Reproduction*. Watson-Guptill, 1981. All the theory and techniques, then nine steps to making a mechanical.

Demoney, Jerry, and Susan Meyer. *Pasteups and Mechanicals*. Watson-Guptill, 1982. Practical and heavily illustrated with close-up photographs.

Graham, Walter. *Complete Guide to Pasteup: A Total System to Prepare Camera-Ready Copy for Reproduction*. Dot Pasteup Supply, 1980. (PO Box 369, Omaha NE 68101.) Lots of good business ideas as well as pasteup techniques and includes 600 design ideas for dozens of printed pieces.

Gray, Bill. *More Studio Tips*. Van Nostrand Reinhold, 1978. Tips about cropping, folding, mechanicals, templates, wax, and many more practical topics.

Gray, Bill. *Studio Tips*. Van Nostrand Reinhold, 1976. Tips about acetate, envelopes, knives, pens, spacing, and many more practical topics.

International Paper Company. *Pocket Pal*. 13th ed. International Paper Company, 1983. Handy guide to printing processes that's been standard since 1933.

Kagy, Frederick, and J. Michael Adams. *Graphic Arts Photography*. Wadsworth Publications, 1983. College textbook with excellent illustrations explaining everything from process cameras to special effects.

Kremer, John. *Directory of Short-Run Book Printers*. Ad-Lib Publications, 1985. (PO Box 1102, Fairfield IA 52556.) Tells capabilities and gives comments about quality and service for book printers in every part of the country.

Lassiter, Frances and Norman. *Screen Printing: Contemporary Methods and Materials*. Hunt Publishing Company, 1978. (1405 Locust Avenue, Philadelphia PA 19102.) Explains automated as well as hand screen printing.

Pickens, Judy. *The Copy-to-Press Handbook: Preparing Words and Art for Print*. John Wiley and Sons, 1985. A business, technical, and artistic manual by a graphic designer.

Saltman, David. *Paper Basics*. Van Nostrand Reinhold, 1978. The most complete book about paper, telling how it is made, purchased, used, and even recycled.

Sanders, Norman. *Graphic Designer's Production Handbook*. Hastings House, 1982. Over 100 short essays about preparation and offset printing. Written by a printer.

Stern, Edward L. *Direct Marketing Marketplace*. Hilary House, 1985. Includes lists of printers, envelope suppliers, and lettershops.

Stockton, James. *Designer's Guide to Color*. (2 volumes) Chronicle Books, 1983 and 1984. Shows thousands of color combinations and comments about using them.

Treweek, Chris, and John Zeitlyn. *The Alternative Printing Handbook*. Penguin Books, 1983. How to prepare and do your own screen, photocopy, mimeo, ditto, and rubber stamp printing.

Books: Reference

R. R. Bowker. *Literary Market Place*. R. R. Bowker, 1985 and annually. The standard guide to the book industry with information about publishers, agents, printers and other suppliers.

Creative Black Book, Inc. *The Creative Black Book*. Friendly Press, annually. Two-volume directory, complete with phone numbers, of designers, illustrators, photographers, and other creative services organized by region. Published every January.

Judd, Karen. *Copyediting: A Practical Guide*. William Kaufmann, 1982. Mostly a style manual, but also tells how to get jobs and handle clients.

Lem, Dean. *Graphics Master 3*. Dean Lem Associates, 1983. (PO Box 46086, Los Angeles CA 90046.) Workbook of planning aids such as a chart of paper sizes, drawings of common folds, and a scaling wheel.

Skillin, Marjorie E. *Words into Type*. Prentice-Hall, 1974. Widely-used style manual covering both general and fine points of grammer, usage, and manuscript production, with comprehensive index.

Stern, Edward L. *Printing and Graphic Arts Buyers Directory*. Hilary House, 1984. Guide to 5,100 buyers, who employs them, and what they buy.

U.S. Government Printing Office. *Style Manual*. Government Printing Office, 1973. Full of hard to find data such as government abbreviations.

University of Chicago Press. *The Chicago Manual of Style*. 13th ed. University of Chicago Press, 1982. Emphasis on style, production, and printing requirements of book writers and editors.

Vance Publishing. *Lockwood's Directory of the Paper and Allied Trades*. Vance Publishing Co., 1985. (122 East 42nd Street, New York NY 10168.) The standard guide to mills, distributors, converters, and related vendors and equipment.

Walden-Mott. *Walden's Handbook for Buyers of Printing Paper*. Walden-Mott Corp. annually. (466 Kinderkamack Road, Oradell NJ 07649.)

Books: Typography

Blumenthal, Joseph. *The Art of the Printed Book 1455-1955*. David R. Godine, 1973. A well-written historical survey with excellent plates.

Chadbourne, Bill. *What Every Editor Should Know about Layout and Typography*. National Composition Association, 1984. (1730 North Lynn Street, Arlington VA 22209.) Booklet with tips about design and how to work with typesetters.

Ernst, Sandra. *The ABC's of Typography: A Practical Guide to the Art and Science of Typography*. Art Direction Book Co., 1984. Tells how to identify, specify, mark up, and copyfit type.

Goodstein, David, and Rosalyn Newhouse. *Typesetting, Computer, and Communications Terms: A Glossary*. National Composition Association, 1983. (1730 North Lynn Street, Arlington VA 22209.) Defines over 800 terms.

Kleper, Michael. *Dictionary of Typographic Communication*. Graphic Dimensions, 1985. (8 Frederick Road, Pittsford NY 14534.) Definitions of 1,000 terms, many illustrated, bridge the gaps between typesetting, word processing, telecommunications, and computers.

Labuz, Ronald. *How to Typeset from a Word Processor*. R. R. Bowker, 1984. Covers all the business and editorial decisions in non-technical terms and with clear examples for both typesetters and type buyers.

Lawson, Alexander. *Printing Types: An Introduction*. Beacon Press, 1971. A brief discussion of the various categories of typefaces in use today including some historical background.

McLean, Ruari. *Typography*. Thames and Hudson, Ltd., 1980. An excellent introductory manual that is very current.

Morison, Stanley. *A Tally of Types*. Cambridge University Press, 1973. A discussion of the Monotype Corporation's type revival and development program in the early twentieth century.

Rasberry, Leslie. *Computer Age Copyfitting*. Art Direction Book Co., 1977. Step-by-step instructions for handling any layout.

Romano, Frank. *The Type Encyclopedia: A User's Guide to Better Typography*. R. R. Bowker, 1984. Type basics in a glossary-like format.

Seybold, John. *The World of Digital Typesetting*. Seybold, 1984. (PO Box 644, Media PA 19063.) In-depth coverage of history and current technology.

Smith, Peggy. *Simplified Proofreading*. National Composition Association, 1984. (1730 North Lynn Street, Arlington VA 22209.) Workbook including simple set of standard marks for training new or occasional proofreaders.

Soloman, Martin. *The Art of Typography*. Watson-Guptill, 1985. Describes aesthetic values of type, tells how to use type properly, and gives exercises for working with tonal value and spacing.

Periodicals

Advertising Age
220 East 42nd Street
New York NY 10017

American Printer
300 West Adams Street
Chicago IL 60606

Business Forms and Systems
North American Publishing Co.
401 North Broad Street
Philadelphia PA 19108

Canadian Printer and Publisher
777 Bay Street
Toronto, Ontario
Canada M5W 1A7

Catalog Age
125 Elm Street
New Canann CT 06840

Communication Arts
410 Sherman Avenue
Palo Alto CA 94303

Design Graphics World
6255 Barfield Road
Atlanta GA 30328

Fine Print
PO Box 3394
San Francisco, CA 94119

Folio
125 Elm Street
PO Box 4006
New Canaan CT 06840

Graphic Arts Abstracts
Graphic Arts Technical Foundation
4615 Forbes Avenue
Pittsburgh PA 15213

Graphic Arts Monthly
875 Third Avenue
New York NY 10022

Graphic Arts Product News
300 West Adams Street
Chicago IL 60606

Graphic Design: USA
120 East 56th Street
New York NY 10022

Graphics Communications World
PO Box 9500
Tallahassee FL 32303

How Magazine
6400 Goldsboro Road
Bethesda MD 20817

Imprint
Advertising Specialty Information Network
PO Box 427
Langhorne PA 19047

In-Plant Reproductions
PO Box 13222
Philadelphia PA 19101

Journal of Graphic Design
American Institute of Graphic Arts
1059 Third Avenue
New York NY 10021

Kodak Magazine
Dept. 661A, Graphic Market Division
Eastman Kodak Company
Rochester NY 14650

Package Printing
North American Publishing Company
401 North Broad Street
Philadelphia PA 19108

Packaging Digest
300 West Adams Street
Chicago IL 60606

Plan and Print
PO Box 879
Franklin Park IL 60131

Print Magazine
355 Lexington Avenue
New York NY 10017

Printing Impressions
North American Publishing Company
401 North Broad Street
Philadelphia PA 19108

Quick Printing
3255 South U.S. 1
Fort Pierce FL 33482

Screen Printing Magazine
407 Gilbert Avenue
Cincinnati OH 45202

Step-by-Step Graphics
6000 North Forest Park Drive
Peoria IL 61656

Studio Magazine
124 Galaxy Boulevard
Toronto, Ontario
Canada M9W 9Z9

Typeworld
15 Oakridge Circle
Wilmington MA 01887

Upper and lower case
International Typeface Corporation
866 Second Avenue
New York NY 10017

Trade Associations

American Advertising Federation
1400 K Street NW #1000
Washington DC 20005

American Book Producers Association
c/o Mountain Lion, Inc.
319 East 52nd Street
New York NY 10022

The American Institute of Graphic Arts
1059 Third Avenue
New York NY 10021

American Paper Institute
260 Madison Avenue
New York NY 10016

American Quick Printing Association
1324 West Clay
Houston TX 77019

Association of College & University Printers
c/o Harvard University Printing Office
219 Western Avenue
Allston MA 02134

Association of Graphic Arts Consultants
1730 North Lynn Street
Arlington VA 22209

Binding Industries of America
200 East Ontario Street
Chicago IL 60611

Book Manufacturers Institute
111 Prospect Street
Stamford CT 06901

Business Forms Management Association
181 SE Division Street
Portland OR 97202

Conference Board of Major Printers
1730 North Lynn Street
Arlington VA 22209

Education Council of the Graphic Arts Industry
4615 Forbes Avenue
Pittsburgh PA 15213

Engraved Stationery Manufacturers Association
PO Box 120539
Nashville TN 37212

Envelope Manufacturers Association
1300 North 17th
Arlington VA 22209

Financial Printers Association
1730 North Lynn Street
Arlington VA 22209

Flexographic Technical Association
95 West 19th Street
Huntington Station NY 11746

Graphic Artists Guild
30 East 20th Street
New York NY 10003

Graphic Arts Association Executives
1730 North Lynn Street
Arlington VA 22209

Graphic Arts Employers of America
1730 North Lynn Street
Arlington VA 22209

Graphic Arts Equipment and Supply
    Dealers Association
1730 North Lynn Street
Arlington VA 22209

Graphic Arts Marketing Information Service
1730 North Lynn Street
Arlington VA 22209

Graphic Arts Technical Foundation
4615 Forbes Avenue
Pittsburgh PA 15213

Graphic Communications Association
1730 North Lynn Street #604
Arlington VA 22209

Graphic Preparatory Association
PO Box 2
Mt. Morris IL 61054

Gravure Education Foundation
60 East 42nd Street
New York NY 10165

Gravure Research Institute
22 Manhasset Avenue
Port Washington NY 11050

Gravure Technical Association
60 East 42nd Street
New York NY 10165

Greeting Card Association
1350 New York Avenue NW
Washington DC 20005

In-Plant Print Management Association
2475 Canal Street #300
New Orleans LA 70119

Institute for Graphic Communication
375 Commonwealth Avenue
Boston MA 02115

International Association
    of Business Communicators
870 Market Street #940
San Francisco CA 94102

International Association
    of Printing House Craftsmen
7599 Kenwood Road
Cincinnati OH 45236

International Business Forms Industries
1730 North Lynn Street
Arlington VA 22209

International Graphic Arts Education Association
4615 Forbes Avenue
Pittsburgh PA 15213

International Prepress Association
552 West 167th Street
South Holland IL 60473

International Printing and Graphics
    Communications Union
1730 Rhode Island Avenue NW
Washington DC 20036

International Reprographics Association
10116 Franklin Avenue
Franklin Park IL 60131

International Thermographers Association
1730 North Lynn Street
Arlington VA 22209

Lasers in Graphics
1855 East Vista Way
Vista CA 92083

Magazine Printers Section/PIA
1730 North Lynn Street
Arlington VA 22209

Magazine Publishers Association
575 Lexington Avenue
New York NY 10022

Master Printers of America
1730 North Lynn Street
Arlington VA 22209

National Art Materials Trade Association
178 Lakeview Avenue
Clifton NJ 07011

National Association of Litho Clubs
PO Box 1074
Passaic NJ 07055

National Association
    of Lithographic Plate Manufacturers
1730 North Lynn Street
Arlington VA 22209

National Association of Printers and Lithographers
780 Palisade Avenue
Teaneck NJ 07666

National Association of Printing Ink Manufacturers
550 Mamaroneck Avenue
Harrison NY 10528

National Association of Quick Printers
111 East Wacker Drive #600
Chicago IL 60601

National Business Forms Association
433 East Monroe Avenue
Alexandria VA 22301

National Catalog Manufacturers Association
444 North Michigan Ave #2000
Chicago IL 60611

National Composition Association
1730 North Lynn Street
Arlington VA 22209

National Paper Trade Association
111 Great Neck Road
Great Neck NY 11021

National Printing Equipment and Supply
   Association
6849 Old Dominion Drive
McLean VA 22101

National Printing Ink Institute
Sinclair Laboratory
Lehigh University
Bethlehem PA 18015

Paper Industry Management Association
2400 East Oakton Street
Arlington Heights IL 60005

Point of Purchase Ad Institute
2 Executive Drive
Fort Lee NJ 07024

Printing Industries of America
1730 North Lynn Street
Arlington VA 22209

Public Relations Society of America
845 Third Avenue
New York NY 10022

Research and Engineering Council
   of the Graphic Arts Industry
PO Box 2740
Landover Hills MD 20784

Screen Printing Association International
10015 Main Street
Fairfax VA 22031

Society of Publication Designers
25 West 43rd Street #711
New York NY 10036

Society for Technical Communication
815 15th Street NW
Washington DC 20005

Society of Typographic Arts
233 East Ontario #301
Chicago IL 60611

Specialty Advertising Association International
1404 Walnut Hill Lane
Irving TX 75038

Tag and Label Manufacturers Institute
PO Box 1333
Stamford CT 06904

Technical Association of Graphic Arts
RIT/T&E Center
PO Box 9887
Rochester NY 14623

Technical Association
   of the Pulp and Paper Industry
PO Box 105113
Atlanta GA 30348

Type Directors Club
545 West 45th Street
New York NY 10036

Typographers International Association
2262 Hall Place NW
Washington DC 20007

University and College Designers Association
c/o Imprint, Inc.
2811 Mishawaka Avenue
South Bend IN 46615

Yearbook Printers Association
1730 North Lynn Street
Arlington VA 22209

APPENDIX D

Metric Information

The market for paper, printing, and color separations is international. People dealing effectively with that market understand the relationships between metric and U.S. measurements.

The metric system of weights and measures is used exclusively in Europe, Central and South America, Japan, and many other nations. It is used frequently in Great Britian, Canada, Australia, and other countries. The metric units most relevant to the graphic arts are grams and kilograms describing weights and millimeters and centimeters expressing linear dimensions.

Consider paper. Mills in the United States make about 20% of the world's paper, but printers in the U.S. use much more than that percentage. Much of the commercial printing paper used in the U.S. is imported from Europe and Asia. It ranges from heavy weight, ultragloss sheets to light weight, wash coated rolls.

Weight of paper made outside the U.S. is expressed in grams per square meter. Metric buyers refer to "grammage" just as U.S. buyers refer to "basis weight." Price books for paper sold internationally show both grammage and basis weight.

The table following this paragraph shows the relationship between some common grammages and basis weights. Unlike the U.S. system, the metric system for describing the weight of paper does not use a concept of basic size or number of sheets. Any paper's grammage is simply the weight in grams of one sheet that measures one square meter. Grammage is usually written "g/sm," the abbreviation for "grams per square meter."

Paper Weight Equivalents

Grammage	Basis weight
34	9# manifold
44	30# book
45	12# manifold
59	40# book
60	16# bond
67	45# book
74	50# book
75	20# bond
81	55# book
89	60# book
90	24# bond
104	70# book/text
105	28# ledger
118	80# book/text
120	32# ledger
135	36# ledger
147	67# bristol
148	100# book/text
150	40# ledger
162	60# cover
163	90# index
163	100# tag
176	65# cover
199	110# index
216	80# cover
218	125# tag
219	100# bristol
270	100# cover
352	130# cover

The table on the previous page gives the impression that there is a grammage equivalent to almost every familiar basis weight. This isn't true in practice, but the variance makes little difference. For example, a 100 g/sm paper is the equivalent of about 67# book or text. The 67# sheet may suit a job just as well as 70# or may be a bonus when compared to 60#. To make the information work for you, pay attention to how you plan to use a paper and not to where it lies in this theoretical system.

Thickness of paper of the same grammage may vary depending on coating and calendering just as it would using the system of basis weights. As with any unfamiliar aspect of a printing job, always ask for a sample of paper that you are considering using. If the paper feels and looks right for the job and you've seen samples printed to your standards of quality, let price and availability guide your decision.

Paper is made in rolls and is easily cut into sheets of any size. Buyers can specify sheet size. Foreign mills ship paper to the U.S. cut to U.S. standard sizes; U.S. mills export paper cut to metric standards. Perhaps the most popular sheet size in the world is 700 x 1000 millimeters (approximately 28 x 40 inches). Much of the paper sold internationally travels as rolls which can be either cut into sheets at the destination or used for web presses.

Although foreign paper cut to U.S. standards is readily available, stock cut to a U.S. standard size may not be the most efficient to run on a specific press. The size of almost every commercial sheetfed press on the market, and the vast majority of presses currently in use, is based on metrics. That means almost every commercial printing job in the U.S. is run on a metric press. For example, printers in the U.S. may refer to a machine as a 40 inch press, but in fact it is typically a 102 centimeter press (40¼ inches).

Of course, metric presses do not have to run paper cut to metric sizes. A 102 centimeter press runs a 25 x 38 inch sheet very efficiently, and that size is by far the most common sheet size imported to the U.S. The press would, however, run a sheet 1000 mm wide slightly more efficiently. The popularity of 102 centimeter presses around the world explains the popularity of 700 x 1000 millimeter paper.

Recognizing that 700 x 1000 millimeter is an efficient size and that U.S. printers are using a lot of foreign paper, some U.S. mills offer sheets to fit a 102 centimeter press. Printers in the U.S. refer to the paper as 28 x 40 instead of 700 x 1000. Paper measuring 28 x 40 inches is not one of the standard U.S. sizes, so we did not include it in the chart on pages 108-109, but it is often available.

Knowing metric paper sizes and weights affects the design and specifications of printing jobs to be done in many nations outside of North America. U.S. buyers often use printers in Europe and Asia, especially for long runs of multicolor and 4-color process jobs. Unless a job is big enough for a mill order made to U.S. specifications, it will run on metric size paper.

The most efficient finish and trim sizes using metric papers are slightly different from those using U.S. papers. For example, 5½ x 8½ inches and 8½ x 11 inches are common book sizes in the U.S. Their most efficient equivalent when printed on standard metric size paper would be 148 x 210 mm (about 5¾ x 8¼ inch) and 210 x 297 mm (about 8¼ x 11¾ inch). Either of those trim sizes would be appropriate for the U.S. book market and would be likely to fit conveniently into packaging and storage systems already developed.

Although most foreign printers use paper cut to metric dimensions, not all the sizes are standard. Japanese mills make a popular sheet at 229 x 304 millimeters, close to both U.S. letterhead and ISO A4 size, and another at 788 x 1091 millimeters. Using these sheets, printers in Japan run a large number of jobs for customers in other countries. Such national variations add to the importance of getting samples and asking about efficient trim sizes.

The International Standards Organization (ISO) developed three series of metric sizes for printing papers known as the A, B, and C series. Each series has within it sheet sizes whose measurements may be found in many reference books. Size A1, for example, is about the same as 23 x 35 inch paper made in the U.S. It is often imported to the U.S. Size A4 is comparable to U.S. 8½ x 11 inch letterhead and is used throughout the world for stationery.

In practice only a few of the ISO sizes are commonly made. Mills in metric countries are more likely to cut sheets to some convenient size for the buyer than they are to use ISO sizes.

Sizes and weights of papers are not the only features to consider when designing or specifying. Foreign papers must also be inspected for their brightness, opacity, and other traits. These traits are measurable and can be expressed in either metric or

U.S. units. Careful examination of samples, however, usually gives enough information to decide which stock to use.

Use of metric units in the graphic arts is not limited to paper and printing. U.S. buyers commonly obtain separations from Hong Kong, Singapore, Germany, and other metric countries. Staff in nations such as these may find inches as cumbersome as many people in the U.S. find centimeters. Using a ruler with metric units while designing can overcome this problem.

Citizens of the United States are more oriented to metric measurements than they often realize. People in many occupations refer to film size by millimeters, ink portions by grams, distances by kilometers, volumes by cubic centimeters, and liquids by liters. People in every occupation use the U.S. monetary system which is organized, similarly to the metric system, in multiples of ten. Graphic arts professionals who are familiar with the metric system of weights and measures can exercise much better control over quality and cost when functioning in the international market.

To convert the units commonly used in the graphic arts from one system to the other, use the following table.

Conversion Equivalents

of inches multiplied by 25.4 = # of millimeters
# of millimeters multiplied by .0394 = # of inches

# of inches multiplied by 2.54 = # of centimeters
# of centimeters multiplied by .3937 = # of inches

lines/inch multiplied by .3937 = # lines/centimeter
lines/centimeter multiplied by 2.54 = # lines/inch

of ounces multiplied by 28.349 = # of grams
# of grams multiplied by .0353 = # of ounces

# of pounds multiplied by .4536 = # of kilograms
# of kilograms multiplied by 2.2046 = # of pounds

CWT multiplied by 45.36 = # of kilograms
# of kilograms multiplied by .022046 = CWT

APPENDIX E

Copy-Ready Forms

The forms on the next six pages appeared earlier in the book slightly reduced in size and filled out with example information. The Printing Job Organizer appeared on pages 17 and 18; the Request for Quotation on pages 23 and 24; and Printer Equipment and Services on pages 165 and 166. Here they are full size, not filled out, and positioned near the back of the book to facilitate photocopying.

There are no standard forms in the graphic arts industry to use for planning jobs, writing specifications, or recording the capabilities of printers. We developed these three forms based on our own experiences and forms that others have found useful.

We hope they will prove useful starting points for your own planning and record keeping. If any of them is too complicated for your routine work, please feel free to change it to suit your needs.

Coast to Coast Books owns the copyright to these forms and its copyright information should be included if they are reproduced. You may make as many copies as you wish as often as you need them. If you change one of these forms and make copies of your new version, we would appreciate a credit line. For example, you might print at the bottom of your new version, "Based on a design in *Getting It Printed*, published by Coast to Coast Books."

Printing Job Organizer

Job Name _____ Coordinator _____ Date _____

Function	Person Responsible	Supplier
Write copy		
Edit copy		
Proofread copy		
Approve copy		
Make rough layout		
Approve rough layout		
Make comp and dummy		
Approve comp and dummy		
Choose typesetter		
Specify type and mark up copy		
Set type		
Proofread type		
Create illustrations		
Create charts, graphs, maps		
Create/select photographs		
Approve visual elements		
Miscellaneous camera work		

Function	Person Responsible	Supplier
Choose production artist		
Paste up mechanicals		
Proofread mechanicals		
Approve mechanicals		
Choose/specify trade services		
Make halftones/separations		
Approve proofs of photographs		
Select paper		
Write printing specifications		
Select possible printers		
Obtain bids from printers		
Choose printer		
Contract with printer		
Approve proofs from printer		
Do printing		
Approve press sheets		
Do bindery work		
Verify job done per specifications		
Verify charges for alterations		
Verify mechanicals and art returned		
Pay printer and trade services		

Request for Quotation

Job name _____ Date _____

Contact person _____ Date quote needed _____

Business name _____ Date job to printer _____

Address _____ Date job needed _____

Phone _____ **Please give** ☐ firm quote ☐ rough estimate ☐ verbally ☐ in writing

This is a ☐ new job ☐ exact reprint ☐ reprint with changes _____

Quantity 1) _____ 2) _____ 3) _____ ☐ additional _____ s

Quality ☐ basic ☐ good ☐ premium ☐ showcase comments _____

Format product description _____

    flat trim size _____ x _____ folded/bound size _____ x _____

    # of pages _____ ☐ self cover ☐ plus cover

Design features ☐ bleeds ☐ screen tints # _____ ☐ reverses # _____ ☐ comp enclosed

Art ☐ camera-ready ☐ printer to typeset and paste up (manuscript and rough layout attached)

    ☐ plate-ready negatives with proofs to printer's specifications

    trade shop name and contact person _____

Mechanicals color breaks ☐ on acetate overlays ☐ shown on tissues # pieces separate line art _____

Halftones ☐ halftones # _____ ☐ duotones # _____

Separations ☐ from transparencies # _____ ☐ from reflective copy # _____ ☐ provided # _____

    finished sizes of separations _____

Proofs ☐ galley ☐ page ☐ blueline ☐ loose color ☐ composite color ☐ progressive

Paper   weight   name   color   finish   grade

    cover _____

    inside _____

    _____ _____

    _____ _____

    ☐ send samples of paper ☐ make dummy buy paper from _____

Printing   ink color(s)/varnish   ink color(s)/varnish

    cover   side 1 _____   side 2 _____

    inside   side 1 _____   side 2 _____

    _____   side 1 _____   side 2 _____

    _____   side 1 _____   side 2 _____

Ink   ☐ special color match   ☐ special ink _____   ☐ need draw down

    coverage is   ☐ light   ☐ moderate   ☐ heavy   ☐ see comp attached   ☐ need press check

Other printing (die cut, emboss, foil stamp, engrave, thermograph, number, etc.) _____

_____

Bindery

    ☐ deliver flat press sheets   ☐ round corner   ☐ pad   ☐ Wire-O

    ☐ trim   ☐ punch   ☐ paste bind   ☐ spiral bind

    ☐ collate or gather   ☐ drill   ☐ saddle stitch   ☐ perfect bind

    ☐ plastic coat with _____   ☐ score/perforate   ☐ side stitch   ☐ case bind

    ☐ fold _____   ☐ plastic comb   ☐ tip in _____

    comments _____

Packing   ☐ rubber band in # ____ s   ☐ paper band in # ____ s   ☐ shrink/paper wrap in # ____ s

    ☐ bulk in cartons/maximum weight ____ lbs   ☐ skid pack   ☐ other _____

Shipping   ☐ customer pick up   ☐ deliver to _____

_____

    ☐ quote shipping costs separately   ☐ send cheapest way   ☐ other _____

Miscellaneous instructions _____

_____

_____

_____

_____

Printer Equipment and Services

Date compiled _____

Printing company _____

      address _____

    city, state, zip _____

Contact _____   or _____

    title _____   title _____

    phone _____   phone _____

Routine quality   ☐ basic   ☐ good   ☐ premium   ☐ showcase

Possible quality   ☐ basic   ☐ good   ☐ premium   ☐ showcase

Comments about samples _____

_____

_____

Type of printer

☐ quick

☐ in-plant

☐ small commercial

☐ medium commercial

☐ large commercial

☐ specialty in _____

Union shop

☐ yes   ☐ no

Sheetfed offset presses

brand _____ max sheet size ___ x ___ min size ___ x ___ # colors ___ ☐ perfector

brand _____ max sheet size ___ x ___ min size ___ x ___ # colors ___ ☐ perfector

brand _____ max sheet size ___ x ___ min size ___ x ___ # colors ___ ☐ perfector

brand _____ max sheet size ___ x ___ min size ___ x ___ # colors ___ ☐ perfector

brand _____ max sheet size ___ x ___ min size ___ x ___ # colors ___ ☐ perfector

Web offset presses

brand _____ maximum roll width ___ cutoff ___ # colors ___

brand _____ maximum roll width ___ cutoff ___ # colors ___

Letterpresses

brand _____ max size ___ x ___ min size ___ x ___ primary function _____

brand _____ max size ___ x ___ min size ___ x ___ primary function _____

Other printing processes (engraving, thermography, photocopy, etc.) _____

_____

Bindery

cutter maximum sheet dimension ___   folder maximum sheet size ___ x ___   min size ___ x ___

folding capabilities _____

_____

binding abilities (wire, paste, saddle stitch, perfect, case, etc.) _____

_____

other bindery abilities _____

Prepress services (halftones, separations, stripping, platemaking, etc.) _____

_____

Miscellaneous in-house services (design, typesetting, pasteup, pick up and delivery, storage, fulfillment,

direct mailing, list management, etc.) _____

_____

_____

Negatives (ownership, storage conditions, insurance, etc.) _____

_____

Credit terms _____

_____

Previous customer references

name _____   name _____

organization _____   organization _____

phone _____   phone _____

Comments _____

_____

_____

_____

_____

Index